The Web of Southern Social Relations

The Web of Southern Social Relations

Women, Family, & Education

EDITED BY

Walter J. Fraser, Jr.
R. Frank Saunders, Jr.
Jon L. Wakelyn

The University of Georgia Press
ATHENS

© 1985 by the University of Georgia Press
Athens, Georgia 30602

All rights reserved

Designed by Kathi L. Dailey
Set in 10 on 12 Linotron 202 Sabon

The paper in this book meets the guidelines for
permanence and durability of the Committee on
Production Guidelines for Book Longevity of the
Council on Library Resources.

Printed in the United States of America

90 89 88 87 86 85   6 5 4 3 2 1

Library of Congress Cataloging in Publication Data

Main entry under title:

The Web of southern social relations.

Includes index.
  1. Southern States—Social conditions—Congresses.
2. Women—Southern States—Social conditions—
Congresses. 3. Education—Southern States—History—
Congresses. 4. Family—Southern States—History—
Congresses. I. Fraser, Walter J. II. Saunders, R.
Frank, 1934–   . III. Wakelyn, Jon L.
HN79.A13W43 1985   306'.0975   85-1054
ISBN 0-8203-0787-4

Contents

v

Contents

Introduction

The essays in this collection were presented during the two-day "Symposium on the South: Education, Family, and Women," held at Georgia Southern College in April 1984. These topics, too long neglected, were selected because they are vital ingredients of the social fabric of the Old and New South.

Only recently have historians of the South become interested in education, family, and women. Indeed, some of the most exciting scholarship has come from practitioners of the "new social history," who are less interested in the "movers and shakers" than in the everyday lives of ordinary people. As its early advocates first proclaimed nearly two decades ago, this approach is "history from the bottom up," the history of common folk, the inarticulate, people who seldom left written records. To seek out this history, new methodologies and sources had to be explored. In so doing, the new social historians have revitalized the American past and have offered fresh insights into areas that provide perspectives on the present.[1]

The essays in this book demonstrate the web of relationships between education, family, and women, past and present, indeed, a matrix of institutions, patterns of thinking, beliefs, and behavior that shaped the culture and the individual lives of southerners. The essays focusing on education in the South, for example, are particularly timely in light of the recent report of the National Commission on Excellence in Education, which proclaims that the United States is "a nation at risk." Scholars have suggested that racial concerns, opposition to outside involvement, and "pride of place" have hindered educational development in the South. Intertwined with the history of education is the study of the family, humanity's most basic and durable institution, which has the awesome responsibility for the rearing of children, the molding of their values, and the transmission of culture from one generation to another. As Allan J. Lichtman has observed: "The study of families can illuminate the workings of an entire society revealing details of people's movement from place to place, or opportunities for social and economic advancement, of relationships between the sexes."[2]

Equally fundamental to an understanding of the southern social fabric is the role of women in social, economic, and intellectual affairs. Virtually neglected until more than a decade ago as a legitimate subject of inquiry, perhaps because men have written most history books, the history of American women is now dominated by a new generation of scholars, mainly female. Only after a long struggle, as Gertrude Himmelfarb has noted, "the victims of history have become its principal agents and actors."[3] Reinterpretations of the male-dominated South have suggested topics necessary for an understanding of everyday life.[4] The essays in this volume cite this recent scholarship and offer additional interpretations and refinements on old themes.

In her essay on the changing status of eighteenth-century Chesapeake women, Lorena Walsh analyzes work patterns, marriages, childbearing, and ownership of land and slaves. Walsh maintains that because of their small numbers, few children, and often early widowhood, seventeenth-century Chesapeake women actually had more control over their own lives than did their daughters. In the eighteenth century, men lived longer and women married younger and had more children than their predecessors. Since women had important household duties, wives were more secure and protected in their marriages. To their detriment, women's status as landholders eroded. For Walsh, the uneven status of women and their subservience to their husbands are the central issues of nineteenth-century southern family life and of women's place in that society.[5]

Where Walsh finds mixed evidence on the declining status of women, Catherine Clinton, enlarging upon the thesis of *The Plantation Mistress,* studies an area in which men indeed dominated. She describes a terrible tale of family impotence in the face of white male sexual exploitation of female slaves. The white planter's wife, who had few options but to accept male behavior, commonly found an outlet for her frustration in the form of brutality toward female slaves. The psychological scars of women at war with women exacerbated racial tensions and confirmed male dominance of women and the family.

In her study of Indian women, Theda Perdue also confirms the power of men in the family. She accepts the standard interpretation that before white and Indian male interference, tribal customs fostered a matrilocal society. Indian women worked the fields, ran the households, and controlled the land; status was passed on to children through the mother.[6] Because they wanted to live in peace with the whites, many Indian leaders forced "civilization" on their women. Indian towns were disbanded; families lived alone and isolated from others. Christianity forced an end to polygamy and imposed formal marriage rites, and the children passed into the father's line of descent. Worst of all for the status of Indian women, Perdue insists, men took control of the land and worked in the fields. Indian women thus became like their white counterparts.

Barbara Bellows describes another set of neglected nineteenth-century southern women, the urban poor and working classes who had to find ways to survive in a male-dominated society. These were women who never married, widows, abandoned women, or those who had to earn part of the family income. These women who fought to keep their families together hardly fitted the stereotype of weak females under the protection of paternalistic males. But Bellows maintains that the town fathers of Charleston, who were dedicated to keeping order, sought to recreate paternal family dominance by controlling the town orphanage and poorhouse. Their "cult of domesticity," however, did not appease the working women, who did their best to provide for themselves and resisted giving up their children.

Carol Bleser captures the tensions between the sexes in her outline of a marriage in an antebellum southern upper-middle-class family. She finds that on the surface, Benjamin F. Perry and his wife had the ideal companionate marriage; they married for love and enjoyed material interests. Their relationship, however, challenges the image of male dominance. Perry was a leading South Carolina politician and was often away while his wife ran the household. Further ambivalence appears in this marriage because her letters to her husband reveal that Elizabeth Perry was actively involved in his political career, even advising him on major decisions.[7]

Another dimension of the paternal planter family emerges in Steven M. Stowe's description of the southern female academies, which he portrays as extensions of the family setting. Young elite women were sent to schools for the purpose of reaffirming the values of the paternal family. Daughters were taught to keep close personal ties to the home, to meet and correspond with proper young men, and to learn how to conduct themselves in married life. In reality, Stowe says, rather than provide young ladies a safe world of shared thoughts while they became women, academies fostered a sisterhood that allowed young women to gain some distance from their families. Although letters home followed the correct pattern of deference, some fathers detected a certain independence of mind. Stowe maintains that the affectionate letters that supposedly revealed the young women's own matrimonial decisions were in reality only literary conventions of the time. In fact, fathers still controlled most options for marriage and used the facade of affection to keep elite families together.

The academic setting as a means of reinforcing paternal power over antebellum southern males is a concern of Jon Wakelyn. He finds that the purpose was flawed from the beginning because many fathers wanted their sons to learn independence at college. These young men, thrown together at an impressionable age, had to make their ways with one another as well as with surrogate father figures in the academic community. Paternal authority was both reaffirmed and denied because the college setting was an extension of the southern family and society, and the pressures of that society did not entirely reflect the paternal theme.

In a historiographical survey, Thomas G. Dyer suggests that most studies of post–Civil War southern colleges are heavily devoted to institutional history and ignore the social, political, and cultural context of higher education. For example, the role of colleges in creating the New South "creed" has been ignored. Likewise, Dyer says, we know almost nothing about student behavior, which also would reveal much about family history.

Bertram Wyatt-Brown argues that recent study of the success or failure of black education during Reconstruction has been too narrowly institutionally evaluated. Wyatt-Brown ties learning to its cultural context, rejects judgments based entirely on class and social bias, and finds other obstacles to black learning. It was not simply the resistance or prejudice of white teachers but cultural confusion that limited pedagogical methods for educating black children. White teachers had a biased concept of black family life and a poor understanding of how blacks functioned. Thus the images they used to communicate were unintelligible to their students. More particularly, black students resisted certain subjects because they feared that learning would separate them from their families and peers. Wyatt-Brown concludes that they had a natural desire to retain the culture they knew, and success in school could ultimately mean leaving familial surroundings.

The Progressive impulse in southern education is studied by Joseph Kett through the role of women in that reform movement. He believes that the New South's women were active in educational reform as a part of their efforts toward independence from the supposedly male-dominated familial social structure. Southerners were individualistic, rural, and dispersed in a period of reform that called for centralized authority. Women, who were sensitive to those values and circumstances, sought reform through education in rural county normal and technical schools.

To appear nonthreatening to white males, the women offered study in home economics. Kett finds tension in their behavior; their activism gave the lie to male dominance, but their teaching chores affirmed the female domestic stereotype.

In a study of black women's activities in social welfare organizations during Reconstruction, Kathleen Berkeley also questions stereotypes of women's status in southern society. The standard view is that the Civil War to some extent freed women from domesticity, but there remain questions as to when and to what extent that occurred.[8] Berkeley explores the impulse that prompted black women to form independent female societies for social welfare. She concludes that most of Memphis's black social activists, who provided food, clothing, and shelter for newly freed persons, had formerly been plantation and town slaves. Therefore, some aspects of life under slavery must have prepared them for their reform activities. Perhaps, says Berkeley, their duties as slaves to nurture and care for others had provided the training and even the independence to provide for others after the war.

Orville Vernon Burton conducted an in-depth study of one community to learn the roles of education and family experience in determining who became leaders in the postwar South. Burton shows that young white men before the war had taken their places as community political and professional leaders, but that for a generation after the war they had held no positions of leadership. Instead, they were replaced by educated blacks with stable home environments. It is possible that former white leaders were devastated by the war experience. Burton suggests that failure to go to college kept some of those whites out of public life. Perhaps also many of those young men were apathetic and indecisive about their future careers because the war had disrupted their family lives.[9]

J. Wayne Flynt questions the traditional interpretation of family life among New South poor whites, who had been driven from landownership and forced into sharecropping or menial jobs. Contemporary observers claimed that most of them lived in poverty, were violent and often drunk, and treated their women and illegitimate children harshly. Flynt depicts their lives in compassionate but realistic terms. He finds, however, that many so-called poor whites held jobs, married, raised and educated their children, had church ties, and often joined the local prohibitionist movement. Even their courtship patterns resembled those of hardworking middle-class families. Flynt rejects the notions of those scholars who viewed poor farmers with nostalgia and claimed that they had all grown up in nuclear families.

Flynt's cautious conclusions are typical of these essays, which attempt to interpret family life, the status and activities of women, and the place of education in the Old and the New South. True, the theme of male dominance or paternalism was central to the values and family structure, at least among the elites of the Old South.[10] Its effect on opportunities for women and on their social-psychological existence could be horrible. Educational institutions supposedly reflected family interests, which were usually synonymous with the interests of fathers. But not all families conformed to the paternalist pattern, and even paternalists at times found their powers thwarted. The same is true for the post–Civil War period, in which Anne Scott has suggested that females at last achieved work and status outside the house.[11] Yet the status of postwar women was ambivalent; something in the home experience must have encouraged women to engage actively in reform. Most of these articles suggest that the judgment that paternal authority as usually defined describes nineteenth-century southern families, women's lives, and educational institutions is only partially correct. Southern families were obviously diverse in attitudes as well as practice.

To make these tentative conclusions, the authors have applied a variety of methodological approaches that might be useful to others at work in the sensitive areas of personal lives. In *Approaches to the History of the Western Family*, Michael Anderson maintains that the family in all its aspects is studied through psychohistory, demography, sentiments (written tests), and household economics such as marriage contracts, land ownership, and wills.[12] Anderson, perhaps unwisely, dispenses with psychohistory and sentiments, which he insists are based on weak evidence and conjecture. He finds that statistical information and the activities in the household offer the best materials for analysis of what family life was like in the past. But the dynamics of interpersonal relations require study of the language and the thoughts and actions behind the sentiments contained in letters, diaries, and other printed matter, which reveal a great deal about style, attitudes, and behavioral conventions. As the essays in this volume demonstrate, the best analysis draws from all of these approaches to the study of the family, women, and the role of education in that society.

Use of demographic data such as age at marriage, length of marriage, and numbers of children allows Walsh to compare women's lives throughout the eighteenth century. Bellows finds in the rich census material much about poverty, single-sex households, and women's occupations to portray the plight of poor women. Berkeley also uses the census data to make quantitative comparisons of career patterns and social class of black women in order to establish the role of former slaves and lower-class black women in reform organizations. Burton finds in census returns much valuable information on college attendance and age of entry into careers. He is then able to compare young blacks and whites during the Reconstruction period to analyze who rose in political and professional circles. Flynt discovers much about lower-class poverty in census information on illiteracy in the New South.

Legal codes, wills, marriage contracts, and dowries, which list household goods, worth, restrictions on women's activities, and what was inherited, allow Walsh to uncover the status of colonial southern women.[13] Clinton finds in wills and court records involving divorce and trials for slave brutality the sordid story of humiliation of white women and savagery toward blacks. Orphan house records reveal to Bellows the similarity between the laws of behavior and the supposed values of family living. Stowe uses school regulations for female behavior and classroom books and assignments to divulge the ways the academies were able to influence elite young women. The organization charts and lists of activities of reform societies gave Berkeley information for comparing household values.

Quantitative information provides the background for social and personal relations. The sentiments expressed in the written word, when carefully interpreted, bring to the foreground the social relationships between the sexes and their place in the sexual world of the South. Bleser reads between the lines of the Perry correspondence and finds in the directness of Elizabeth Perry's contempt for her husband's political mistakes female frustrations related to status. Stowe posits a typology of sentiments in letters between student daughters and their families to show the tensions between the conventions of contentment and the romance of the sisterhood. He uses the school's formal guides to letter writing to interpret much about the values of that society. Wyatt-Brown's comparison of textbook images to the actual lives of former slaves reveals why classroom instruction was so often difficult for young black students. Kett examines curricula in the community training colleges so that he can compare what the women teachers taught with their actual domestic situation. Oral interviews and the records of the Works Progress Administration are used by Flynt to reconstruct differences among poor whites by examining their responses to questions about their lives.

These authors also use psychological analysis to clarify often tense personal relationships. Clinton infers much about the contempt of white women for blacks from the shadowy records of a court system that hardly wanted to dwell on violence among women. Burton turns statistics on occupation into a world of family fears that reflected loss of nerve by many young white men. Bellows uses codes of orphanage behavior to infer the restiveness of white male elites in the face of an undisciplined poor class. Bleser reads beneath the surface of supportive personal letters to see a tense family situation. After all, what was Elizabeth Perry hiding when she chose not to publish her letters to her husband? Wyatt-Brown goes beyond the surface of his evidence to find black students fearful of continued change in their lives. Stowe says that the conventions in the letters home from daughters actually showed a suppression of real feelings. Suppression of feelings seemed to predominate in that nineteenth-century Victorian society so famous for its supposedly romantic and open literary expression.[14]

The variety of materials used and the interpretations made in these essays naturally suggest areas for further study and research into the private and personal lives of nineteenth-century southerners. Scholars have only begun to use quantitative data available on women and the family. Jane Turner Censer has made a model test for a particular group of elites in marriage age, numbers of children, longevity, years of education, and wills, but similar information needs to be gathered for other regions and people. Bleser has begun the process of understanding the roles of women in politics. Recently the Genoveses showed that in the writings of Louisa McCord there was a women's world of politics.[15] This subject should be pursued further. In *The Women of Petersburg,* Suzanne Lebsock has placed women in the changing antebellum urban work force. Other towns require such careful analysis. Rural poor women, white and black, also need to be studied. The suggestions about the activities of female slaves call for another look at slave quarters. Walsh's interpretation of the mixed status of colonial women requires us to analyze status over a long period. Lebsock, for one, says that gains from the antebellum period did not necessarily carry over into the New South, despite the hopes that Anne Scott had held for women's gains during the war period. In short, the meaning of status and other aspects of female relations in family and institutional lives over the course of the nineteenth century requires much further study before we can understand the female response to paternalism.

In his thoughtful analysis of earlier studies on higher education, Dyer offers an entire field for study of institutional-cultural history. His work also suggests that the roles in southern life of other institutions and organizations, such as churches and reform groups, need to be evaluated. Such works as those of E. Brooks Holifield and Anne Loveland on professionalization of clergy and church-led reforms suggest fertile areas for scholarly endeavor.[16] Dyer maintains that those institutions also reflected society and that we should know how.

The essays in this collection on family and women call into question how we have looked at the menfolk. Although one hesitates to ask for more work on the planter, books such as James Oakes's *The Ruling Race* suggest that interest in family concerns can clarify our understanding of male lives.[17] Professional people also inhabited the South. If they were not as numerous as planters and farmers, their lifestyles may have been sufficiently different that their world-view, especially their attitudes toward the opposite sex, might provide comparison to that of the planter paternalists. And lest we forget, many of the essays in this volume suggest that much can be learned from looking at southern youth. Perhaps a study of growing up in the South, the counterpart to Joseph Kett's *Rites of Passage,* would unlock some of the secrets about southerners, both female and male.

Besides understanding these people over time, place, class, and status, more research is needed on the southern value system, especially concerning gender. Philip Greven's provocative *The Protestant Temperament* compares colonial family lifestyles based on varieties of religious beliefs and attachments.[18] Essays in this volume have disclosed enough ambivalence in family relations among elites, the middle class, and the poor that perhaps someone should attempt a similar model for the nineteenth-century South. Certainly there were enough Souths or southern types of a different stripe, even with the binding force of slavery and religious fundamentalism, to suggest the usefulness of such a model. Perhaps such a model would help to clarify the different constraints on relationships that determined the status of women in the southern family.

The following essays are meant to provoke questions for all students of southern society, especially for those who want to know more about ordinary lives. They demonstrate how the study of the many aspects of family life contribute to our understanding of the entire social system. The seamless web of southern social relations encompasses all facets of family life, not for prurient motives or to satisfy those who would snoop into private lives, but for a more sensitive understanding of the South. What we ask about class and status we must also ask about gender relations. This volume has concentrated on family, women, and education. It is our hope that other volumes will emerge from this beginning. Indeed, a criterion in evaluating the worth of any book is the degree to which it influences future scholarship.

The "Symposium on the South" out of which this book grew was supported by a grant from the National Endowment for the Humanities through the Georgia Endowment for the Humanities and cash contributions from private individuals, businesses, and historical societies of the region. It was designed to introduce an audience of both laymen and scholars to some of the most creative research currently under way in southern history. We are indebted to Ronald Benson, Georgia Endowment for the Humanities, Dale Lick, president of Georgia Southern College, who encourages the undertaking of such projects in the humanities, and Warren F. Jones, Jr., dean of the School of Arts and Sciences, who helped in providing release time from normal academic duties so that faculty members could undertake and conduct the symposium. We are grateful to those who recommended topics and scholars for the conference. We wish to thank Betty Reaves and Sharon T. Hodges for patiently and efficiently handling tedious secretarial chores, and we also gratefully acknowledge the assistance of Julius Ariail, director of the Georgia Southern College Library, in preparation of the index. Most of all we appreciate the cooperation of the participants, whose contributions made this volume possible.

WALTER J. FRASER, JR.
R. FRANK SAUNDERS, JR.
JON L. WAKELYN

Notes

1. Peter N. Stearns, "The New Social History: An Overview," in James B. Gardner and George Rollie Adams, eds., *Ordinary People and Everyday Life: Perspectives on the New Social History* (Nashville: American Association for State and Local History, 1983), pp. 3–18.

2. Allan J. Lichtman, *Your Family History* (New York: Vintage Press, 1978), p. 5.

3. Quoted in ibid.

4. Jane Turner Censer, *North Carolina Planters and Their Children* (Baton Rouge: Louisiana State University Press, 1984); Bertram Wyatt-Brown, *Southern Honor* (New York: Oxford University Press, 1982); Dorothy Ann Gay, "The Tangled Skein of Romanticism and Violence in the Old South: The Southern Response to Abolitionism and Feminism, 1830–1860" (Ph.D. dissertation, University of North Carolina, 1975); Catherine Clinton, *The Plantation Mistress* (New York: Pantheon Books, 1982); Suzanne Lebsock, *The Free Women of Petersburg* (New York: Norton, 1984); the best recent historiographical essay is

Mary Beth Norton, "The Evolution of White Women's Experience in Early America," *American Historical Review* 89 (June 1984): 593–619.

5. See the classic work of Julia C. Spruill, *Women's Life and Work in the Southern Colonies* (Chapel Hill: University of North Carolina Press, 1938).

6. Jon A. Schlenker, "An Historical Analysis of the Family of the Choctaw Indians," *Southern Quarterly* 13 (July 1975): 323–34.

7. For another study of a wife in politics, see W. Conrad Gass, "A Felicitous Life: Lucy Martin Battle, 1805–1874," *North Carolina Historical Review* 52 (October 1975): 61–73.

8. See Anne F. Scott, *The Southern Lady: From Pedestal to Politics* (Chicago: University of Chicago Press, 1970); Lebsock, *Free Women of Petersburg,* pp. 239–49; Lebsock, "Radical Reconstruction and the Property Rights of Southern Women," *Journal of Southern History* 43 (May 1977): 195–216; Jonathan M. Wiener, "Female Planters and Planters' Wives in Civil War and Reconstruction," *Alabama Review* 30 (April 1977): 135–49.

9. For economic background see Steven Hahn, *The Roots of Southern Populism* (New York: Oxford University Press, 1983).

10. The most forceful argument for the paternalist family theme is in Wyatt-Brown, *Southern Honor,* esp. pp. 174–76, 199–226, 291.

11. See Scott, *Southern Lady,* chap. 5.

12. Michael Anderson, *Approaches to the History of the Western Family* (Bristol, England: MacMillan Press, 1980).

13. See Gloria L. Main, "Probate Records as a Source for Early American History," *William and Mary Quarterly,* 3d ser., 32 (January 1975): 89–99; Carole Shammas, "Constructing a Wealth Distribution from Probate Records," *Journal of Interdisciplinary History* 9 (Autumn 1978): 297–308.

14. See Mel Albin, ed., *New Directions in Psychohistory* (Lexington, Mass.: Lexington Books, 1980).

15. Elizabeth Fox-Genovese and Eugene Genovese, "Antebellum Political Economists and the Problem of Slavery in a Worldwide Capitalist Mode" (Paper presented at the Organization of American Historians Annual Meeting, Los Angeles, April 1984).

16. E. Brooks Holifield, *The Gentlemen Theologians* (Durham: Duke University Press, 1978); Anne C. Loveland, *Southern Evangelicals and Social Order, 1800–1860* (Baton Rouge: Louisiana State University Press, 1980).

17. James Oakes, *The Ruling Race* (New York: Knopf, 1982).

18. Philip J. Greven, *The Protestant Temperament* (New York: Knopf, 1977). Greven has little to say about the South.

The Web of Southern Social Relations

The Experiences and Status of Women in the Chesapeake, 1750–1775

Lorena S. Walsh

In the third quarter of the eighteenth century, the maturation of colonial society in the Chesapeake had many implications for the character and quality of women's existence. First, changes in the makeup of the population, in marriage patterns, and in the degree of economic opportunity, as well as increased longevity, helped to shape new life courses for women. Second, new relationships emerged within the family, which for white women meant coping with the increasingly patriarchal attitudes of fathers and husbands. Black women had to find ways to raise children in a slave society that enabled them to rely on the help of many kinfolk but might result in their arbitrary separation from their mates and adolescent offspring.

These women's lives differed markedly from those of earlier generations of Chesapeake women. Until the end of the seventeenth century most had immigrated from Britain or from Africa by way of the West Indies while in their late teens or early twenties. The great majority had come to work, either involuntarily for life as slaves or voluntarily for a term of four to five years as servants. In the Chesapeake they were subject to hazards they might have avoided by staying at home: death from "seasoning" as they became exposed to a new disease environment; for white women constant hoeing in the tobacco and corn fields instead of, or in addition to, household duties; and a greater likelihood of bearing an illegitimate child in a land where white servants could not marry during their contracted term and where slave unions might be severed by their owners.

For white women who survived their term of service, opportunities had been great. Men heavily outnumbered women—three to one among immigrants across much of the seventeenth century—so they were certain to find husbands. The typical former servant woman had married in her mid-twenties and consequently would bear her husband a small number of children—on average only three to four—because she had remained single for up to ten years of her childbearing life. In the harsh disease environment of the colonial Chesapeake, many infants died, and adults had short life spans as well. Since men often did not marry until their late twenties or early thirties, immigrant women tended to outlive their first husbands and frequently took second mates. In part because they usually brought valuable assets to a second marriage and were the link that joined households composed of children of one or more marriages, wives' power within the family was generally greater than it would have been elsewhere.[1]

Immigrant slave women, in contrast to their white counterparts, had limited opportunities to marry and raise families. Before the 1690s, many belonged to masters who owned only a few other blacks. By the early eighteenth century, when slaves were more heavily concentrated on large estates, they still lived in scattered quarters that seldom housed more than twenty to thirty men, women, and children. With freedom of movement off the plantation restricted, some may never have found acceptable partners. Although, as among whites, black men outnumbered women well into the eighteenth century, African women in the Chesapeake were slow to choose mates and begin bearing children, perhaps because of isolation, a diversity of tribal origins and languages, chronic ill health, and extreme alienation. African-born women had, on the average, only three children, at least one of whom would die in infancy.

Girls born to immigrant mothers both black and white had quite different experiences. The daughters of white immigrants—girls coming of age in the 1670s through the 1730s—tended to marry at a young age, often well below twenty. Pressures for early weddings were great because men continued to outnumber women and couples found it relatively easy to accumulate enough assets to set up a household. Although early death remained the fate of most, women wed so young in the first half of the eighteenth century, and usually to men in their early twenties, that their marriages lasted longer—twenty to twenty-five years on average compared to nine to thirteen years for their mothers. Consequently, they had more children—six overall and nine if the mother survived to the end of her childbearing years. Afro-American girls coming of age in the early eighteenth century found a large surplus of both Creole and African males, and they chose partners and began having children in their late

2

teens. Thus their families were nearly three times as large as those of immigrant black women.[2]

As many as half of these girls had lost at least one parent before they came of age, and many had lost both and consequently had spent some years in the homes of stepparents, guardians, masters, or, in the case of blacks, perhaps unrelated slave women. Therefore, marrying early and setting up their own households may have seemed especially attractive. Often there were no parents to interfere with their choice of mates, and high rates of premarital pregnancy among native white girls suggests that their courting was little supervised. A major difference from the immigrant generation was that most had one or more siblings living nearby. Perhaps in part because they lacked other kin, Creole brothers and sisters tended to form close ties that were retained throughout their lives.[3]

By the 1750s, few English women chose to immigrate to the Chesapeake. White female servants were an increasingly less visible part of the labor force and a very small proportion of the adult female population. As in earlier years, a former servant's chance to rise in status lay in marriage. But there was no longer a shortage of women, and probably few former servants, especially the increasing proportion who had come as convicts, were able to contract advantageous matches. From the beginning of the eighteenth century, the region's white population was predominantly native-born, sharing common beliefs and habits that provided the norm to which newcomers had to adjust. Newly enslaved Africans continued to augment the numbers of blacks, but by midcentury the majority of them as well had been born and raised in the Chesapeake. Consequently, the remainder of this essay will deal only with the experiences of Creole women.

White women marrying in the 1750s, 1760s, and 1770s spent more time at home before becoming wives and mothers than did their predecessors. Fewer married in their teens, and most married between the ages of twenty and twenty-four. Their spouses also tended to be older, usually in their late twenties. This disparity in age was in part attributable to a more nearly equal sex ratio and reflected changing cultural ideals and economic constraints as well. More parents survived to see their elder offspring educated and raised to maturity and were able to supervise their courtships and advise them in their marriages. Parents may also have encouraged daughters to delay marriage until their chosen partners had established themselves, which apparently was becoming increasingly difficult for poorer whites in tidewater areas, for the daughters of tenant farmers tended to marry about two years later than did the offspring of landowners. Some daughters of small planters also must have had to marry

3

downward into the class of tenant farmers because their families were increasingly unable to provide the dower assets that would permit unions with more propertied spouses. In contrast, women living in newly settled piedmont areas, where economic opportunity was greater, continued to marry at younger ages.[4]

Despite these changes, marriage still offered almost the only way for a woman to enhance her status and make her future secure. If she remained single, she was likely to spend most of her life as a servant to others or as a little-respected dependent in someone else's house, and she might well fall mercy to charity or poor relief when she could no longer support herself.

The benefits of marriage were clear—being mistress of her own household, fulfilling community and family expectations, raising children in a secure environment, and certain entitlement to a sizable portion of her husband's estate if he died first. To the modern eye, the attendant costs also seem high. At common law, the husband and father had nearly absolute authority over his wife and children, including the right to administer physical correction. A wife was unable to make contracts or to own property unless she negotiated a premarital contract, and she could not make gifts or write a will without her mate's consent. She owed her husband total obedience, and he could do what he wished with any property she brought unencumbered to the marriage or that they accumulated together. He also controlled the management and took the profits of any property in which she had a life interest, and he could appropriate any wages she might earn.

Common law restrictions did not, however, fully describe reality. Except in very wealthy households, the wife was of critical importance to the household economy, and her wishes had to be taken into account. Husbands usually recognized their wives' joint authority in raising the children, and some granted their spouses much more latitude in running the family's economic affairs than the bare law suggests. Clearly both husbands and the community as a whole usually had faith in the wife's capacity to manage children and property. Most men who made wills named their wives as executors, and if there was no will the courts made the widow the administrator if she wished to be. When there were minor children they were almost always left to the care of their mother whether by direction in a will or by the court's decision.[5]

The prevailing legal and societal restrictions did mean, however, that the nearly inevitable decision to marry had graver consequences for women than for men. If a woman made an unfortunate choice of a husband or if she found normative pressures demanding wifely submission and subordination distasteful, she was nonetheless trapped. Absolute divorces could not be gotten in either Virginia or Maryland. Legal separations were difficult to obtain and left the woman unable to remarry and unlikely to be able to collect any support payments awarded her if her partner decided to run off. Although a man was legally no freer to escape a bad marriage than was his wife, he could much more easily arrange to spend most of his time away from home and at the same time had full use of her property as well. If a wife deserted her husband, she was committing a final act of desperation, leaving her a social and economic outcast.

Given these difficulties, one might expect that women would have taken steps to protect themselves before they married. Marriage contracts that used third-party trusts to bypass the penalties of coverture and were enforceable in courts of equity might have permitted a married woman to control the property she brought to the marriage. A recent study shows, however, that these were little used in Maryland for a girl's first marriage, and there is scant reason to believe that Virginia women were any more prudent. Apparently young women (and/or their fathers or guardians) believed that their dower rights offered them sufficient protection, or perhaps they tended to trust that their mates would not act contrary to their interests.[6]

Nonetheless, the restrictions imposed by coverture did adversely affect some married women. Disagreements about the management or disposition of dower property were a major cause of legal separations and must have troubled many marriages that remained intact. If a husband could not disinherit his wife at death, he could waste her property during his lifetime. Chesapeake law offered some protection by preventing husbands from selling away land without the wife's consent. Maryland courts seem to have interpreted a law that required two justices of the peace to ascertain her wishes in private very strictly. This was probably the case, too, in much of tidewater Virginia, where many men did not consider themselves free to proceed with transfers until their wives also agreed to the sale. Some other Virginia county courts, however, especially those in the newer piedmont areas, apparently often neglected to get the wife's consent before a sale was completed, thereby leaving her little effective say in the matter. The wife had either to give pro forma assent or openly oppose her spouse's dealings. Nor was there anything to prevent a husband in either colony from coercing his wife into a dower release.[7]

Certainly a number of women who survived their first husbands were unwilling to surrender their autonomy so totally a second time. Many more widows than single girls negotiated premarital contracts that occasionally permitted them some control of their property and even more frequently provided for its ultimate division among their children.

Clearly there was little in a white girl's upbringing that would have encouraged the self-confidence required to insist on special measures for her later protection. As very young children, daughters and sons probably received equal shares of family attention and affection, but when children reached the age of about five or six, some segregation of the sexes began. Boys started to help their fathers in the fields and at other outside work, while girls began to aid their mothers with more specifically feminine domestic chores in the kitchen, laundry, dairy, vegetable garden, poultry house, and sickroom. The degree of work segregation differed with the level of family affluence. In small planter households, there were undoubtedly times when all members of the family did their turn in the fields. Among the wealthy, slaves increasingly performed the most laborious plantation chores, leaving to the planter's wife and daughters supervision of household help and the less arduous tasks of food preparation, washing, sewing, gardening, poultry raising, and child care. By the mid-eighteenth century, more spacious and better-furnished upper-class houses required more time to maintain and enclosed the females of the family in a more clearly defined domestic space.[8]

White parents at every wealth level seem almost universally to have expected that all their daughters would eventually become wives, and their training was tailored accordingly. Directions for education made by fathers in their wills or stipulations by county courts when orphans were bound out reveal something of the norms and expectations for daughters. Some concerned kinfolk hoped that little girls would be spared sheer drudgery—"working at the hoe," "tending corn and tobacco," and "pounding the mortar." Whereas their brothers were often to learn a trade, special training for girls was limited to the domestic arts of sewing and "other huswifery" and increasingly, carding and spinning. York County, Virginia, tailor Reginald Orton, for example, stipulated in his will of 1752 that his son William have "sufficient schooling" but only that his daughters Mary and Elizabeth "be brought up in a Godly decent and genteel manner."[9]

Orphan indentures providing for schooling show lesser expectations for the education of poor girls—only one year of formal schooling if schooling was required at all (just enough "to learn to read distinctly in the Bible") and almost never training in writing. From the 1720s nearly all bound female orphans in Maryland counties were supposed to learn to read. In Virginia, a law of 1705 required guardians of minor children

6

to teach all their charges to read and write. But the degree to which this law was enforced—especially for the girls—is questionable, for many Virginia women were still unable to write in the later eighteenth century.[10]

Still, as parents lived longer and there were more friends or relations available and willing to take in orphaned children, fewer girls ended up bound out by the courts. Those who did were usually orphaned at less vulnerable ages and had the benefit of legal protections established in an earlier period, when many more young children had needed community protection to an even greater degree. Apprenticed orphans could not be sold to other masters without the permission of the court, and they could complain if they were ill-treated.

It is difficult to judge how effective these protections were. Male orphans and immigrant female servants did turn to the court for redress, but Creole girls seldom did so. We do not know whether poor orphan girls were usually well treated or whether many were not but were too intimidated to complain. Flagrant cruelty could hardly be long concealed from watchful neighbors, but simple neglect or harsh but not vicious treatment must sometimes have gone unreported. Similarly, some guardians of better-off, orphaned girls took great pains to dress and educate them as befitted their family's status, but others seem to have badly neglected their wards. Unless there were male relatives to intervene, these girls had little chance for remedy until they reached majority (sixteen in Maryland, twenty-one in Virginia unless a lesser age had been specified).

Even when parents survived, and often when they were in a position to school all their children, conceptions of "education as is suitable for Woomen" remained limited. Fathers making provisions for minor children by will often directed that the girls spend only a year or so at school, yet their brothers were often to have an additional six months to a year learning writing as well as reading. This restriction was no severe handicap so long as many men remained unlettered and most important economic transactions were negotiated by word of mouth. In these circumstances women were usually privy to most of their husbands' affairs. Once sons began to get appreciably better educations than daughters, however, women found themselves at a decided disadvantage.

In less affluent households, later eighteenth-century daughters may have had little formal schooling, but they did spend more time learning the art of housekeeping—a task that was becoming more complex as families became larger and women spent more time in home care, needlework, gardening, dairying, poultry-raising, brewing, cooking, preserving, and soap- and candle-making. By the 1750s they were also making

7

greater contributions to family prosperity through textile production. In most parts of the Chesapeake, carding and spinning of wool and cotton and hackling and spinning of flax were uncommon until midcentury. Thereafter women more frequently made yarn, thread, and coarse cloth that substituted for expensive imports and allowed the family to spend any surpluses that might be accumulated on a greater variety of foreign manufactured goods.[11]

Not surprisingly, very rich fathers were more likely than poorer men to provide some education for their daughters. Wealthy fathers often engaged tutors who provided some advanced learning for all the children. For instance, in 1774 the girls of the affluent Carter family at Nomini Hall did not learn Latin as did their brothers, but they were reading in a variety of sources, writing, and even learning arithmetic. Time was devoted as well to the social graces—dancing, music, and polite conversation—that were essential to the increasingly formalized and intricate courtship ritual. Although by the end of the colonial era, some Chesapeake women were still totally illiterate, a substantial number had not learned to write, and even among the elite, daughters were still getting an unequal education compared to sons, most women were better educated than their mothers had been, and some were demonstrably better educated.

Although later eighteenth-century Creole girls were more mature when they married than their mothers had been, they were hardly encouraged to develop well-rounded personalities. The increasingly sharp differentiation of male and female roles permitted only a very limited sphere in which girls could exercise their new skills and learning. Women were increasingly advised to cultivate only the passive aspects of their temperaments. To secure a husband, they had to appear modest and amiable, and once married, they were expected to be in every way submissive and accommodating to their spouses. They were taught that their intellects were inferior to men's, that their powers of reasoning were weaker, and in general that their sex was inferior, much in need of the protection of more powerful males.[12]

Single, adult daughters of small planters may have gained increasing experience in managing on their own. Fathers who willed girls a house, ground to plant a garden and to raise flax and corn, and pasture for their livestock (rather than instructing their brothers to support them) clearly thought the daughters could (and would prefer to) take care of themselves. A poorer girl who had been bound out had often acquired skills that would enable her to hire herself out as a housekeeper or earn some income from sewing, spinning, or weaving until she found a husband.

8

Daughters who were to inherit more valuable assets probably seldom controlled their property before marriage. Arrangements for leasing land and hiring out slaves were surely most often made by stepfathers, brothers, or male guardians.

Parents expected their daughters to choose husbands wisely, not to "join in marriage with some undeserving fellow as a degradation of herself and family." Although there is little evidence of matches arranged solely by the parents, undoubtedly most girls did seek the advice of parents or guardians before marrying, and those under age had to do so. An increasingly high proportion of marriages between cousins suggests the strong power of family ties. Girls who disregarded their relatives' wishes faced severe disapproval and sometimes outright disinheritance. William Byrd II, for example, concurred with Mary Randolph Fleming's distress and rage when her daughter married her uncle's overseer. The man, Byrd stated, "has not one visible qualification except impudence to recommend him to a female's inclinations." Had the daughter "run away with a gentleman or a pretty fellow there might have been some excuse for her, though he were of inferior fortune; but to stoop to a dirty plebian without any kind of merit is the lowest prostitution."[13]

Courtship practices among the eighteenth-century elite are well documented. A round of dances, barbecues, fish feasts, musicals, dinners, and more casual visits afforded young people opportunity to assess one another's merits. For common planter families courting is less well described, although harvest frolics, country dances, and meetings at horse races, cockfights, and church must have served the same purpose as the more carefully arranged pastimes of the upper classes.[14]

Comte de Rochambeau observed that Chesapeake "girls enjoy the utmost freedom until they are married . . . once married they give themselves entirely to their new authority."[15] Undoubtedly the early freedom he observed was largely illusory. Unless women lived in one of the few Chesapeake towns and possessed the business skills necessary to run a tavern or a shop, they had only a somewhat augmented freedom to choose a suitable mate before they reached an age that branded them "old maids." Their main destiny was to catch a husband—and family connections and assets helped to determine what sort of husband a girl could attract.

Providing for daughters' portions was just one part of a family's strategy for passing assets from one generation to the next. The interests of spouses and sons also had to be considered, and these were often foremost in a father's mind. In any event, daughters' portions were intended not to supply an independent support but to enable them to become "better provided for by marriage." Men who failed to make wills relegated their daughters to the provisions of the laws of intestacy that afforded them an equal share of personal property with their younger brothers after the mother's dower had been deducted but awarded all the land to the eldest son. Fathers who wrote wills could divide assets differently. In fact, the majority of will-makers were men with land who wanted to divide the family's acres between a greater number of heirs. In the seventeenth century propertied fathers often gave land to daughters as well as sons, a practice attributable both to the abundance of land and to the need for sure resources to maintain young girls in a place where they might have no relatives.

By the eighteenth century, among the better off, the nature of property to be transmitted had shifted from land as the single major valuable asset to both land and slaves. As settlement thickened, land was no longer plentiful in older areas, and fathers increasingly awarded family acres only to male heirs. The numbers of slaves continued to grow, however, and more and more daughters received slaves as part of their dowries along with the traditional beds, pots, and livestock. Even on the frontier, later eighteenth-century fathers were likely to divide their more abundant acres only among their sons, probably in part because slaves now made a suitable dowry for a daughter in need of a husband. Property devolution thus became increasingly segregated by sex. Land became a predominantly male inheritance, but slaves were distributed among daughters as well as sons. Often sons inherited fewer laborers than they needed to farm their estates. New economic units had then to be assembled through a series of strategic marriages. This scheme worked to retain land more consistently within the family lineage. Daughters could attract propertied mates with valuable human dowries and no longer had to be given land that would then pass outside the family.[16]

Once a woman married, she became a fully responsible member of the community with the duty of supervising her own household. This could indeed be an onerous task, and it was supposed to occupy her time fully. Wives who aspired to be "notable women" almost universally meant no more than that they intended to become exemplary household managers. Only near the end of the century did the majority of farmers own slaves, and even then, most slaveowners commanded so few blacks that they must have employed their laborers almost exclusively in the fields, including very probably a number of families who considered themselves gentry. In households just above the average level of wealth, the mistress was probably directly responsible for feeding and clothing the family's slaves besides caring for her own children. Only the local aristocracy, less than 10 percent of the white population, could spare slaves for waiting at table, cooking elaborate meals, or looking after the master's and mistress's wardrobes. Married women then must have looked forward to the time when their daughters became old enough to take over some of the burden of routine household chores.[17]

A wife usually conceived soon after her wedding and could expect to be pregnant every other year until her early forties, should she survive to that age—and more often if a child was stillborn or died soon after birth. The typical woman marrying after 1750 would bear six or seven children. (Achieved family size is always smaller than the maximum number of children—ten to twelve—who might potentially be conceived. Not all women married at exactly the same age, and not all survived to the end of their reproductive years.) Despite this increasing burden, most colonial Chesapeake women chose to nurse their infants unless illness required that they engage a poor white or slave wetnurse. These frequent pregnancies tended to sap a woman's strength and left her vulnerable to disease and especially susceptible to attacks of malaria as well as periodically exposing her to the risks of death in childbirth or from childbed infections. Despite these hazards, by the 1750s more women were surviving to age forty than had women of their mothers' generation. Still, they were well aware that they were more likely to die during their twenties and thirties than were men. Almost all had known relatives and friends who had met such a fate. So most were justly apprehensive about the dangers of giving birth. In addition, infant and childhood mortality improved but little. The deaths of one out of five children before their fifth birthday and of another before age twenty took a heavy emotional toll. [18]

Since most married women were soon encumbered with pregnancy, nursing, and caring for young and often sick children, their chances for getting far from home were limited. Their spouses could escape the monotony of daily routine with trips to stores, militia musters, the county court, or the capital, or with visits to friends and business associates. Women had to content themselves with visits to nearby plantations—usually to farms no more than five miles distant—or with longer exchanges with relatives where arrangements could be made for child care. As one Virginia planter explained when declining an invitation to visit friends, "Ladies who have Children to teach, and cloth to weave, & poultry to raise, and the Kitchen and Dairy, and Store Room, and Dining room to attend to, can only visit at particular seasons." Consequently, although extending hospitality to a stream of visitors added greatly to the housewife's burdens, it also provided her a welcome change and a chance to see fresh faces.[19]

As more women learned to read and write, they also had greater opportunities to maintain contact with childhood friends and relatives who lived farther away. Although marriage frequently continued to demand that a woman leave family and friends behind, she was more often able to maintain contact with other women whose fortunes and support were important to her.[20]

Because married white women appear only infrequently in the legal records that are most likely to have survived, we have to infer much about how their husbands regarded them from evidence that came as the marriage was ending and the husband wrote his will. Comparable studies of testamentary practices in England are rare, but it does seem clear that the English precedents selected in the Chesapeake made the legal framework there more favorable than it was in England. A woman's dower rights to freehold land were more certain than were her rights to land held under a greater variety of tenures in England. She had an enhanced right as well to a substantial share of the personal estate, although there were differences between Maryland and Virginia law as to how much she might claim.

Maryland had perhaps the most liberal dower law of all the mainland colonies, allowing the widow to renounce her husband's will and claim thirds of personal as well as real property. (By the end of the seventeenth century, English women had lost the right to claim dower in personalty if their spouses willed them less.) Arrangements in Virginia were somewhat less liberal. There widows could claim a third of the slaves for life only and were not able to sell or give them away, as widows could do in Maryland. In addition, a Virginia widow got only a child's portion of other personal property if there were more than two children. Still, dower rights awarded the wife a substantial share of family property if there was no will and established the minimum that a man could bequeath his spouse if he wrote a will.

In England at this time, many men were making wills in part to restrict the amount of family property their widows would inherit. In contrast, the majority of Chesapeake husbands chose to give their widows more than their dower rights in real and personal property. This inheritance was often in the form of a life estate in the dwelling plantation and in the seventeenth century was rarely restricted either to the children's minority or to widowhood. During the eighteenth century widows on the whole lost ground. They were less likely than earlier to receive more than a dower share of property, although they also more often renounced wills that offered less and took their dower instead. More important, the interest bequeathed wives in land began to be contingent on their remaining unmarried, and there was an increasing tendency as well to restrict the widow's use of personalty to life or sometimes to widowhood. More husbands came to think like a man who provided generously for his widow so long as she remained single but directed that if she remarried, she "may have her due and begone." Although the majority of testators continued to appoint their wives as executors, here too women lost ground. A growing proportion of husbands excluded them altogether, and sons or other male relatives were more often made coexecutors.

These more restrictive arrangements still guaranteed the widow's immediate provision but without risking improper use of the children's shares by stepfathers or postponing distribution of property to children beyond the time their mother required it for comfortable support. By the 1750s wives were likely to be in their forties or fifties when their husbands died, and some of their offspring would already be of age. Because there was less necessity for them to take new husbands—and with more balanced sex ratios, fewer chances to remarry even if they wished to do so—widowhood restrictions may have been acceptable to many older women. A widow's comfort must have depended a good deal on whether her settlement gave her control over her own household. Unless his wife was very elderly, the husband always gave her property rather than instructing his children to provide her with maintenance. If she received the dwelling plantation for life or widowhood, however, she might have to share it with an inheriting son, who might well demand the management of it. Perhaps most women who had thus far lived their lives in male-dominated households felt ill-equipped to take up running a farm in late middle age, but some must surely have wished to do so.[21]

For much of the period between 1750 and 1775, black women shared the doubtful advantages of greater equality with black men—usually the equal privilege of working with hoes and axes in the tobacco, corn, and grain fields. Increasingly, economic diversification offered black males more time at tasks such as carting, plowing, cutting timber, sowing grain, mowing, ditching, and the more skilled jobs of shoemaking, blacksmithing, coopering, gardening, fishing, erecting farm buildings, and running mills. To the extent that there was occupational differentiation, black women were assigned slightly less arduous but low-status jobs like grubbing swamps and grassy, fallow fields; hand weeding; building fences; gathering and spreading manure; and cleaning harvested grain. No wonder slaves looked forward to times when all worked together—at the grain harvest, corn husking, and tobacco stripping, for example.

The fate of most eighteenth-century black women was almost uninterrupted field labor. Some adolescent girls were sent to the great house to care for white children and to wait on the adults. But about the time they bore their first child, most would be sent back to the fields to work until old age or ill health no longer permitted it. Most older black women and those who managed to escape the fields entirely were assigned to domestic production—spinning, weaving, dairying, and poultry raising, or to service tasks like cooking and washing. Few apparently had much role in household management—poor white women were hired as housekeepers when these were deemed necessary.[22]

Black women continued to marry early and usually bore a total of six to eight children, although one-quarter of the children would die in their first year and almost as many again before age fifteen. These grievous losses were undoubtedly attributable both to low birth weights among slave babies brought on by the mother doing continual heavy field labor during pregnancy and to the poor care black mothers were allowed to give their offspring after they were born. Most had to return to the fields soon after delivery and were allowed only limited time to nurse their infants. Once weaned, the youngsters were left to the care of slightly older children or to old women while the parents worked.[23]

Many slave women were of necessity primarily responsible for raising their children. Those living on large estates often found husbands on the same plantation and with time were usually allowed to share a cabin with their mates. Many masters encouraged marriages within the plantation community, recognizing that women and men separated from their mates often worked less willingly and might even run off to visit their spouses at critical times in the plantation calendar. Thomas Jefferson, for example, gave couples who married on the plantation a bed and a pot but awarded no such advantages to those who chose mates who belonged to other masters.

Women who were owned by small planters or who lived on isolated quarters must often have had to choose partners who lived elsewhere. The woman usually moved out of her mother's cabin and into one of her own when her first child was born. Her husband normally could visit only on occasional weekends and so could not help with the day-to-day upbringing of the children. Joseph Ball of Lancaster County, for example, directed that his slave man Jo have the use of a horse to visit his wife once a month. "If his wife and he are so fond of one another," he added, "she must come at other times to him."[24] Thus it was often largely up to the mother to pass on to the child the history of her people and appropriate strategies for surviving in slavery. But if a woman's spouse was often absent, she almost always had a number of kinfolk living in the same quarter. She could turn to her mother, sisters, brothers, uncles, aunts, or cousins for companionship, a limited degree of protection from the master, and help with childrearing.

Most slaveowners apparently tried to keep mothers and young children together, but black family life was always less secure than that of whites. In addition to the possibility that one of the parents might die young, division of an estate, the forced sale of slaves for debt, or a master's decision to establish a new quarter on the frontier all could separate wives from husbands and mothers from older children.[25]

The position of black women in the Chesapeake improved only slightly in the later eighteenth century. They did come to live with a number of supportive kinfolk, and almost all could find mates and have children. Their lives, however, might always be disrupted by the actions of their owners. As slaves, they were not allowed to do much to improve their material conditions. Some slave women may have earned small sums of money by selling poultry or garden produce that they raised, and the few who worked in and around the master's dwelling occasionally received tips from visitors. Such bits and pieces were probably soon spent for food or clothing because Chesapeake slaves (unlike those in South Carolina, for example) were usually not allowed to own valuable livestock or to pass inheritances to their children. Finally, to the extent that male and female work roles diverged, black women were increasingly relegated to the most monotonous and least desirable farm chores.[26]

In many of the ways that we measure well-being, white women, in contrast, gained in the later eighteenth-century Chesapeake. They increasingly grew up in more stable families, enjoyed somewhat longer life spans, received some or better education, and most had access for the first time to some conveniences and amenities in the home. Growing differentiation of men's and women's occupations exempted white women from some of the worst sorts of drudgery. At the same time they continued to enjoy a more favorable legal position than did women in England and in many other mainland colonies. In other ways, however, their status was eroding. As fathers and husbands lived longer, men were in a better position to maintain a more authoritative role in managing the family, while daughters and wives were relegated to a more clearly articulated subordinate status. Earlier, free women had often exercised unusual power in the family largely as a result of demographic accidents. By the later eighteenth century, the patterns of their lives were more secure and more protected but at the cost of smaller chances to manage property or to assume an equal rather than a subordinate role in marriage.

Notes

1. This material is presented and documented in Lois Green Carr and Lorena S. Walsh, "The Planter's Wife: The Experience of White Women in Seventeenth-Century Maryland," *William and Mary Quarterly*, 3d ser., 34 (1977): 542–71 (hereafter *WMQ*).

2. See Russell R. Menard, "The Maryland Slave Population, 1658–1730: A Demographic Profile of Blacks in Four Counties," *WMQ*, 3d ser., 32 (1975): 29–54.

3. Darrett B. Rutman and Anita H. Rutman, "Now-Wives and Sons-in-Law: Parental Death in a Seventeenth-Century Virginia County," in Thad W. Tate and David L. Ammerman, eds., *The Chesapeake in the Seventeenth Century: Essays on Anglo-American Society* (Chapel Hill: University of North Carolina Press, 1979); Rutman and Rutman, *A Place in Time: Middlesex County, Virginia, 1650–1750* (New York: Norton, 1984), chap. 4; Rutman and Rutman, *A Place in Time: Explicatus* (New York: Norton, 1984), chaps. 4, 5, 6, and 8; Russell R. Menard and Lorena S. Walsh, "The Demography of Somerset County, Maryland: A Progress Report," in *The Newberry Papers in Family and Community History* (Chicago: Newberry Library, 1981).

4. For later demographic developments see Allan Kulikoff, "Tobacco and Slaves: The Development of Southern Cultures in the Chesapeake Colonies, 1680–1780," manuscript in preparation kindly shared by the author. See also Nancy Oberseider, "A Socio-Demographic Study of the Family as a Social Unit in Tidewater Virginia, 1660–1776" (Ph.D. dissertation, University of Maryland, 1975).

5. This discussion is more fully presented in Lois Green Carr and Lorena S. Walsh, "Woman's Role in the Eighteenth-Century Chesapeake," paper presented at a conference on Women in Early America, November 1981, Williamsburg, Virginia.

6. Marylynn Salmon, "The Property Rights of Women in Early America: A Comparative Study" (Ph.D. dissertation, Bryn Mawr College, 1980).

7. The issue of dower release merits systematic investigation. Kulikoff, "Tobacco and Slaves," and Lorena S. Walsh, "Till Death Us Do Part: Marriage and Family in Seventeenth-Century Maryland," in Tate and Ammerman, eds., *The Chesapeake in the Seventeenth Century*, provide examples of the disputes that might arise over property. See also Helen Mast Robinson, "The Status of the Femme Covert in Eighteenth-Century Virginia" (M.A. thesis, University of Virginia, 1971).

8. Daniel Blake Smith, *Inside the Great House: Planter Family Life in Eighteenth-Century Society* (Ithaca: Cornell University Press, 1980), and Jan Lewis, *The Pursuit of Happiness: Family and Values in Jefferson's Virginia* (New York: Cambridge University Press, 1983), discuss childrearing practices and their implications. For changes in work patterns see Cary Carson and Lorena S. Walsh,

"The Material Life of the Early American Housewife," paper presented at a conference on Women in Early America, November 1981, Williamsburg, Virginia.

9. York County Wills and Inventories, liber 20, f. 434. Educational provisions are discussed in Lorena S. Walsh, "Child Custody in the Early Colonial Chesapeake: A Case Study," paper presented at the Fifth Berkshire Conference, June 1981; in Carr and Walsh, "Women's Role"; and in Thomas K. Bullock, "Schools and Schooling in Eighteenth-Century Virginia" (Ed.D. dissertation, Duke University, 1961). For courts see Evelyn McNeill Thomas, "Orphans' Courts in Colonial Virginia" (M.A. thesis, College of William and Mary, 1964), and Lois Green Carr, "The Development of the Maryland Orphans' Count, 1654–1715," in Aubrey C. Land, Lois Green Carr, and Edward C. Papenfuse, eds., *Law, Society, and Politics in Early Maryland* (Baltimore: Johns Hopkins University Press, 1977).

10. Kenneth Lockridge, *Literacy in Colonial New England: An Inquiry into the Social Context of Literacy in the Early Modern West* (New York: Norton, 1974). Rutman and Rutman, *A Place in Time: Explicatus,* chap. 11, present similar findings and show in addition that daughters of poor men were much less likely to be literate than were their brothers.

11. Carson and Walsh, "The Material Life of the Early American Housewife." Julia Cherry Spruill, *Women's Life and Work in the Southern Colonies* (1938; rpr. New York: Norton, 1972), remains the best published source.

12. Women's perceptions of inferiority are well documented in Mary Beth Norton, *Liberty's Daughters: The Revolutionary Experience of American Women, 1750–1800* (Boston: Little, Brown, 1980).

13. Louis B. Wright, ed., *The Prose Works of William Byrd of Westover* (Cambridge, Mass., Harvard University Press, 1966), p. 342.

14. Jane Carson, *Colonial Virginians at Play* (Williamsburg: Colonial Williamsburg Foundation, 1965), discusses recreational and social activities.

15. Charles Sherrill, ed., *French Memories of Eighteenth Century America* (New York: Charles Scribner's Sons, 1915), p. 65.

16. Inheritance practices are discussed in Lois Green Carr, "Inheritance in the Colonial Chesapeake," paper presented at the Social Science History Association, Bloomington, 1982.

17. Carson and Walsh, "The Material Life of the Early American Housewife."

18. The demographic evidence is summarized in Kulikoff, "Tobacco and Slaves." See also Darrett B. Rutman and Anita H. Rutman, "Of Agues and Fevers: Malaria in the Early Chesapeake," *WMQ*, 3d ser., 33 (1976): 31–60.

19. Cocke Deposit, MSS, Alderman Library, University of Virginia, quoted in Boyd Coyner, "John Hartwell Cocke of Bremo," (Ph.D. dissertation, University of Virginia, 1961), pp. 57–58. Women's geographic networks are discussed in Lorena S. Walsh, "Women's Networks in the Colonial Chesapeake," paper presented at the annual meeting of the Organization of American Historians, Cin-

cinnati, 1983. See also John Robert Sellers, "The Leisure Time of the Plantation Mistress in Colonial Virginia" (M.A. thesis, Tulane University, 1964).

20. See Norton, *Liberty's Daughters,* and Smith, *Inside the Great House.* Linda K. Kerber, *Women of the Republic: Intellect and Ideology in Revolutionary America* (Chapel Hill: University of North Carolina Press, 1980), discusses changes in women's education and attitudes toward it in the revolutionary era.

21. The literature on women and inheritance is extensive. See especially Carr and Walsh, "The Planter's Wife" and "Women's Role"; Smith, *Inside the Great House;* and Linda Speth, "Southern Women and Probate Records: The Transfer of Property and Authority in Southside Virginia, 1735–1775," paper presented at the Fifth Berkshire Conference, June 1981. For an excellent discussion of problems and approaches see Toby Lee Ditz, "Ownership and Obligation: Family and Inheritance in Five Connecticut Towns, 1750–1820" (Ph.D. dissertation, Columbia University, 1982). James W. Deen, Jr., "Patterns of Testation in Four Tidewater Counties in Colonial Virginia," *American Journal of Legal History* 16 (1972): 154–76; and Joan R. Gundersen and Gwen Victor Gampel, "Married Women's Legal Status in Eighteenth-Century New York and Virginia," *WMQ,* 3d ser., 39 (1982): 114–34, are relevant to some of the issues discussed.

22. Carole Shammas, "Mammy and Miss Ellen in Colonial Virginia?" paper presented at a conference on Women in Early America, November 1981, Williamsburg, Virginia. These points will be further developed in a joint essay by Carr and Walsh on women's work.

23. Robert William Fogel, "Without Consent or Contract: The Rise and Fall of American Slavery," manuscript in preparation kindly shared by the author; Kulikoff, "Tobacco and Slaves."

24. Joseph Ball to Joseph Chinn, August 30, 1746, Joseph Ball Letterbook, MSS, Library of Congress.

25. For black family life see Herbert G. Gutman, *The Black Family in Slavery and Freedom, 1750–1925* (New York: Pantheon, 1977); Allan Kulikoff, "The Beginnings of the Afro-American Family in Maryland," in Michael Gordon, ed., *The American Family in Social Historical Perspective,* 2d ed. (New York: St. Martin's Press, 1978); Kulikoff, "A 'Prolifick' People: Black Population Growth in the Chesapeake Colonies, 1700–1790," *Southern Studies* 16 (1977): 391–428; Kulikoff, "The Origins of Afro-American Society in Tidewater Maryland and Virginia, 1700–1790," *WMQ,* 3d ser., 35 (1978): 226–59; and Joseph Douglas Deale, "Race and Class in Colonial Virginia: Indians, Englishmen, and Africans on the Eastern Shore during the Seventeenth Century" (Ph.D. dissertation, University of Rochester, 1981).

26. On slave work see Gerald W. Mullin, *Flight and Rebellion: Slave Resistance in Eighteenth-Century Virginia* (New York: Oxford University Press, 1975); Philip David Morgan, "The Development of Slave Culture in Eighteenth Century Plantation America" (Ph.D. dissertation, University of London, 1977); and Kulikoff, "Tobacco and Slaves."

Caught in the Web of the Big House: Women and Slavery

Catherine Clinton

I n Pauli Murray's absorbing account of her family's history, *Proud Shoes*, she provides a rare and compelling perspective on slavery and its human consequences. Weaving together oral accounts and traditional historical records, she introduces an intriguing cast of characters. Murray's moving recollections of her grandmother, Cornelia Smith, especially illuminate the complexity of antebellum southern race relations.

Born in North Carolina in 1844, the child of a slave mother and a white father, Cornelia Smith was obsessed with her ancestors. Her granddaughter recalls that tales of illustrious forefathers bolstered Cornelia's self-image during her later years. Murray recalled her grandmother's admonition: "Hold your head high and don't take a back seat to nobody. You got good blood in you—folks that counted for somebody—doctors, lawyers, judges, legislators. Aristocrats, that's what they were, going back seven generations right in this state."[1] It was not until she was older that Murray was able to decode the contempt with which her aunts and grandfather treated these accounts of white ancestors. For as she matured, Pauli Murray discovered that this aristocratic pedigree carried a price.

When her grandmother dissolved into sorrow recounting the experiences of her own mother, Harriet, Pauli Murray's appreciation of the ambivalence of these emotions increased. Harriet was a fifteen-year-old mulatto slave of indeterminate racial mixture when she was bought in 1834 by the prestigious Smith family of Orange County, North Carolina.

Dr. Francis Smith owned a home in Hillsboro, a family plantation, Price's Creek (a fourteen-hundred-acre spread within three miles of Chapel Hill), and two dozen slaves. Smith, a member of the state legislature, was one of the most influential men in the county and also served as a trustee of the nearby University of North Carolina. Dr. Smith bought Harriet as a maid for his daughter, Mary Ruffin Smith, the eldest of his three children. The two younger siblings, sons Frank and Sidney, were attending college.

Harriet proved a model servant for her mistress. Only after her marriage in 1839 to a local free-born mulatto, Reuben Day, did she relinquish her sleeping pallet outside Mary Smith's door. When Harriet chose a mate, the doctor gave his permission for the couple to marry. Day was given rights to visit Harriet in the cabin the Smiths assigned her on their Hillsboro lot. In 1842 their son Julian was born.

Day was a thrifty and energetic artisan who might have been able to purchase freedom for his wife and child if events had not intervened. When the Smith boys returned home after completing their educations, harmony within the household disintegrated. Mary Smith watched with alarm as her two brothers competed for the attention of her maid. One day, when Sidney lunged for Harriet and the ensuing fracas was heard by the entire household, Francis warned his brother to keep his hands off her. The Smith parents, embarrassed by their sons' rivalry, ignored the matter, and Mary was unable to influence her brothers' behavior.

Shortly thereafter, Sidney threatened Harriet's husband, ordering him not to return to her cabin. In 1843, after a severe beating and a death threat from both brothers, Day fled the county, leaving behind his wife and child. By now the Smith brothers' pursuit was the subject of town gossip. Abandoned by her husband, unprotected by both her mistress and the household patriarch, Harriet was at the mercy of not one but two malicious predators. Each evening, she nailed her door shut, barricading herself in her cabin. Unfortunately, these precautions failed to protect her.

One night Sidney broke into Harriet's cabin and raped her. This practice became a nightly ritual—the smashing of the door, the sound of a woman screaming, the cries for mercy, the beating, the moans, and finally silence. Members of the slave community turned a deaf ear to Harriet's shrieks, and the Smiths ignored the nocturnal disturbances. Then one evening, as Sidney left Harriet's cabin, Frank attacked his brother. The next morning a slave found Sidney unconscious in the yard, soaked in his own blood. Sidney was slow to recover from the head injury he had suffered and took to drink. After this fraternal battle, however, Sidney never again molested Harriet.

Within months Harriet gave birth to a daughter whom she named Cornelia. Although Dr. Smith and his wife were ashamed and Mary Smith was "mortified," Sidney became boastful about his slave progeny. As if this scandal were not enough, Frank soon began to visit Harriet's cabin. The slave woman did not put up a struggle; she apparently was resigned to the situation. Harriet gave birth to three more daughters within the next eight years, all fathered by Frank Smith.

The births of these mulatto babies threw the Smith family into a serious crisis. If they sold Harriet and her children, the Smiths would rightly be accused of selling their own blood. Yet these illegitimate offspring were a stain upon the honor of the Smith name. Indeed, after the second daughter was born, the family moved out of town onto the plantation to escape neighborhood gossip. Not surprisingly, Mary Smith was the most guilt-ridden of the owner family, caught between morality and her pride. The entire white household suffered the consequences. Pauli Murray effectively conveys the contradictions: "Conscience is a ruthless master and the Smiths were driven into an enslavement no less wasteful than Harriet's. They were doomed to live with blunted emotions and unnatural restraints, to keep up appearances by acting out a farce which fooled nobody and brought them little comfort."[2]

Murray finishes the saga by describing the white family's increasing isolation from society. Frank, Sidney, and Mary never married, spending their lives involved in polite "charade." The mulatto daughters were not raised in the slave quarters but within the white household. As Murray comments, "The Smiths were as incapable of treating the little girls wholly as servants as they were of recognizing them openly as kin."[3] Indeed, Cornelia and her sisters looked to Mary Smith rather than to Harriet for guidance and approval. Their aunt increasingly took control of their supervision, becoming a surrogate mother. Yet these Smith daughters remained inferiors, required to sit in the "negro balcony" of the University of North Carolina Chapel of the Cross when their aunt took them to church. Even though she took great pains with their upbringing, having them trained in the Episcopal faith before their baptism in the campus chapel (indeed, confirmed alongside the daughter of the university president), Mary Smith clearly had mixed emotions about raising these girls. A legacy of pain and ambivalence accompanied advantages of birth and rearing.[4]

The various strands of intimacies and blood which wove together black and white in the Old South created a tangle of issues that is enormously difficult to unravel. Even the passage of time does not give us enough distance from these explosive topics. Nevertheless, it is essential for our understanding of women's lives and especially for exploring sexuality in the Old South that we address these important topics.

Many complexities and myriad contradictions were apparent at the time. A survey of antebellum southern travel literature reveals references to relationships between masters and their female slaves.[5] Not only did observers mention these illicit liaisons, but several commented on the hypocrisy such connections reveal. Fanny Kemble, the famed English actress, who married a wealthy Georgia slaveowner, provides sharp commentary about her months on her husband's sea island plantation:

> Nobody pretends to deny that, throughout the South, a large proportion of the population is the offspring of white men and colored women. . . . Mr —— (and many others) speaks as if there were a natural repugnance in all whites to any alliance with the black race; and yet it is notorious, that almost every Southern planter has a family more or less numerous of illegitimate colored children. . . . If we are to admit the theory that the mixing of the races is a monstrosity, it seems almost as curious that laws should be enacted to prevent men marrying women toward whom they have an invincible natural repugnance.[6]

Kemble criticizes southerners who make racist claims about the inferiority and repulsiveness of blacks, observing tartly that despite owners' complaints that their slaves were foul-smelling, many still managed to share the beds of female chattel. She does not imagine slaves would smell any worse if they were freed.[7] Kemble, like other British critics of slavery, harps on the theme of hypocrisy.[8]

Members of the southern planter class who recorded their critiques of slavery did not often attack the immorality of owners. Most bemoaned the immorality of slaves.[9] The few who acknowledged that male planters could and did fall from grace treat the matter casually, offering a variety of lame excuses ranging from black female promiscuity to protection of white women from sexual licentiousness.

Few scholars have bothered to explore this question systematically, and, as I have argued elsewhere, their efforts have been feeble.[10] New records are available, however, and black voices—from slave narratives, from Works Progress Administration (WPA) interviews, and from documents collected by the Freedmen's Bureau—testify to the inaccuracy of "whitewashing" the slave experience. Even a cursory survey of the published nineteenth-century narratives and the WPA interviews of the twentieth century reveals scores of black descriptions of sexual connections between white masters and slave women. The passion and bitterness of this black testimony ring true.

Lewis Clarke, a former slave during the antebellum era, lectured a northern audience on behalf of abolitionism: "How you would like to have *your* sisters, and *your* wives, and *your* daughters, completely, tee-totally, and altogether, in the power of a master.—You can picture to yourselves a little, how you would feel; but oh, if I could *tell* you!" He then confessed the cruel dilemma of his sister: "She was whiter than I am, for she took more after her father. When she was sixteen years old, her master sent for her. When he sent for her again, she cried, and didn't want to go. She told mother her troubles, and she tried to encourage her to be decent, and hold up her head above such things, if she could. Her master was so mad, to think she complained to her mother, that he sold her right off to Louisiana; and we heard afterward that she died there of hard usage."[11]

Her sad fate was not uncommon. Madison Jefferson, another emancipated slave, told a similar tale: "Women who refuse to submit themselves to the brutal desires of their owners, are repeatedly whipt to subdue their virtuous repugnance, and in most instances this hellish practice is but too successful—when it fails, the women are frequently sold off to the south."[12] Jefferson went on to describe his own abusive owner, a member of the Methodist church, who beat one of his slaves senseless: "At length [he] accomplished his purpose, while she was in a state of insensibility from the effects of a felon blow inflicted by this monster."[13]

Sexual abuse of young slave girls, especially those who worked within the big house, was a crime of which many slaves complained.[14] Herbert Gutman's research indicates that these patterns of exploitation persisted past slavery. The records of the Freedmen's Bureau reveal that white men were slow to break the habit of abusing black women.[15]

Sexual abuse manifested itself in various ways. "Slave breeding" was an indignity of which many slaves complained. Slaves bitterly resented masters' attempt to control mating by matching up couples. In addition to manipulating pair bonding, some masters might rent or borrow men for stud service, subjecting their female slaves to forced breeding or rape. These inseminators appear in the slave narratives in the guise of "stock-men," "travelin' niggers," or "breedin' niggers." Casual references and the slang terms used to describe these men give credence to the commonality of such practices. One former slave recalled that stockmen were "weighed and tested." On the other extreme, a former slave recalled castrations and that "runty niggers" were operated on like hogs, "so dat dey can't have no little runty chilluns." Although Paul Escott, discussing his research on the slave narratives, warns that evidence of such incidents was rare, he argues that "mere numbers cannot suggest the suffering and degradation they caused, and it is likely that reticence caused some underreporting."[16]

Masters attempted to control reproduction in other ways. Slave women were expected to bear children as frequently as possible. If they failed to give birth, they might be sold. Barren women were shunned by their communities and punished by their owners. All of these factors impaired slave sexuality and crippled the stability of traditional family structure.

Evidence from both blacks and whites indicates that forced interracial sex was more common than slave breeding.[17] Blacks often were coaxed before they would reveal sexual exploitation. One exchange with a former slave from Alabama reflects this syndrome: " 'Granny,' I said, 'did your master harm you in another way?' She did not understand at once, then as she gained my meaning, she leaned over and answered, 'did you see dat girl in de house below here? Dat's my chile by him. I had five, but dat de only one livin' now. I didn't want him, but I couldn't do nothin'. I uster say "What do yer want of a woman all cut ter pieces like I is?" But 'twant no use.' "[18]

It is also important to note that blacks were reluctant to discuss such matters, especially with racial and sexual factors inhibiting responses. In fact, evidence from the appendixes of Escott's survey of the WPA interviews indicates that the sex and race of the interviewer influenced the frequency of former slaves' revelations concerning interracial sex. For example, more than 13 percent of the WPA interviewees confessed to having a white father when interviewed by a black female, although only 5.3 percent of those interviewed by white males responded yes to the question and only 4.4 percent of those questioned by a white woman. Concerning queries about forced sex, these ratios are even more dramatic: white female interviewers reported that only 6.1 percent of their respondents claimed slaves were sexually exploited and only 8.6 percent of those interviewed by white males. But 13 percent of those questioned by 65 black male interviewers reported forced sex and 18 percent of the former slaves interviewed by black females. If we assume that former slaves were more honest with interviewers of their own race—and indeed black women might have been more comfortable to reveal such practices to a woman than to a man—we might conclude that forced sex was a problem on roughly one out of five plantations.

An interview with former slave Harry McMillan was equally revealing.

When asked about the morality of slave women, he confessed that although most were church members, girls were more likely to succumb to sexual temptation than were boys. McMillan reported, "Sometimes the Masters, where the Mistress was a pious woman, punished the girls for having children before they were married. As a general thing the Masters did not care, they like the colored women to have children." When an interviewer directly asked McMillan, "Suppose a son of the Master wanted to have intercourse with the colored women, was he at liberty?" the former slave demurred that white owners were "not at liberty" because it was considered a stain "on the family." But he admitted that "there was a good deal of it." McMillan remembered masters who kept "one girl steady," others who maintained "sometimes two on different places," regardless of whether they were married or unencumbered by white wives. His vivid recollection—"if they could get it on their own place it was easier, but they would go wherever they could get it"—demonstrates that, as a rule, white males in slave society were at liberty to exploit slave women, despite family or Christian obligations to the contrary.[19]

McMillan was not depicting his own or his family's encounters with sexual exploitation. Many blacks discussed the abuse of other slaves on the plantation, perhaps unwilling to recount the indignities to which their own kin were subjected.[20] Their revelations reflect genuine horror when they describe the practice of masters who auctioned off their own offspring.[21]

Another category of cruelty was reported as "miscegenation." In other words, slaves perceived the coercive forces at work within plantation society as exploitive as well. This exploitation is more subtle and, as a result, more difficult to extract from historical records. But nonetheless, not only must the glaring contradictions of slavery be brought to light, but the shadowy and elusive inconsistencies that continue to confound us. There are clues to these closeted practices as well.

As we saw with the complex tale of Pauli Murray's ancestry, white men and enslaved women could and did form long-term liaisons, which may not have been founded on mutual feeling but often grew into relationships that demonstrated fidelity and devotion. The records show that not all black female–white male liaisons were maintained or even initiated by brute force.

Perhaps most remarkable within the spectrum of interracial connection was the system of *plaçage*, which developed in New Orleans. This port city was renowned for its unique Franco-American culture, particularly the European influence on sexual and social mores. In addition, with the excessive ratio of free women of color to free men of color within this southern city (one hundred women to fifty-seven men in 1850),[22] contractual concubinage flourished. The system that developed guaranteed these women both male protectors and financial support for illegitimate children. The city was famous for its "quadroon" or "fancy girl" balls at which the refined, cultivated daughters of the *gens de couleur libres* were put on display for the dandies of Louisiana society. The balls, attended only by free mulatto women and white men, provided the means for matching up *placées* with protectors. After brief courtship, a formal contract between the girl's family and her protector was signed. *Plaçage* guaranteed financial security for these women of color and perpetuated concubinage. A quadroon *placée* often groomed her octoroon daughter to follow her example; sons were encouraged to pursue artisanal trades. This elaborate system of codification was peculiar to New Orleans, although evidence of legal protection of concubines and their children appears in Charleston and Mobile as well, and owner-slave liaisons developed throughout the South.

The offspring of these interracial unions, slave or free, were referred to as "natural children." They appear in the wills of planters, often along with their mothers, as beneficiaries of their fathers' generosity.[23] The fate of slave concubines and their natural children following an owner's death most often depended upon whether white relatives honored the will. A white widow or legitimate children were likely to ignore the wishes of the testator for their own financial advantage.[24]

Many slave concubines improved the status of themselves and their offspring through their involvements with wealthy owner-lovers. In his *Yazoo, or on the Picket Line of Freedom in the South,* A. T. Morgan, a northern planter who married a black woman and settled in Mississippi after the Civil War, described the phenomenon. Morgan argued that because colored concubines achieved prestige "according to the rank of their white 'sweethearts,'" the kept women of color reigned within "black society" in Yazoo City, Mississippi. A daughter often followed in her mother's footsteps, and upon extreme occasion, "*in her very tracks.*" Ironically, if a woman of color was freed and married a black, her status was lowered within "colored society."[25]

As in many other instances, slavery reinforced the rule of white supremacy. Slave women involved in illicit relationships with white men were accorded more privilege than those who contracted regular unions with black men. Because both sets of relations were outside the law, the woman's status depended solely upon the rank of the man with whom she shared her bed and had no relation to any attempts to replicate traditional patterns of virtue and legitimacy. Evidence indicates that mulatto concubines might wield more influence than free women of color because of the complex perversities fostered by slavery.

So slave women, given the limited options they faced within severely circumscribed spheres, might improve their lots by liaisons with owners, as Lewis Clarke, in his lecture to a white audience, acknowledged: "A woman's being a slave, don't stop her having genteel ideas; that is, according to their way, and as far as they can. They know they must submit to their masters; besides, their masters, maybe, dress 'em up, and make 'em little presents, and give 'em more privileges, while the whim lasts."[26] The divorce records and wills of slaveowners provide testimony of the power and influence many black concubines possessed.[27]

Despite the abundant evidence of warmth and even affection between concubines and owners, these liaisons also provoked instability and conflict. Harriet Jacobs recalled in her autobiography, *Incidents in the Life of a Slave Girl* (1861), that at the age of sixteen she deliberately contracted a relationship with a "Mr. Sands" and became pregnant by him. She confessed, "It seems less degrading to give one's self, than to submit to compulsion."[28] Jacobs's affair was part of a complicated chain of circumstances. After being harassed by her own master for more than a year and persecuted by her watchful mistress, she succumbed to the attentions of a white gentleman who expressed sympathy about her dilemma. Jacobs confided: "I knew the impassable gulf between us but to be an object of interest to a man who is not married and not her master is agreeable to the pride and feelings of a slave." When her owner began to build a cottage outside of town where he intended to keep her as his sexual companion, Jacobs became pregnant by her lover and hoped her master would sell her to him.

This plan collapsed when her mistress accused Jacobs of sleeping with her master and her white lover failed to buy her (although he eventually purchased their two children after his marriage). This case demonstrates the utter powerlessness of these women, who more often were pawns than agents in the complex network of interracial affairs.

Former slave Sella Martin described an even more perverse scheme. Her white father was manipulated into a liaison with a quadroon slave by his aunt:

Mr. Martin, her brother's only child, and her only heir, was destined by the old folks in both families to marry a young lady of wealth and position, who was some eight years his junior; and that this purpose might not be thwarted by her nephew forming attachments elsewhere while the girl was a minor,

Mrs. Henderson, by methods known only to the system of slavery, encouraged, and finally secured a relationship between Mr. Martin and my mother, of which my sister Caroline and myself were the fruits. She had a separate establishment set up for her on the estate; that is, she had a cabin all to herself, which is very rare, except in such cases. Her duties about the house were merely nominal, and her fare was from the table of her mistress.[29]

Although exceptional, this case is another example of the way slavery could distort sexual relations.

Many examples can be found of white women on plantations attempting to prevent interracial liaisons. The burdens of humiliation and responsibility seem to have fallen more heavily on women than men. One black woman described the rude awakening of her grandmother, Mathilda:

She were near thirteen-year old, behind the house tee-teein when young marster came up behind her. She didn't see him, but he put his hand up her dress and said, "Lay down, Tildy." . . . And so this thing happened, and her stomach began to get big. One day, grandma and old mistress, they was putting up clean clothes. Old mistress had a pair of socks in her hand. She said, "Tildy, who been messin wit you down there?" Grandma say, "Young marster." Old mistress run to her and crammed these socks in her mouth and say, "don't you ever tell nobody. If you do, I'll skin you alive."[30]

The violent reaction of the mistress and her attempt to silence any testimony of a sexual connection are the most common responses within the records of plantation slavery. Wives as often as mothers agonized over illicit interracial affairs.

Owner-slave liaisons not only wreaked havoc within black families, they created violence and resentment among members of white families as well. Lacking the power to prevent sexual activities between male owners and slaves, white women on plantations struggled to discourage sons, shame brothers, and conceal marital infidelities. The jealousy and hatred many white women harbored for the slave women to whom their husbands were attached was legend within the Old South.

White southern women uniformly scorned black women's physical attributes. Mary Chesnut's diary illuminates her prejudices: "There will never be an interesting book with a negro heroine down here. We know them too well. In fact they are not picturesque—only in fiction do they shine. Those beastly negress beauties. Animals—tout et simple." In a later entry she describes a "beautiful mulatress" but qualifies her judgment: "that is, as good-looking as they ever are to me. I have never seen a mule as handsome as a horse—and I know I never will."[31] Complaining about the "unattractiveness" of black women was perhaps an unconscious defense mechanism against the "attraction" many white men acted upon within southern society. An undertone of hysteria appears in many diaries of plantation mistresses when black women are discussed. Some women pathetically clung to the notion that owners slept with their slaves, as one woman claimed, "by no other desire or motive but that of adding to the number of their slaves," neglecting the reality that there was no shortage of black men available for this purpose.[32]

Travelers, observers, court records, and slave narratives all testify to the hostility many white women felt toward black concubines. In these situations they may have felt equally at the mercy of white men. Harriet Jacobs's mistress, the slave confessed, "watched her husband with unceasing vigilance; but he was well practised in means to evade it."[33] Southern masters, used to ruling unchallenged in sexual matters as single men, were loath to bridle their licentiousness after marriage, even to please their wives.[34]

Plantation matrons had few options when confronted with their husbands' infidelities with a slave. Some might beg their husbands' fathers for assistance, and others might look to their own parents for comfort, but generally women were expected to turn a blind eye toward these dalliances.[35] Under extreme circumstances, if a husband abused his privilege by flaunting an affair, a wife might demand that the slave be sold. If her husband refused, she could retaliate by petitioning for divorce, citing infidelity as legal grounds for dissolution. Although the very wealthiest of slaveowners were not often sued for divorce (the upper ranks of society rarely allowed their names to be soiled by scandal), many divorce petitions filed during the antebellum era demonstrate the humiliations to which white wives might be subjected.

Evidence from the county records of Virginia reveals the scope of the problem. An Augusta woman complained in 1814 that her husband took her slave Milly "in his own wife's bed." Milly gave birth to a mulatto shortly thereafter. A Henry County wife reported in 1820 that her husband took to bed with him, night after night for three months, a female slave—in the same bedroom with his wife. In an 1837 petition from King William County an abused wife revealed that not only was her spouse smitten with a hired female slave but he "suffered and even encouraged the said negro woman, Grace, to use not only the most insolent language, but even to inflict blows upon the said Elizabeth, his wife."[36]

And in a detailed 1848 petition from Henry County, a wife provided testimony from friends to verify her husband's extreme cruelty. One witness confided that the husband "frequently slept with her, the said negro servant girl—sometimes on a pallet in his wife's room and other times in an adjoining chamber. He often embraced and kissed her in my presence." Another visitor to the household testified: "He directed the said servant girl to seat herself at the table from which I had just risen—to which Mrs. N. objected, saying to the girl, if she seated herself at that table that she would have her severely punished. To this Mr. N. declared that in that event he would visit her [Mrs. N] with a like punishment. Mrs. N then burst into tears and asked if it was not too much for her to stand."[37]

Perhaps some of these situations led to the explosive violence that sometimes occurred within the big house. Certainly the sexual liaisons between black women and white men stirred up anger and resentment within the slave cabins and provoked equal disharmony among members of the white family, most notably injuring women within the planter household. In an interview, J. W. Lindsay described such discord: "Sometimes white mistresses will surmise that there is an intimacy between a slave woman & the master, and perhaps she will make a great fuss & have her whipped, & perhaps there will be no peace until she is sold."[38]

The presence of a slave concubine and, secondarily, her bastard children promoted conflict within the plantation household. Such women's mere existence would cause pain for most wives, but their constant presence was a burden few women could tolerate. Most responded by lashing out at the helpless victims—the slave women. Evidence suggests that mistresses were free with the whip when dealing with women and children. It is futile to advance any single causal factor, but women's need to attack their rivals and their husbands' illegitimate offspring surely inspired some violence. Fears and suspicion played as large a role as fact in motivating many white women.[39]

In the vast records of slavery, not just the papers of slaveowners and white institutions but also slave narratives, both whites and blacks confirm that mistresses attempted to enforce Christian principles and to deal morally with a very brutal and dehumanizing system. Yet how are we to explain the barbarity of white women torturing and even killing slaves? Former slave James Curry reported to his abolitionist audience: "I could relate many instances of extreme cruelty practised upon plantations in our neighborhood, instances of *woman* laying heavy stripes upon the back of *woman*, even under circumstances which should have removed every feeling but that of sympathy from the heart of *woman*, and, which was sometimes attended with effects most shocking."[40] Curry might have been referring to the fact that the whipping of pregnant women could and did result in miscarriages. Murderous assaults might have been provoked by jealous rage. Appreciation of the dynamics at play can broaden our understanding of antebellum households.

Mary Armstrong of Houston, Texas, at the age of ninety-one, still remembered her first mistress:

> Old Polly, she was a Polly devil if there ever was one, and she whipped my little sister what was only nine months old, and just a baby, to death. She come and took the diaper offen my little sister and whipped till the blood just ran—just cause she cry like all babies do, and it kilt my sister. I never forgot that, but I got some even with that Old Polly devil and it's this-a-way.
>
> You see, I'se 'bout ten year old and I belongs to Miss Olivia, what was that old Polly's daughter, and one day Old Polly devil comes to where Miss Olivia lives after she marries, and tries to give me a lick out in the yard, and I picks up a rock about as big as half your fist and hits her right in the eye and busted the eyeball, and tells her that's for whippin' my baby sister to death. You could hear her holler for five miles, but Miss Olivia, when I tells her, says, 'Well, I guess Mama has learnt her lesson at last.' "[41]

This story is remarkable not only for the barbarity it describes but for the vengeance Mary Armstrong wreaked and the response of her second mistress, Polly's daughter. One can only wonder what emotional conflicts influenced this strange series of events.

Historical records abound with senseless acts of cruelty. Elizabeth Sparks recounted that her mistress's mother beat her with a broom or a leather strap and that severe whippings were inflicted for such trifles as burning bread. Susan Merrit described being knocked in the head for trying to learn to read and being forced to walk barefoot through a bed of coals after being accused of carelessness. Several slaves reported that abusive mistresses administered daily whippings as morning rituals.[42] Therefore, despite the general goodwill she supposedly maintained toward her charges and despite the positive impact the majority of slaves claimed she had on their lives,[43] the plantation mistress could and did succumb to the cruelties fostered by southern slavery.

Although many cruelties may have been motivated by the existence of concubines and illegitimate mulattoes, it is also possible that white women, like white men, sometimes perpetrated violence without any rational cause. Scholars sensitive to the complexities of human motives realize that there are many events that can never be fully reconstructed and many facets of a given circumstance that may never be fathomed. Yet we must attempt to explore below the surface of historical records, to reveal the deeper meanings of people's experiences.

Perhaps we will never be able to determine causal factors for either

31

individual or even group behavior within slave society. By looking at the "darker side" of the system of slavery, however, at the dynamics that have been obscured by modesty or distorted for numerous motives, we may discover some lost insights into this complex chapter of the southern past. It may be essential to place gender and sexuality in the foreground of our portrait of the Old South in order to sharpen our focus on some important areas of exploitation and suffering. The prolonged emphasis on slavery as an economic system has blurred our ability to understand the critical dynamics of slavery as a social system.

Women, both black and white, were ensnared within the confines of southern slave society. Color and class gave white women the privilege to exercise control over their lives, but evidence demonstrates that many were nevertheless victimized by a system that subjected them to prolonged humiliation and severe psychological stress. The problems of white women pale in comparison to those that plagued slave women in white households and black women within southern society. In some cases the anguish and frustration of white women compounded black women's difficulties, resulting in the physical and emotional abuse of slave mothers and children. Even though they were pitted against one another by a racist sexual ideology, black and white women were often trapped in similar situations: both were at the mercy of male will. Southern women have rarely been able to identify their common interests, to recognize that they were "sisters under the skin," until the modern era.

We need to investigate the complex past attuned to many of the issues that emerge from my opening vignette: Cornelia Smith's divided loyalties and mixed heritage. Scholars are quick to chronicle the tales of whips and chains but less eager to tackle more subtle forms of exploitation. Pauli Murray encourages us to see that both sexes and both races were trapped, struggling in vain against barely visible restraints. We must illuminate the web that entangled black and white, men and women, to reconstruct the bonds of blood and emotion that drew white and black together as well as bringing them into competitive conflict. Only by examining these critical aspects of sex and race will we be able to gauge the impact of slavery and its continuing legacy.

Notes

The author wishes to thank the members of the Harvard History Dinner Group for their comments.

1. Pauli Murray, *Proud Shoes* (New York: Harper & Row, 1978), p. 33.
2. Ibid., p. 47.
3. Ibid., p. 49.
4. It was doubtless a great triumph for Pauli Murray when she was first ordained as an Episcopal minister in 1977. Becoming an official of the church as a woman and indeed a woman of color was a private victory as well as a public accomplishment; one month after her ordination, she conducted the service in the same church where her grandmother Cornelia had been baptized in 1854.
5. Marquis de Chastellux, *Travels in North America*, 2 vols. (Chapel Hill: University of North Carolina Press, 1961), 2:241; Ferdinand Bayard, *Travels of a Frenchman in Maryland and Virginia* (Ann Arbor: University of Michigan Press, 1950), p. 20; William N. Blane, *An Excursion through the United States and Canada* (1824; rpt. New York: Negro University Press, 1969), p. 204.
6. Fanny Kemble, *Journal of a Residence on a Georgian Plantation in 1838–1839* (1964; rpt. Chicago: Afro-Am Press, 1969), pp. 14–15.
7. Ibid., p. 23.
8. J. S. Buckingham, *The Slave States of America*, 2 vols. (London: Fisher, Son & Co., 1842), 2:241.
9. Susan Nye Hutchinson Diary, July 29, 1815, and September 6, 1829, Southern Historical Collection, University of North Carolina, Chapel Hill; letter in Bumpas Papers, August 15, 1844, ibid.
10. See Catherine Clinton, *The Plantation Mistress: Woman's World in the Old South* (New York: Pantheon, 1982), pp. 212–13, 220–21.
11. John Blassingame, ed., *Slave Testimony: Two Centuries of Lectures, Speeches, Interviews and Autobiographies* (Baton Rouge: Louisiana State University Press, 1977), p. 156.
12. Ibid., p. 221. See also Dorothy Sterling, ed., *We Are Your Sisters: Black Women in the Nineteenth Century* (New York: Norton, 1984), pp. 26–27.
13. Blassingame, *Slave Testimony*, p. 221.
14. Ibid., pp. 128, 279–80, 347, 382.
15. Herbert Gutman, *The Black Family in Slavery and Freedom* (New York: Pantheon, 1976), pp. 83–84, 395–99.
16. Paul Escott, *Slavery Remembered: A Record of Twentieth Century Slave Narratives* (Chapel Hill: University of North Carolina Press, 1980), p. 45.
17. Ibid., p. 43.
18. Blassingame, *Slave Testimony*, p. 540.
19. Ibid., p. 382.
20. Escott, *Slavery Remembered*, p. 44.
21. See "Testimony of Tabb Gross," in Blassingame, *Slave Testimony*, p. 347.
22. Sterling, ed., *We Are Your Sisters*, p. 27. Although one might be tempted to argue that an imbalanced sex ratio of white men to white women contributed significantly to the institution of *plaçage,* evidence indicates that the codification of these interracial liaisons rarely appears outside of a few urban ports—New Orleans and to a lesser extent Mobile and Charleston. The cultural climate of

these cities fostered a distinctly European cosmopolitanism, which must be seen as a more crucial factor shaping race relations than mere demographics. The higher ratio of men to women was more acute in the Mississippi and Alabama interior, an area in which there is no evidence that *plaçage* was common or recognized, although illicit liaisons were frequently and informally established.

23. Ibid., pp. 29–31; Clinton, *Plantation Mistress*, pp. 213–14.

24. See James Hugo Johnston, *Race Relations in Virginia and Miscegenation in the South, 1776–1860* (1937; rpt. Amherst: University of Massachusetts Press, 1970), p. 232; Clinton, *Plantation Mistress*, pp. 214, 217.

25. Gutman, *Black Family*, pp. 392–93.

26. Blassingame, *Slave Testimony*, p. 157.

27. Sterling, ed., *We Are Your Sisters*, pp. 26, 30–31; Johnston, *Race Relations*, pp. 232, 239, 247.

28. Sterling, ed., *We Are Your Sisters*, p. 23.

29. Blassingame, *Slave Testimony*, p. 702.

30. Sterling, ed., *We Are Your Sisters*, p. 25.

31. C. Vann Woodward, ed., *Mary Chestnut's Civil War* (New Haven: Yale University Press, 1982), p. 243.

32. See Clinton, *Plantation Mistress*, pp. 91, 190, 211.

33. Sterling, ed., *We Are Your Sisters*, p. 21.

34. Kemble, *Journal*, p. 228; Edward Abdy, *Journal of a Residence and Tour of North America*, 3 vols. (London: John Murray, 1835), 2:93; Charles Elliot, *The Sinfulness of Slavery in the United States*, 2 vols. (Cincinnati, 1857), 2:69, 152.

35. See Clinton, *Plantation Mistress*, pp. 81, 211–12, 214–15.

36. Johnston, *Race Relations*, pp. 239, 241, 245–46.

37. Ibid., p. 247.

38. Blassingame, *Slave Testimony*, pp. 400–401.

39. Sterling, ed., *We Are Your Sisters*, pp. 21, 23; Solomon Northup, *Twelve Years a Slave* (Buffalo, N.Y.: Orton & Mulligan, 1854), pp. 198–99.

40. Blassingame, *Slave Testimony*, p. 138.

41. Norman Yetman, ed., *Voices from Slavery* (New York: Holt, Rinehart and Winston, 1970), pp. 18–19.

42. Ibid., pp. 297–98, 225, 252.

43. Clinton, *Plantation Mistress*, pp. 187–89.

Southern Indians and the Cult of True Womanhood

Theda Perdue

S outhern Indians stand apart culturally and historically from other native Americans.[1] Building of temple mounds, an elaborate ceremonial life, a complex belief system, riverine agriculture, and matrilineal descent characterized their aboriginal culture. Southern Indians embraced European culture with such enthusiasm and success that they came to be known as the "five civilized tribes." They acquired this sobriquet in the half-century after the ratification of the United States Constitution, a time when many southern Indians came to believe that their physical survival depended on adopting an Anglo-American lifestyle and value system. These Indians gradually abandoned hunting and subsistence agriculture, the practice of blood vengeance, their traditional religious beliefs and practices, and other aspects of their aboriginal way of life. Some individual Indians succeeded so well that they became culturally indistinguishable from their white neighbors. They owned large plantations, operated successful businesses, attended Christian churches, promoted formal legal and judicial systems, and wrote and conversed in the English language.[2]

An integral part of this cultural transformation was a redefinition of gender roles. Just as men could no longer follow their aboriginal pursuits of hunting and warfare, women could no longer behave in what was perceived to be a "savage" or "degraded" way.[3] Instead, they had to attempt to conform to an Anglo-American ideal characterized by purity, piety, domesticity, and submissiveness.[4] By the second quarter of the nineteenth century, the glorification of this ideal had become so pervasive in American society that the historian Barbara Welter has called it the "cult of true womanhood." A true woman was essentially spiritual rather than physical. She occupied a separate sphere apart from the ambition, selfishness, and materialism that permeated the man's world of business and politics. Her proper place was the home, and because of her spiritual nature, she imbued her home with piety, morality, and love. The home was a haven from the outside world, and in its operation a true woman should excel. Openly submissive to men, a true woman influenced them subtly through her purity and piety.

Traditionally southern Indians had a very different view of womanhood. Indian women occupied a separate sphere from that of men, but they had considerable economic, political, and social importance. While men hunted and went to war, women collected firewood, made pottery and baskets, sewed clothes, cared for children, and cooked the family's food. These tasks certainly fell within the nineteenth-century definition of domesticity, but the sphere of Indian women extended beyond home and hearth to encompass economic activities that seemed far less appropriate to their sex. In particular, women farmed in a society that depended primarily on agriculture for subsistence, and women performed most of the manual labor with men assisting only in clearing fields and planting corn. This inequitable division of labor elicited comments from most Euro-American observers. In 1775, Bernard Romans described the women he encountered on a journey through east and west Florida: "Their strength is great, and they labor hard, carrying very heavy burdens great distance." On his 1797 tour of the Cherokee country, Louis-Philippe, who later would become king of France, observed: "The Indians have all the work done by women. They are assigned not only household tasks; even the corn, peas, beans, and potatoes are planted, tended, and preserved by the women." In the economy of southern Indians, therefore, women did what Euro-Americans considered to be work—they farmed—while men did what was considered sport—they hunted.[5]

This arrangement was amazing in that women did not seem to object to doing most of the work. In the early nineteenth century, a missionary commented on the willingness with which the women toiled: "Though custom attached the heaviest part of the labor of the women, yet they were cheerful and voluntary in performing it. What others have discovered among the Indians I cannot tell, but though I have been about nineteen years among the Cherokees, I have perceived nothing of that slavish, servile fear, on the part of women, so often spoke of." One reason women may have worked so gladly was that they received formal recognition for their economic contribution and they controlled the fruit of their labor. In the Green Corn Ceremony, the southern Indians' most important religious event, women ritually presented the new crop, which was sacrificed to the fire, and when Europeans occasionally purchased corn from Indians in the eighteenth century, they bought it from women.[6] Women may also have labored without complaint because farming was one of the determinants of gender. Southern Indians distinguished between the sexes on other than merely biological grounds. Women were women not only because they could bear children but also because they farmed, and men who farmed came to be regarded sexually as women. Men hunted, therefore, because hunting was intrinsically linked to male sexuality; women farmed because farming was one of the characteristics that made them women.[7]

The matrilocal residence pattern of southern Indians probably contributed to the association of women and agriculture. A man lived in the household of his wife's lineage, and buildings, garden plots, and sections of the village's common field belonged to her lineage. A man had no proprietary interest in the homestead where he lived with his wife or in the land his wife farmed. Nor was a husband necessarily a permanent resident in the household of his wife's lineage. Polygamy was common, and he might divide his time between the lineages of his wives. Furthermore, southeastern Indians frequently terminated their marriages, and in the event of divorce, a man simply left his wife's household and returned to his mother's house and his own lineage. Because southeastern Indians were also matrilineal, that is, they traced kinship only through the female line, children belonged to the mother's lineage and clan rather than to the father's, and when divorce occurred, they invariably remained with their mothers. Men, therefore, had no claim on the houses they lived in or the children they fathered.[8]

John Lawson tried to explain matrilineal lineage, which he considered an odd way of reckoning kin, by attributing it to "fear of Imposters; the Savages knowing well, how much Frailty possesses *Indian* women, betwixt the Garters and the Girdle."[9] Women in southern Indian tribes did enjoy considerable sexual freedom. Except for restraints regarding incest and menstrual taboos, Indian women were relatively free in choosing sexual partners, engaging in intercourse, and dissolving relationships. All southern Indians condoned premarital sex and divorce, which were equally female or male prerogatives, but attitudes toward adultery varied from one tribe to another.

Indian women usually displayed a sense of humor and a lack of modesty regarding sexual matters. One member of Lawson's expedition took an Indian "wife" for a night. The couple consummated their marriage in a room occupied by other members of the company and guests at the wedding feast. In the morning the groom discovered that both his bride and his shoes were gone.[10] So brazen and skilled were most Cherokee women that Louis-Philippe concluded that "no Frenchwomen could teach them a thing." When his guide made sexual advances to several Cherokee women in a house they visited, he recorded in his journal that "they were so little embarrassed that one of them who was lying on a bed put her hand on his trousers before my very eyes and said scornfully, *Ah, sick.*"[11]

Compared to the other southern Indians, Louis-Philippe decided, the Cherokees were "exceedingly casual" about sex. Although all southern Indians had certain common characteristics—they were matrilineal and matrilocal, women farmed, and both sexes enjoyed some sexual freedom—Cherokee women had the highest degree of power and personal autonomy. The trader James Adair maintained that the Cherokees "have been a considerable while under a petticoat-government." In Cherokee society, women spoke in council and determined the fate of war captives. Some even went on the warpath and earned a special title, "War Woman."[12] In fact, Cherokee women were probably as far from the "true women" of the early nineteenth-century ideal as any women Anglo-Americans encountered on the continent. When the United States government and Protestant missionaries undertook the "civilization" of native Americans in the late eighteenth century, however, the Cherokees proved to be the most adept at transforming their society.[13] Because the Cherokees provide the greatest contrast between the aboriginal role of women and the role that emerged in the early nineteenth century as a consequence of civilization, I will examine the impact of the cult of true womanhood on the status of Cherokee women.

Until the late eighteenth century, Europeans had few relations with Cherokee women other than sexual ones. Europeans were primarily interested in Indian men as warriors and hunters and considered women to be of little economic or political significance. After the American Revolution, native alliances and the deerskin trade diminished in importance. All the Indians still had that Europeans valued was land. George Washington and his advisers devised a plan which they believed would help the Indians recover economically from the depletion of their hunting grounds and the destruction experienced during the Revolution while making large tracts of Indian land available for white settlement. They hoped to convert the Indians into farmers living on isolated homesteads much like white frontiersmen. With hunting no longer part of Indian economy, the excess land could be ceded to the United States and opened to whites.

The Cherokees traditionally had lived in large towns located along rivers. These towns were composed of many matrilineal households containing several generations. A woman was rarely alone: her mother, sisters, and daughters, with their husbands, lived under the same roof, and other households were nearby. Beyond the houses lay large fields which the women worked communally. Originally, these towns had served a defensive purpose, but in the warfare of the eighteenth century, they became targets of attack. In the French and Indian War and the American Revolution, soldiers invaded the Cherokee country and destroyed towns and fields. As a result, Cherokees began abandoning their towns even before the United States government inaugurated the civilization program. When a government agent toured the Cherokee Nation in 1796, he passed a number of deserted towns; at one site he found a "hut, some peach trees and the posts of a town house," and at another there was only a "small field of corn, some peach, plumb and locust trees."[14]

Agents appointed to implement the civilization program encouraged this trend. They advised the Cherokee to "scatter from their towns and make individual improvements also of cultivating more land for grain, cotton &c. than they could while crowded up in towns." The Cherokees complied: "They dispersed from their large towns,—built convenient houses,—cleared and fenced farms, and soon possessed numerous flocks and herds." By 1818 missionaries complained that "there is no place near us where a large audience can be collected as the people do not live in villages, but scattered over the country from 2 to 10 miles apart." The breaking up of Cherokee towns resulted in a very isolated existence for women because new households often consisted of only one nuclear family. This isolation occurred just at the time when the work load of women was increasing.[15]

In a letter of 1796, George Washington advised the Cherokees to raise cattle, hogs, and sheep. He pointed out that they could increase the amount of corn they produced by using plows and that they could also cultivate wheat and other grains. Apparently addressing the letter to the men, Washington continued: "To these you will easily add flax and cotton which you may dispose of to the White people, or have it made up by your own women into clothing for yourselves. Your wives and daughters can soon learn to spin and weave."[16] Washington apparently knew nothing about traditional gender roles, and the agents he sent usually had little sympathy for the Indian division of labor. They provided plows to the men and instructed them in clearing fields, tilling soil, and building fences. Women received cotton cards, spinning wheels, and looms.

The women, politically ignored in the eighteenth century and bypassed in the earlier hunting economy, welcomed the opportunity to profit from contact with whites. In 1796, agent Benjamin Hawkins met with a group of Cherokee women and explained the government's plan. He reported to

Washington that "they rejoiced much at what they had heard and hoped it would prove true, that they had made some cotton, and would make more and follow the instruction of the agent and the advice of the President." According to a Cherokee account, the women proved far more receptive to the civilization program than the men: "When Mr. Dinsmore, the Agent of the United States, spoke to us on the subject of raising livestock and cotton, about fifteen years ago, many of us thought it was only some refined scheme calculated to gain an influence over us, rather than to ameliorate our situation and slighted his advice and proposals; he then addressed our women, and presented them with cotton seeds for planting; and afterwards with cards, wheels and looms to work it. They acquired the use of them with great facility, and now most of the clothes we wear are of their manufacture." Two censuses conducted in the early nineteenth century reveal the extent to which women accepted their new tasks. In 1810 there were 1,600 spinning wheels and 467 looms in the Cherokee Nation; by 1826 there were 2,488 wheels and 762 looms.[17]

In 1810, one Cherokee man observed that the women had made more progress toward civilization than the men: "The females have however made much greater advances in industry than the males; they now manufacture a great quantity of cloth; but the latter have not made proportionate progress in agriculture; however, they raise great herds of cattle, which can be done with little exertion." At the same time, women continued to do most of the farming, and many even raised livestock for market. This extension of woman's work concerned government agents because many men were not acquiring the work habits considered essential to "civilized" existence.[18] They had not been able to accomplish a shift in gender roles merely by introducing the tools and techniques of Western culture. Gender roles as well as many other aspects of Cherokee culture proved extremely difficult to change.

Cultural change came more easily, however, among Cherokees who already had adopted the acquisitive, materialistic value system of white Americans. Turning from an economy based on hunting, they took advantage of the government's program and invested in privately owned agricultural improvements and commercial enterprises. They quickly became an economic elite separated from the majority of Cherokees by their wealth and by their desire to emulate whites. In the early nineteenth century, members of this economic elite rose to positions of leadership in the Cherokee Nation because of the ease and effectiveness with which they dealt with United States officials. Gradually they transformed Cherokee political institutions into replicas of those of the United States.[19] This elite expected Cherokee women to conform to the ideals of the cult of true womanhood, that is, to be sexually pure, submissive to fathers and husbands, concerned primarily with spiritual and domestic matters, and excluded from politics and economic activities outside the home. In 1818, Charles Hicks, who later would become principal chief, described the most prominent men in the nation as "those who have kept their women & children at home & in comfortable circumstances."[20] Submissive, domestic wives were a mark of prominence.

Cherokees learned to be true women primarily through the work of Protestant missionaries whom tribal leaders welcomed to the nation. In 1800 the Moravians arrived to open a school, and in the second decade of the nineteenth century Congregationalists supported by the inter-denominational American Board of Commissioners for Foreign Missions, Baptists, and Methodists joined them. Except for the Methodists, missionaries preferred to teach children in boarding schools, where they had "the influence of example as well as precept." In 1819 President James Monroe visited the American Board's Brainerd mission and approved "of the plan of instruction; particularly as the children were taken into the family, taught to work, &c." This was, the president believed, "the best, & perhaps the only way to civilize and Christianize the Indians."[21] For female students, civilization meant becoming true women.

Mission schools provided an elementary education for girls as well as boys. Either single women or the wives of male missionaries usually taught the girls, but all students studied the same academic subjects, which included reading, writing, spelling, arithmetic, geography, and history. Examinations took place annually and were attended by parents. The teachers questioned students in their academic subjects as well as Bible history, catechism, and hymns, and "the girls showed specimens of knitting, spinning, mending, and fine needlework."[22]

Mastery of the domestic arts was an essential part of the girls' education because, according to one missionary, "all the females need is a proper education to be qualified to fill any of the relations or stations of domestic life." The children at the mission schools performed a variety of tasks, and the division of labor approximated that in a typical Anglo-American farming family. The boys chopped wood and plowed fields, and the girls milked, set tables, cooked meals, washed dishes, sewed clothing, knitted, quilted, did laundry, and cleaned the houses.[23] Because their fathers were wealthy, many students were not accustomed to such menial labor. Missionaries endeavored to convince them that "the charge of the kitchen and the mission table" was not degrading but was instead a "most important station," which taught them "industry and economy."[24]

The great advantage of teaching Cherokee girls "industry and economy" was the influence they might exert in their own homes. One girl wrote: "We have the opportunity of learning to work and to make garments which will be useful to us in life." Another girl expressed gratitude that missionaries had taught the students "how to take care of families that when we go home we can take care of our mothers house." A missionary assessed the impact of their work: "We cannot expect that the influence of these girls will have any great immediate effect on their acquaintance—but I believe in each case it is calculated to elevate the families in some degree, with which they are connected." Although missionaries and students expected the domestic arts learned in the mission schools to improve the parental home, they believed that the primary benefit would be to the homes the girls themselves established. Missionary Sophia Sawyer specifically hoped to "raise the female character in the Nation" so that "Cherokee gentlemen" could find young women "sufficiently educated for companions." In 1832 missionaries could report with satisfaction that the girls who had married "make good housewives and useful members of society."[25]

The marriages missionaries had in mind were not the Cherokees' traditional polygamous or serial marriages. Louis-Philippe had believed that such a marriage "renders women contemptible in men's eyes and deprives them of all influence." A monogamous marriage was supposedly liberating to women because these "serve exclusively to heighten the affections of a man."[26] Although the Cherokee elite accepted most tenets of Western civilization, some balked at abandoning the practice of polygamy. The chief justice was one who had more than one wife, but these marriages differed from traditional ones in which a man lived with his wives in their houses. Polygamous members of the elite headed more than one patriarchal household. They recognized the desirability of monogamous unions, however, encouraged others to enter into them, and sent their children to mission schools where they were taught that polygamy was immoral.

In practice, religious denominations confronted the problem of polygamy in different ways. Moravians apparently allowed converts to keep more than one wife. The American Board required a man "to separate himself from all but the first." Perhaps because some of their chief supporters were polygamists, the governing body in Boston advised missionaries in the field to be "prudent and kind" when dealing with this "tender subject" and to instruct polygamous converts "in the nature and design of marriage, the original institution, and the law of Christ, that they may act with an enlightened conviction of duty." American Board ministers sometimes remarried in a Christian service couples who had lived for years in "a family capacity." Missionaries also rejoiced when they united in matrimony young couples of "industrious habits & reputable behavior" who were "very decent and respectable in their moral deportment."[27]

Achieving "moral deportment" at the mission schools was no simple matter, but missionaries considered the teaching of New England sexual mores to be one of their chief responsibilities. According to some reports, they enjoyed success. In 1822, American Board missionaries reported: "Mr. Hall thinks the moral influence of the school has been considerable. . . . The intercourse between the young of both sexes was shamefully loose. Boys & girls in their teens would strip & go into bathe, or play ball together naked. They would also use the most disgustingly indecent language, without the least sense of shame. But, when better instructed, they became reserved and modest." To maintain decorum, the missionaries tried to make certain that girls and boys were never alone together: "When the girls walk out any distance from the house they will be accompanied by instructors." Male and female students normally attended separate classes. When Sophia Sawyer became ill in 1827 she reluctantly sent the small girls to the boys' school but taught the larger girls in her sickroom. Miss Sawyer so feared for the virtue of the older girls that she asked the governing board "could not the boys at Brainerd be at some other school." The Moravians did resort to separate schools. The American Board, however, simply put locks on the bedroom doors.[28]

Even with these precautions, difficulties arose. In 1813 the Moravians recorded in their journal: "After prayer we directed our talk toward Nancy, indirectly admonishing her to abstain from the lust which had gripped her. She seemed not to have taken it to heart, for instead of mending her ways she continues to heap sin upon sin." Nancy Watie later moved to an American Board mission along with her cousin Sally Ridge. Their fathers were prominent in the Cherokee Nation, and they had left strict instructions that their daughters be supervised constantly and their purity preserved. A problem occurred when teenage boys in the neighborhood began calling on the girls at the mission. At first, the young people decorously sat in front of the fire under the watchful eyes of the missionaries, but soon the conversation shifted from English to Cherokee, which none of the chaperons understood. Suspecting the worst, the missionaries ordered the suitors to "spend their evenings in some other place." A year later, however, the missionaries reported that despite their care, the girls "had given themselves up to the common vices."[29]

The missionaries did not, of course, intend to cloister the young women to the extent that they did not meet suitable young men. Sophia Sawyer observed: "Like all females they desire the admiration of men.

They can easily be shown that the attention, or good opinion of men without education, taste, or judgement is not worth seeking, & to gain the affection or good opinion of the opposite character, their minds must be improved, their manner polished, their persons attended to, in a word they must be qualified for usefulness." Attracting the right young men was permissible and even desirable.[30]

The girls' appearance was another concern of the missionaries. Ann Paine related an attempt to correct the daughter of a particularly prominent Cherokee: "Altho' her parents supplied her with good clothes, she was careless and indifferent about her appearance.—I often urged her attention to these things and offered as a motive her obligation to set a good example to her nation as the daughter of their chief. Told her how the young ladies of the North were taught to govern their manners and tempers and of their attention to personal appearance. She never appeared more mortified than in hearing of her superiority of birth, and of the attention she ought to pay to her personal appearance." Paine soon had "the satisfaction of witnessing her rapid improvement." Four years later, Sophia Sawyer complained about the female students in general: "I have had to punish several times to break bad habits respecting cleanliness in their clothes, books, & person—I found them in a deplorable situation in this respect. The largest girls I had in school were not capable of dressing themselves properly or of folding their clothes when taken off." Sometimes concern for the students' appearance went beyond clothing. One girl wrote a correspondent: "Mr. Ellsworth told me I had better alter my voice. He said I spoke like a man."[31]

In addition to a neat, feminine appearance, respectable men presumably also admired piety in young women and probably expected them to be more pious than they themselves were. The missionaries clearly believed that the female students in mission schools were more serious about religion than the male students, and they encouraged this emotion. Nancy Reece wrote her northern correspondent that "after work at night the girls joined for singing a special hymn Mr. Walker wrote for them & then go to worship services." Many of the girls wrote about their spiritual lives. A ten-year-old confided in a letter that "some of the girls have been serious about there wicked hearts and have retired to their Chambers to pray to God. . . . I feel as though I am a great sinner and very wicked sinner."[32]

The piety of the girls at the mission station was manifest in other ways. They organized a society to raise money to send missionaries into heathen lands. The American Board agreed to pay them for clothing they made, and they in turn donated the money to mission work. They also sold their handwork to local Cherokee women. The piety of the girls extended beyond the school and into the community. Once a month, neighboring women would gather at the mission for a prayer meeting "that missionary labors may be blessed." One missionary reported with satisfaction that "the females have a praying society which is well attended, and they begin to do something by way of benevolence."[33]

Of the several hundred Cherokee girls who attended mission schools, the best example of "true womanhood" was Catharine Brown. She was sixteen or seventeen years old when she arrived at the Brainerd mission. She had some European ancestry, and although she had grown up in a fairly traditional Cherokee household, she spoke and read a little English. The missionaries reported that, despite the absence of a Christian influence in her childhood, "her moral character was ever good." Her biographer added: "This is remarkable, considering the looseness of manners then prevalent among the females of her nation, and the temptations to which she was exposed, when during the war with the Creek Indians, the army of the United States was stationed near her father's residence. . . . Once she even fled from her home into the wild forest to preserve her character unsullied." When she applied for admission to Brainerd, the missionaries hesitated because they feared that she would object to the domestic duties required of female students. They later recalled that she was "vain, and excessively fond of dress, wearing a profusion of ornaments in her ears." Catharine "had no objection" to work, however, and shortly after her admission, her jewelry disappeared "till only a single drop remains in each ear." After she became a part of the mission family, Catharine became extremely pious: "She spent much time in reading the Scriptures, singing, and prayer." She attended weekly prayer meetings and helped instruct the younger girls in the Lord's Prayer, hymns, and catechism. In 1819, Catharine received baptism. Her intellectual achievements were also remarkable, and soon the missionaries sent her to open a female school at the Creek Path Mission station. There she fulfilled not only her spiritual and educational responsibilities but also her domestic ones. Visitors reported: "We arrived after the family had dined, and she received us, and spread a table for our refreshment with the unaffected kindness of a sister." When her father proposed to take the family to Indian territory, Catharine was appropriately submissive. Although she did not want to go, she acquiesced to his wishes and prepared to leave for the West. Catharine's health, however, was fragile. She became ill, and "as she approached nearer to eternity her faith evidently grew stronger." In July 1823, "this lovely convert from heathenism died."[34]

Few women in the Cherokee Nation could equal Catharine Brown, and perhaps the majority of Cherokee women had little desire to be "true women." The historical record contains little information about the Cherokee masses, but from the evidence that does exist, we can infer that many Cherokees maintained a relatively traditional way of life. Continuing to exist at the subsistence level, they rejected Christianity and mission schools and relied on local councils rather than the central government dominated by the elite. Borrowing selectively from the dominant white society, a large number of women also maintained a semblance of their aboriginal role. As late as 1817, a council of women petitioned the Cherokee National Council to refrain from further land cessions, and in 1835 at least one-third of the heads of households listed on the removal roll were women.[35] Some probably were like Oo-dah-less who, according to her obituary, accumulated a sizable estate through agriculture and commerce. She was "the support of a large family" and bequeathed her property "to an only daughter and three grand children."[36] Other women no doubt lived far more traditionally, farming, supervising an extended household, caring for children and kinsmen, and perhaps even exercising some power in local councils.

Although the feminine ideal of purity, piety, submissiveness, and domesticity did not immediately filter down to the mass of Cherokees, the nation's leaders came to expect these qualities in women. Therefore, the influence of the cult of true womanhood probably far exceeded the modest number of women trained in mission schools. The Cherokee leaders helped create a new sphere for women by passing legislation that undermined matrilineal kinship and excluded women from the political process. In the first recorded Cherokee law of 1808, the national council, which apparently included no women, established a police force "to give their protection to children as heirs to their father's property, and to the widow's share." Subsequent legislation gave further recognition to patrilineal descent and to the patriarchial family structure common among men of wealth. In 1825 the council extended citizenship to the children of white women who had married Cherokee men, another act that formally reordered descent. Legislation further isolated women by prohibiting polygamy and denied women the right to limit the size of their families by outlawing the traditional practice of infanticide. In 1826 the council decided to call a constitutional convention to draw up a governing document for the tribe. According to legislation that provided for the election of delegates to the convention, "No person but a free male citizen who is full grown shall be entitled to vote." Not surprisingly, when the convention met and drafted a constitution patterned after that of the United States, women could neither vote nor hold office. The only provisions in the Cherokee legal code reminiscent of the power and prestige enjoyed by aboriginal women were laws that protected the property rights of married women and prohibited their husbands from disposing of their property without consent.[37]

The elite who governed the Cherokee Nation under the Constitution of 1827 regarded traditionalists with considerable disdain. Having profited from the government's civilization program, most truly believed in the superiority of Anglo-American culture. Some leaders and, to an even greater extent, United States officials tended to question the ability of traditionalists to make well-informed, rational decisions. This lack of faith provided a justification for those highly acculturated Cherokees who in 1835, without tribal authorization, ceded Cherokee land in the Southeast contrary to the wishes of the vast majority of Indians.[38] The failure of many Indian women to conform to the ideals of womanhood may well have contributed to the treaty party's self-vindication. Perhaps they believed that the land could have little meaning for the Cherokees if women controlled it, that the Indians must still depend primarily on hunting if women farmed, and that the Indians had no notion of ownership if men had no proprietary interest in their wives.

Of all the southern tribes, the Cherokees provide the sharpest contrast between the traditional role of women and the role they were expected to assume in the early nineteenth century. In this period, the Cherokees excluded women, who originally had participated in tribal governance, from the political arena. Women in other tribes had been less active politically; consequently, their status did not change as dramatically. All southern nations, however, did move toward legally replacing matrilineal with patrilineal descent and restricting the autonomy of women. In 1824, for example, the Creeks passed one law prohibiting infanticide and another specifying that upon a man's death, his children "shall have the property and his other relations shall not take the property to the injury of His children."[39]

Men of wealth and power among the Creeks, Choctaws, and Chickasaws as well as the Cherokees readily accepted the technical assistance offered through the government's civilization program and gradually adopted the ideology it encompassed. Although these changes occurred at different rates among southern Indians, women began to fade from economic and political life in the early nineteenth century. Just as the traditional female occupation, farming, became commercially viable, men took over and women became only secondarily involved in subsistence. Women, of course, still had their homes and families, but their families soon became their husbands' families, and domesticity brought

47

influence, not power. Similarly, purity and piety seemed almost anachronistic in a culture and age that tended to value the material above the spiritual. Perhaps all that remained for women was what historian Nancy Cott has called "bonds of womanhood," but Indian women did not even develop closer ties to other women.[40] Living a far more isolated existence than ever before, they no longer shared labor and leisure with mothers, daughters, and sisters. Instead they spent most of their time on remote homesteads with only their husbands and children.

This separate sphere in which Indian women increasingly lived in the nineteenth century could hardly give rise to a women's rights movement, as some historians have suggested it did among white women, because true womanhood came to be associated with civilization and progress.[41] Any challenge to the precepts of the cult of true womanhood could be interpreted as a reversion to savagery. Ironically, by the end of the century, some white Americans had come to view the traditional status of Indian women in a far more favorable light. In 1892 the author of an article in the *Albany Law Review* applauded the revision of property laws in the United States to protect the rights of married women and noted that such a progressive practice had long existed among the Choctaw and other southern Indians.[42] This practice, however, was only a remnant of a female role that had been economically productive, politically powerful, and socially significant but had been sacrificed to the cult of true womanhood.

Notes

1. For studies of the aboriginal Southeast, see John R. Swanton, *The Indians of the Southeastern United States* (Washington, D.C.: Bureau of American Ethnology, 1946), and Charles Hudson, *The Southeastern Indians* (Knoxville: University of Tennessee Press, 1976).

2. Works on the "five civilized tribes" include Henry T. Malone, *Cherokees of the Old South: A People in Transition* (Athens: University of Georgia Press, 1956); Theda Perdue, *Slavery and the Evolution of Cherokee Society, 1540–1866* (Knoxville: University of Tennessee Press, 1979); Arrell M. Gibson, *The Chickasaws* (Norman: University of Oklahoma Press, 1971); Angie Debo, *The Rise and Fall of the Choctaw Republic* (Norman: University of Oklahoma Press, 1934); Angie Debo, *The Road to Disappearance* (Norman: University of Oklahoma Press, 1941); Michael D. Green, *The Politics of Indian Removal: Creek Government and Society in Crisis* (Lincoln: University of Nebraska Press, 1982); Daniel F. Littlefield, Jr., *Africans and Creeks: From the Colonial Period*

to the *Civil War* (Westport, Conn.: Greenwood Press, 1979); Edwin C. McReynolds, *The Seminoles* (Norman: University of Oklahoma Press, 1957). Acculturation was limited among the Seminoles.

3. Mary E. Young, "Women, Civilization, and the Indian Question," in Mabel E. Deutrich and Virginia C. Purdy, eds., *Clio Was a Woman: Studies in the History of American Women* (Washington D.C.: Howard University Press, 1980).

4. Barbara Welter, "The Cult of True Womanhood, 1820–1860," *American Quarterly* 18 (1966): 151–74. Although Welter begins her discussion in 1820, the "cult" had been emerging since the mid-eighteenth century.

5. Bernard Romans, *A Concise Natural History of East and West Florida* (Facsimile reproduction of the 1775 edition, Gainesville: University of Florida Press, 1962), p. 62; Louis-Philippe, *Diary of My Travels in America*, trans. Stephen Becker (New York: Delacorte Press, 1977), p. 73. For details of women's work, see James Adair, *Adair's History of the American Indian*, ed. Samuel Cole Williams (Johnson City, Tenn.: Watauga Press, 1927), pp. 434–41, 447, 453–56; William Bartram, "Observations on the Creek and Cherokee Indians, 1789," *Transactions of the American Ethnological Society* 3, pt. 1 (1853): 31, 82; Samuel Cole Williams, ed., *Early Travels in the Tennessee County, 1540–1800* (Johnson City, Tenn.: Watauga Press, 1928), pp. 100–101, 257–58, 478; John Lawson, *Lawson's History of North Carolina*, ed. Francis Lathan Harris (Richmond: Garrett and Massie, 1937), pp. 199, 220.

6. The comment about the attitude of women toward work was made by Daniel Butrick of the American Board of Commissioners for Foreign Missions, John Howard Payne Papers, 4:27, Newberry Library, Chicago. For a description of the Green Corn Ceremony, see Adair, *History*, pp. 105–17.

7. I base this assertion on Cherokee mythology, the role assigned to women in the Green Corn Ceremony, the reaction of southeastern Indians to men who did not hunt or go to war, and the presence of transvestites among the Choctaws and Chickasaws (and perhaps other groups as well). See James Mooney, *Myths of the Cherokee* (Washington, D.C.: Bureau of American Ethnology, 1900), pp. 242–48; Adair, *History*, pp. 109, 163; Romans, *Concise Natural History*, pp. 70, 83.

8. Bartram, "Observations," pp. 40, 66; Lawson, *History*, pp. 184, 195–96; Louis-Philippe, *Diary*, p. 77; Williams, ed., *Early Travels*, p. 261; Adair, *History*, p. 462. Also see John R. Swanton, *Social Organization and Social Usages of the Indians of the Creek Confederacy* (Washington, D.C.: Bureau of American Ethnology, 1928); John Phillip Reid, *A Law of Blood: Primitive Law of the Cherokee Nation* (New York: New York University Press, 1970); and Alexander Spoehr, *Changing Kinship Systems: A Study in the Acculturation of the Creeks, Cherokee, and Choctaw* (Chicago: Field Museum of Natural History, 1947).

9. Lawson, *History*, pp. 37–38, 197–98.

10. Ibid., pp. 37–38.

11. Louis-Philippe, *Diary*, pp. 84–85.

12. Adair, *History*, pp. 152–53; Pat Alderman, *Nancy Ward: Cherokee Chieftainess* (Johnson City, Tenn.: Overmountain Press, 1978).

13. The major study of United States policy in this period is Francis Paul Prucha, *American Indian Policy in the Formative Years: The Indian Trade and Intercourse Acts, 1790–1834* (Cambridge, Mass.: Harvard University Press, 1962). For mission work, see Robert F. Berkhofer, Jr., *Salvation and the Savage: An Analysis of Protestant Missions and American Indian Response* (Lexington, Ky.: University of Kentucky Press, 1965), and William G. McLoughlin, *Cherokees and Missionaries, 1789–1839* (New Haven: Yale University Press, 1984).

14. Payne Papers, 4:34; William L. McDowell, *Documents Relating to Indian Affairs, May 21, 1750–Aug. 7, 1754* (Columbia, S.C.: South Carolina Archives Department, 1958), pp. 246–47, 149; Benjamin Hawkins, *Letters of Benjamin Hawkins, 1796–1806* (Savannah: Georgia Historical Society, 1916): 16–18.

15. Payne Papers, 9:53; Brainerd Journal, December 29, 1818, American Board of Commissioners for Foreign Missions Papers, Houghton Library, Harvard University, Cambridge, Mass.

16. The *Cherokee Phoenix* printed the letter March 20, 1828.

17. Hawkins, *Letters*, p. 20; John Norton, *The Journal of Major John Norton, 1816*, ed. Carl F. Klinck and James J. Talman (Toronto: Champlain Society, 1970), p. 36; Elias Boudinot, *An Address to the Whites* (Philadelphia: W. F. Geddes, 1826), p. 8.

18. Report from Willstown, October 10, 1828, American Board Papers; Hawkins, *Letters*, pp. 20–21.

19. William G. McLoughlin and Walter H. Conser, Jr., "The Cherokees in Transition: A Statistical Analysis of the Federal Census of 1835," *Journal of American History* 64 (1977): 678–703; Malone, *Cherokees of the Old South*.

20. Ard Hoyt, Moody Hall, William Chamberlain, and D. S. Butrick to Samuel Worcester, July 25, 1818, American Board Papers.

21. Cyrus Kingsbury to Samuel Worcester, November 28, 1816, Brainerd Journal, May 27, October 29, 1819, ibid.

22. Payne Papers, 8:10–12; William Potter to Jeremiah Evarts, August 16, 1826, American Board Papers.

23. Sophia Sawyer to Jeremiah Evarts, August 21, 1824, Appendix to Memoranda of the Cherokee Mission, May 16, 1822, Brainerd Journal, December 14, 1822, June 11, 1823, American Board Papers; Payne Papers, 8:6, 9, 11, 18, 39.

24. Brainerd Journal, June 19, 1818, August 2, 1821, Memoranda of the Cherokee Mission No. 2, May 1822, Ann Paine to Jeremiah Evarts, November 8, 1821, American Board Papers; Payne Papers, 8:51.

25. Sophia Sawyer to Jeremiah Evarts, August 21, 1824, Elizur Butler to Evarts, August 3, 1829, Lucy A. Butler to Daniel Green, September 29, 1832, American Board Papers; Payne Papers, 8:34, 49.

26. Louis-Philippe, *Diary,* p. 72.

27. Samuel Worcester to Ard Hoyt, November 11, 1818, Moody Hall's Journal, April 21, 1824, Brainerd Journal, February 9, 1820, September 18, 1823, American Board Papers; McLoughlin, *Cherokees and Missionaries,* pp. 204–5.

28. Memoranda Relative to the Cherokee Mission No. 1, April and May 1822, D. S. Butrick to Jeremiah Evarts, October 17, 1824, Sophia Sawyer to Evarts, August 11, 1825, October 19, 1827, American Board Papers; "Diary of the Moravian Mission at Spring Place," trans. Carl C. Mauleshagen, typescript, Georgia Historical Commission, Department of Natural Resources, Atlanta.

29. Moravian Mission Diary, April 11, 1813; Frederick Ellsworth to Jeremiah Evarts, May 25, August 12, 1825, American Board Papers.

30. Sophia Sawyer to Jeremiah Evarts, August 21, 1824.

31. Ann Paine, Notebook 2, December 20, 1820, Sophia Sawyer to Jeremiah Evarts, June 25, 1824; Payne Papers, 8:39.

32. Brainerd Journal, August 9, 1818, American Board Papers; Payne Papers, 8:1, 20, 41.

33. Payne Papers, 8:9, 16; William Chamberlain to Jeremiah Evarts, January 8, 1829, American Board Papers.

34. Rufus Anderson, *Memoir of Catharine Brown, a Christian Indian of the Cherokee Nation* (Boston: S. T. Armstrong and Crocker and Brewster; New York: J. P. Haven, 1825).

35. Kingsbury Journal, February 13, 1817, American Board Papers; Census of 1835, Indian Affairs, Record Group 75, National Archives, Washington, D.C. Cherokee speaker Robert Bushyhead kindly provided the gender for names on the census.

36. *Cherokee Phoenix,* July 2, 1828.

37. *Laws of the Cherokee Nation: Adopted by the Council at Various Times, Reprinted for the Benefit of the Nation,* vol. 5 of *The Constitutions and Laws of the American Indian Tribes* (Wilmington, Del.: Scholarly Resources, Inc., 1973), pp. 3, 4, 5, 10, 53, 57, 73, 79, 120–21, 142–43.

38. In "Letters and Other Papers Relating to Cherokee Affairs," treaty signer Elias Boudinot wrote: "We can see strong reasons to justify the action of a minority of fifty persons—to do what the majority *would do* if they understood their condition" (Theda Perdue, ed., *Cherokee Editor: The Writings of Elias Boudinot* [Knoxville: University of Tennessee Press, 1983], p. 162).

39. Antonio J. Waring, ed., *Laws of the Creek Nation,* University of Georgia Miscellaneous Publications, No. 1 (Athens: University of Georgia Press, 1969), pp. 19, 24.

40. Nancy F. Cott, *The Bonds of Womanhood: "Woman's Sphere" in New England, 1780–1835* (New Haven: Yale University Press, 1977).

41. Ibid., pp. 197–206; Aileen S. Kraditor, *Up from the Pedestal* (Chicago: Quadrangle Books, 1968).

42. "Current Topic," *Albany Law Journal* 45 (1892): 199.

"My Children, Gentlemen, Are My Own": Poor Women, the Urban Elite, and the Bonds of Obligation in Antebellum Charleston

Barbara L. Bellows

On almost any evening during the years before the Civil War, well-dressed gentlemen might have been seen ranging the back alleys of Charleston, gingerly picking their way through filthy, unpaved streets. They knocked at the doors of crowded boardinghouses, climbed steps to third floor garrets, and stopped laborers to question them about their neighbors. Neither census takers nor bill collectors, these were members of the city's elite inquiring into the state of the poor. Moved by the same sense of moral stewardship that motivated northern men of standing, the elite of Charleston living amid a black majority had a particular interest in creating a community of obligation among all white citizens. By serving as commissioners of municipal charities, leaders of the aristocratic old city involved themselves intimately in the lives of the poor.[1]

The closest associations developed between the fathers of the town and the city's poor women, who of all the urban denizens endured the "greater portion of extreme wretchedness." Widowed, abandoned, or single women sought employment in a society that equated labor with servitude and embraced the myth that white women were ill suited for any duties unrelated to housekeeping or childraising. Most lived like Jane Brownwell, "entirely dependent upon her own exertions and the charity of the world." Although these women approached the upper classes with the deference demanded by the etiquette of poverty, their letters of petition to the commissioners of the city charities suggest that they also refused to truckle before them. Poor women bearing the responsibility for their children's welfare understood and asserted their claims to the benevolence extended by the urban patriarchs.[2]

The formal relationship between the poor and the town's leaders evolved from the first provisions for public relief passed by the colonial assembly in 1712. More significant than the adoption of the principles of the English Poor Laws, though, was the desire among the rising elite to model themselves after the paternalistic British gentry. In addition to following the ritual of laying out plantations and building town houses, they felt obligated to serve the community as Anglican vestrymen, assessing and collecting taxes and judging the worthiness of applicants for charity. Colonial Charlestonians' reputation for liberal disposition toward the lower and potentially disaffected classes may be credited in part to a Whiggish tradition in local politics that idealized the harmonious community and strove for consensus.[3] By being generous with relief to the infirm and unemployed, public-spirited men of property hoped to convince poor whites that the elite were concerned with their interests. From 1736 until the twentieth century, Charleston supported a poorhouse and hospital; an orphanage established in 1790 during the early republican zeal for institution building won praise from reformers for its generous and enlightened treatment of orphaned and derelict children.

In 1825, Robert Mills noted the existence of more than thirty private and religious societies and the generous municipal expenditure for poor relief and observed that "no city abounds in so many benevolent institutions, in proportion to population, as Charleston." Mills neglected to mention the great need that existed among even the working classes. Only 5 percent of the city's laborers could claim any assets in 1860; women suffered the most of all. Those without skills found their experience much like that of Margaret Ryan, who had two children and by "working late and early, she could not make over 25 to 30 cts. a day." Independence was scarcely possible at such wages; the city jailer received at least fifty cents a day just to feed each of his charges.[4] By 1860, Charleston had the greatest disparity in the distribution of wealth of any southern city, with the largest class enjoying riches and, correspondingly, the largest class suffering deprivation.[5]

Described by Michael P. Johnson as the "ideal-typical" patriarchs, Charleston's urban elite shared a sense of responsibility that went beyond caring for their own families and slaves to include the unemployed laborer, husbandless woman, and fatherless child. They accepted the direc-

53

torships of public institutions; the commissioners of the Alms House, the Orphan House, Shirras Medical Dispensary, and Roper Hospital all bore such honored local names as Aiken, Ravenel, Moultrie, and Desaussure. In keeping with family and community expectations, they assumed the mantle of public men not only serving as advocates for the poor but also standing for public office, directing benevolent and religious societies, participating in social clubs, and sitting as trustees on the boards of banks and railroads. The Orphan House commissioners, especially, spent long hours in weekly meetings, interviewing the mothers of applicants for admission and inspecting the asylum. Men of wealth in other coastal southern cities shared a paternalistic attitude. George Greenhow, one of Richmond's overseers of the poor, compared his relationship to the city's white indigent population to that of a "cautious, prudent, industrious master, who has a large, and for the most part, helpless family to bring up, support and Educate."[6]

Concern over rewarding the virtuous poor while punishing the idle and vicious, curbing intemperance, and purging the streets of begging children and enticing prostitutes burdened city fathers, North and South, but the southerners' task was complicated by their desire to regulate but not alienate the poor whites.[7] They were torn between their revulsion for the "lawless ignorant and drunken man" and his "squalid and filthy woman," and their desire that the working and dependent classes find an identity within the white community.[8] In the southern city, the idea of uplift extended beyond moral improvement to include bolstering the poor to help maintain the grand illusion of white supremacy.[9] The immigrants who made up one-fifth of the city's population and three-fourths of its welfare recipients shared the degradation of poverty with the urban Negroes. They also lived near one another in areas where rent was cheap and the police not too diligent, tended one another's children, and competed for dollar-a-day jobs as laborers. Charleston's working class, which was over half (58 percent) either northern or foreign-born, shared little in common with the town elite except race.

Although familiarity with the poor did not necessarily breed contempt, it did little to reduce the prejudices felt by the rich for the poor or vice versa. As a visitor for several benevolent societies as well as a commissioner of the poor, William H. Gilliland kept a notebook in which he recorded all his distributions of cash and random observations about those petitioning his aid. He was moved to great sympathy for some and could hardly disguise his distaste for others. No matter how personally repulsive, though, he seldom turned a woman away. When the police arrested a Mrs. O'Neal, she sent for Gilliland to speak to the authorities on her behalf. He negotiated her release and sent her on her way with two dollars. That evening, Gilliland confided to his journal his dislike for the woman, especially the way "she makes poor mouth," and added, "I don't much believe in her." When Eliza Bingin, who lived with her unemployed, alcoholic husband, asked Gilliland for a handout, he acquiesced with disgust: "I think she drinks. She is Irish, has been here for 20 years. . . . I don't much like her looks or talk."[10] Clearly, however, Gilliland and others did not reserve their charity for the virtuous and the worthy among the white population.

Gilliland's less than chivalric attitude toward the immigrant women typified that of many of the elite, for whom association with the lower classes was unsavory though obligatory. Women of wealth often shared a feeling of duty toward the poor, but the plight of powerless women frequently evoked in them an empathy that superseded class distinctions. Members of Charleston's Ladies Benevolent Society, founded in 1813, all belonged to the city's most prominent families, but they defied the stereotype of the society dames who descended upon the huts of the poor, deposited a bag of sugar, some tea, and an inspirational tract, and left feeling virtuous. Instead, they visited the sickbeds of lepers, arranged for nurses to assist the curably ill, and interceded on the behalf of poor women who were sometimes reluctant to ask the gentlemen commissioners for assistance directly. A typical experience was that of Sarah Russell, a leading member of Charleston society, who answered a summons from a brothel in the city's Tenderloin District on a February night. There she found a prostitute in the last throes of death, who begged Russell to take her child away from the iniquitous house and have the commissioners place her in the city's Orphan House.[11]

Even among women who lived in great luxury, few owned their own wealth; thus they understood the precariousness of the lives of working-class women. Associations run by women for women typically encouraged the poor to become self-sufficient rather than fostering dependence with an occasional handout. Whether this approach may be attributed to the typically small budgets of female societies or to a deliberate attempt to help poorer women escape the bonds of dependence upon men is unclear, but women usually imposed much more demanding requirements in return for relief than did the male societies. The Sisters of Charity, operated by the female communicants of Charleston's prestigious St. Michael's Episcopal Church, withheld their support from all but that "class of industrious poor who prefer earning a livelihood for themselves and their families." Annually the society assisted about forty families headed by women who agreed to do sewing in their homes for patrons solicited by the women of the church.[12]

The Charleston Ladies' Seamen Friend Society aided women who suffered deprivation while their husbands sailed on long, hazardous voyages. When the women of the society visited the mean quarters of the sailors' wives, they found them sewing the coarse cloth distributed by the local "slop shops" that specialized in the mass production of cheap clothing. After they worked up rough shirts and trousers at home, the seamstresses took the goods back to the slop dealer, who paid them by the finished piece. The women of the society were so "pained" and outraged at the pittance these workers received that they determined to rob the slop shops of their monopoly and open a store in which poor women could sell their goods at fair prices. Members of the Ladies' Seamen Friend Society spent long hours cutting out patterns for the poor seamen's wives to stitch in their homes. Most considered their contribution to the operation of the Seamen's Bethel Clothing Shop well worth the effort because they had "made many to feel that a new channel is opening to them from which they may receive the means of earning an honest living."[13]

Although the response of poor women to such programs was often gratifying, the husbands of those who were married were often resentful over intrusions into their households and resented their wives' feelings of found independence. A. Toomer Porter, who ran a sewing society at a Charleston Episcopal church, admitted that he sometimes had to replace clothing that his parishioners had sent to be mended because a "drunken husband had resented the intrusion into his domestic circle and had thrown the goods in the fire."[14]

Many women's societies believed that women could have control over their own lives, not merely be dependents of men, either their husbands or the town patriarchs. Women, even if poor, could make contributions and had a legitimate claim to the charity of the city to help them become useful to themselves and the community. The constitution of Richmond's Female Humane Association expressed this sentiment best. Its members pledged themselves to saving the city's women from the degradation that often accompanied poverty, not because those women were the source of the next generation or to protect the moral tone of the town but because every woman was also a "valuable citizen."[15]

The fallacy, of course, in the philosophy of the women's groups that urged self-help was that even the most industrious unskilled women supported themselves only with great difficulty and found raising a family without assistance almost impossible. There was much truth in an observation by a Charleston urban missionary that "misfortunes and afflictions fall with a heavier blow" upon a woman because she is "excluded by her position in Society from all active and lucrative occupations." In 1860, 6 percent of the white women in the four lower wards of the city claimed employment outside of their homes, but with the exception of the few who ran small stores or were trained milliners or skilled dressmakers, most did very menial work such as taking in laundry or sewing. Forty percent found work as domestics, which often required them to leave their families and live in their employers' households.[16] Thomas Stien observed the struggles of his neighbor, a widow with four children, in 1852 and concluded: "Tis impossible for a woman left alone in the cold world to sustain herself and her children at the wash tub, thrice within the last two months has she been brought to the borders of the grave through excessive labour striving to work for bread for her children."[17]

Although the constant stream of applications to the commissioners of the Charleston Orphan House from indigent mothers unable to find work that paid enough to support their children should have been ample evidence of the need for female training and education, they did little to break the cycle of poverty that trapped many of the city's women. Like the boys of the asylum, the girls were apprenticed sometime between their fourteenth and sixteenth birthdays, but their training usually suited them only for marriage and domestic work. A few went to work for milliners or dressmakers, but most moved from the asylum into Charleston homes and became maids. Unlike the boys, who were given the opportunity to attend the high school and even college or professional schools if they seemed talented, the girls' formal education ended when they had mastered the most basic skills.

In 1855, the Committee on Discipline of the Charleston Orphan House revised the girls' educational program to give them more time in the laundry and sewing room at the expense of classroom time but made no corresponding changes in the boys' schedules. Under the new arrangement, the older girls spent seven to eight hours doing the work of the institution and no longer studied grammar or geography except "in their leisure time." The curriculum for boys and girls began running on parallel tracks, one instilling independence, the other perpetuating dependence and servility. Boys competed for academic prizes; girls hoped to win commendation for their domestic achievements. Every Saturday, each girl put her name on the stack of clothes she had mended, washed, ironed, starched, and folded during the week and hoped to be singled out for praise when the lady commissioners completed their inspection. During the 1850s, the most accomplished girls tended to remain in the institution past their eighteenth birthdays. They received room, board, and a small stipend as teaching assistants, if clever, or sewing instructors, if skilled.[18]

Mothers of sons often asked the commissioners to take their children into the institution so they might receive a good education, but the mothers of daughters seldom did so. Many were like Lydia Crafts, who was forced to commit her daughter when abandoned by her husband. After a few very difficult years and with "great exertions," she was able to give up the city rations and live independent of charity. She then petitioned the commissioners for custody of her child. Besides desiring her daughter's company, she wanted to oversee her education personally so that she would grow up learning to be self-reliant and independent of men, either the commissioners or her husband: "I wish above all things in this world . . . to have her finish her education and to learn her to be useful to herself that she may if left as I was with her know how to do as well as I have done for her and [am] still doing."[19]

The benign paternalism of the Orphan House encouraged a thoroughgoing dependence that sometimes persisted, even after the girls left the institution. Some of the young women learned to play upon the patriarchal feelings of the commissioners to their own best advantage. Always couching their requests in the most extravagant language of respect, a skill well rehearsed during their Orphan House stay, they tugged upon the ties that bound them to the commissioners, reminding them of their parental obligations.

Caroline Street, who had been born in New York, spent a few years in the Charleston asylum until she was apprenticed in 1848 as a housekeeper. When she was about to be married at age twenty, two years after her apprenticeship was completed, she wrote to the commissioners suggesting that because she had once been their ward, her welfare remained their responsibility and asking them for "a little pecuniary assistance" to help buy her wedding clothes: "Confiding in your uniform generosity to us Orphans in all our difficulties and necessities, I take the Liberty to beseech your aid at this important juncture in my existence." She closed her request by describing herself as "Your humble and Grateful Child."[20]

The claims of the former girls of the house were not limited to the frivolous requests of brides wanting fashionable clothing. In 1863, a Mrs. Jenkins turned to the commissioners to relieve her of the difficulties brought by her own personal tragedies, which had been exacerbated by the Civil War. At age thirty-three, she had been twice married, twice widowed, and was now unable to support her two children on the "mere pittance which she forces herself to earn by dragging out a miserable existence in drudgery of different kinds." Her application received particular attention because her claim was not only that of the poor upon the rich but also one of a child upon a parent. The commissioners readily agreed to accept her daughter, a second-generation dependent of the city, viewing it as natural that this woman should look "to her alma mater for assistance in bringing up properly her little girl," and permitted her to keep her three-year-old son "as company and solace."[21]

When Catherine Taylors was widowed in 1830, she also asked the institution where she had received care to take in her four children. Writing in the third person, she solicited for her own children all the "blessings of an Institution from whence she herself has derived the protection and support of her Infancy; she therefore commits to a Guardianship with which she is well acquainted, and will forever honor and Respect, her children with the greatest confidence and hope of their future welfare and safety."[22] Just as the obligation to serve the community evolved from one generation to the next, so, too, did the habits of dependency.

Even for those women who were long removed from their Orphan House experience the years they spent in the institution sometimes assumed a nostalgic quality and represented a time when they enjoyed the thoughtless dependency associated with childhood. Mary Kains Spearing maintained a mental tie with the asylum throughout her life. To her, the institution and its commissioners represented not only security but also authority and equity. Orphaned in 1836, she came to the Charleston asylum with her brother and sister when she was eight years old. At sixteen, she moved in with her sister, who had married and left the institution. When this situation proved unsatisfactory, she returned to the Orphan House until she was apprenticed to an umbrella maker, who later failed to provide her with what the commissioners considered a proper home. She left the Orphan House a third time for a position described as "assistant in domestic duties" in a minister's home. She soon tired of the drudgery of that work and asked to return once more to her childhood home, but the board found she had insufficient cause for discontent and refused her request.[23]

Mary Kains continued to seek contact with the Board of Commissioners. After being refused readmittance to the asylum, she rented a room and did what many eighteen-year-old girls who had no skills did— she found a husband. Even though she had not displayed model behavior in the asylum, the commissioners voted to "promote the marriage and allow her thirty dollars for clothing." She returned once more to the institution to be married in the chapel; twenty-two years later she still remembered the names of the commissioners who attended the ceremony.[24]

After her marriage, Mary Kains Spearing moved away and lost touch with the asylum until 1870. Then, widowed, in ill health, and financially ruined by the war, she wrote to the Orphan House Board asking them to honor a pledge made to her as a youth. She reminded them that Henry Desaussure, who had served as a commissioner for forty years, promised her that if she was ever in trouble she must "come to the Orphan House, it would protect me." Desaussure had helped her in 1836 by employing the city attorney to secure a small inheritance left by her mother for the three Kains children. She now entertained a vague notion that there was property yet to be claimed and asked the city to act once again on her behalf. What she really wanted was affirmation that she still enjoyed the protection of the benevolent community in which she was raised. Her plea, "Please help me for I have no home, act for me as though I was still in your house," may be interpreted as a reversion to the dependence upon the fathers of the town instilled by their paternalistic policies.

Women who had lived under the authority of the Orphan House accepted and often welcomed the commissioners' involvement in their lives; their acquiescence often worked to their short-range benefit. Women who had not been raised as part of that community of obligation were more reluctant to acknowledge the right of public men to intervene in their domestic affairs. When a woman fell into need, the relationship with the agents of the city charities was fairly straightforward. She could apply for rations and live at home or ask for a room in the poorhouse and agree to follow the rules of that institution. If she was truly wanting, had no husband, and committed no flagrant breaches of community morality, the commissioners of the poor would likely assist her.

When women of the lower classes had children they wanted to commit to the Orphan House either from necessity or for their own convenience, the relationship between these women and the town fathers became more complex. Before the city accepted responsibility for a child, a commissioner first investigated the child's background and the circumstances of the home, and if he gave his consent, the parent had to renounce all claims to the child through a legal indenture that was equivalent to the contract struck between apprentice and master. In the case of the Orphan House, the children were "apprentices to education." Any contact between parent and child thereafter was strictly at the pleasure of the commissioners. They decided visiting hours, apprenticeships to trades, and, if the circumstances of the parent improved, whether the child should return home. Reunion of parent and child was not automatic. If a parent attempted to steal a child back after the indenture was drawn, the commissioners could call upon the city police to pursue the parent and the city attorney to press charges. Also, any woman who persisted in an immoral manner of life and was reported to the city authority risked having her child taken from her without a hearing.

The commissioners enforced such stringent measures from a mixture of motives. Humanitarianism caused them to be vigilant over the welfare of powerless children and rescue them from possible parental abuse. They also imagined that the Charleston Orphan House, which they designed as a substitute for the "mother's knee, the father's countenance, the hearth, the social board, and the conventional rule," offered an environment vastly superior to that afforded by a German maid or an Irish washerwoman. In fact, the commissioners often failed to acknowledge that lower classes valued their families; their doubts were reinforced when poor women turned their children over to the city. The deliberateness with which many women sought to regain their children suggests that most continued to perceive them as their own property even if they could not support them. When Susan Ridley remarried and was able to take care of her children she explained to the commissioners that she shared the "natural desire of every parent to have their children under their particular care." In 1854, Andrew Carson ran away from the asylum and convinced his widowed mother to apply for his custody and that of his brother. She wrote to the commissioners "To beg you if you please as to be so good as to give me back my sons," reminding them that poverty did not diminish the ties between parents and children: "Thanks be to God i have got well and harty again abel to work for them a support. now gentlemen you no that they ain't one of you that would like to part with your child."[25]

Undeniably, some women did regard their offspring as nuisances when small and servants when grown. For these women the Orphan House served as a convenience, where their children would be fed and clothed, nursed through illnesses, educated, and then returned when they were old enough to make a contribution to the household. In 1842, Ann Kimmy asked the commissioners if they would allow her to exchange her twelve-year-old daughter, who had been in the institution for some years, for her son, who was nearly six: "My reason for the exchange is that Eliza can now be of Servis to me whereas Gustis in onley a burdin and a grate troble to keep out of the street." The number of women sharing Ann Kimmy's sentiments was probably equaled by those who felt like Catherine Biggs. She asked for a job as a nurse in the Orphan House because "I have three children in the institution who are very dear to me."[26]

The right and even the duty of the city's public men to involve themselves with the children of the poor was outlined by Thomas Smith Grimké, who enjoyed high esteem in both the legal and social circles of the conservative southern city. The same fervor that moved his sisters, Sarah and Angelina, to take their unpopular stands propelled Grimké toward an advocacy of Sunday schools and other reforms aimed at the moral improvement of the lower classes.[27]

The force of his reasoning continued to influence the commissioners of the Orphan House throughout the antebellum period. Grimké contended that the bond between parents and children (presumably only of the lower classes) was not a sacred one ordained by God. Although he believed "Family Government the foundation of Society," he did not interpret this principle to mean that parents exercised exclusive control over their children for "every child belongs first to God, next to his Country, and lastly to his Parents or other Guardians," who served as "merely Trustees." If natural parents were but the nurturers and keepers of the next generation of Christians and Americans, that trusteeship could easily be transferred or forfeited by a relative to those most able to assume the responsibility, who also had a strong claim upon these future citizens, without disrupting any divine order. Grimké reasoned that whenever, through God's plan, a child was left parentless, the responsibility of the city became clear and binding: "The Community becomes their parents; and is bound to discharge the duties of one." "You," Grimké charged the commissioners of the Orphan House in an 1825 address, "are the agents" of the community. It was through this agency that the commissioners believed they had the right not only to take in parentless children but to take under their control the children of the unfit.[28]

What Grimké failed to tell the commissioners was how to convince the poor women of the city that they were God's agents, empowered to judge the women's fitness as mothers. Irishwoman Margaret Boggs did not hesitate to confront the fathers of the town when they intruded upon her private life. Although an excellent seamstress and able to provide for her children, Margaret Boggs also was a chronic drinker and occasionally spent a night in the city jail for being drunk in public. When she returned from a jail stay in the spring of 1827, she discovered that neighbors had reported her as a negligent and unfit mother and the steward of the Orphan House had taken the children from her rooms without her knowledge or consent. She immediately wrote to the commissioners, beginning her letter with the customary humility, promising "an entire change and reformation," but her anger swelled as she wrote and she ended up frankly venting her feelings about their violation of her home: "What was at the time by you considered as a duty (though my children were taken off from me by surprise) . . . may be deemed oppression now that I can prove my ability to keep my children, free from encumbrance to the public." Boggs acknowledged the right of the city to intervene if a mother's negligence might cause the children or herself to become a public burden, but she emphatically denied that it had the right to rule on her fitness as a mother upon moral grounds. The relationship between mother and child, she contended, superseded any claim of the city: "My children, Gentlemen, are my own and I am their mother. They are the only link which binds me to this world; judge then of my lacerated feelings to live separated from them both."[29]

The commissioners remained unmoved by Boggs's pleadings and retained custody of her children until a respected man from her neighborhood vouched for her sincerity, both in her love for her children and her willingness to reform. For three months she had kept an oath not to drink, made "before God and the townspeople," and had agreed to send her children faithfully to the free school. Thus, he explained, she had followed as closely as possible "the requisite conditions prescribed to her, by your wisdom; having thus fulfilled your demands of her Duty towards you, she requires you, Gentlemen, to fulfill yours towards her by restoring to her bosom what only makes life dear to her. If contrary to her most sanguine expectations, you persist in your refusal, nothing will remain to her, but to quite this world of misery."[30]

The commissioners agreed to reunite Boggs's family, thus upholding their part of the bargain with Boggs, which resembled the larger contract between the lower classes and the town elite. They pledged to let the poor live their lives without undue control in exchange for the acknowledgment that that control did exist.

Other women denied the right of the city to regulate their relationship with their children but were less willing than Margaret Boggs to confront the commissioners of the Orphan House. They took the less direct but equally eloquent approach and hid their children or stole them from the asylum. When the husband of a Charleston woman had to be taken to the insane asylum in Columbia, a member of the German Fusiliers benevolent society encouraged the city to investigate the condition of her children. Neighbors warned the woman that representatives from the Orphan House had been making inquiries, so she quietly left town. After her husband died, Clara Gorge Haggamore was unable to support her children, so she legally bound them to the Orphan House for their wellbeing. After a year, her youngest, four-year-old Eliza, died in the institution of dropsy. Although the mortality rate of the orphanage was very low, the mother feared for the safety of her two sons and "stole" the boys by refusing to return them to the asylum after a visit. Whenever the master of the Orphan House called to reclaim them, "she always kept them locked up and denied that they were with her." The commissioners considered offering her free rations from the city market if she returned the boys, then decided they did not want to negotiate because the law was on their side. Instead, they discussed having her committed to the cells of the Alms House, for she was clearly deranged.[31]

The majority of single parents who bound their children to the Charleston Orphan House, as well as those who later tried to retrieve them, were women, but one case heard before the commissioners in 1852 involving a father's claim to his children is instructive for the contrast it presents with the official attitude toward the rights of mothers. John Smythe and his family had enjoyed a comfortable living from his upholstery and furniture shop until he became so intemperate and negligent that his business declined. He lost his store and could no longer support his children. When his wife became ill and entered the hospital ward of the Poor House for treatment, she requested that the children be accepted into the Orphan House, where their welfare would be assured. One of the commissioners paid the obligatory call and found a penitent Smythe, who had taken an oath of temperance before a Catholic priest as the first step toward reformation. Although Smythe's wife continued to press for the children's admission, having been too often disappointed by the promises of an alcoholic, the commissioners took the side of the father, who refused to give up his children. Henry A. Desaussure wrote in his report that "for the present, I would recommend that the children be not forcibly taken from the Father's control against his wishes. If children become or remain, a burthen upon the public bounty they may then be transferred to the Orphan House." Not only were the father's wishes given precedent over his wife's, but intemperance in the male was viewed with much less moral indignation than the same failing in a woman.[32]

Some women resisted placing their children in the Orphan House because it implied the shame of being unfit. But to women who had no alternatives and were desperate for a safe home for their children, the Orphan House was literally an asylum. When these anxious mothers approached the commissioners, it was to assert their right, not to keep their child in their home but to claim the city's benevolence.

Few women stated the case for their children in as sophisticated fashion as Elizabeth Whitney, who described herself as "a lone and poor widow." Writing in a very matter-of-fact manner, she argued that because her parents and her late husband's parents had paid taxes most of their lives, a percentage of which went to the support of the Orphan House, she and her four children had a legitimate claim upon the charity of the city. Even though those taxpayers were now dead, she contended, their contribution should be considered as a sort of insurance policy binding the city to care for their heirs: "If then you refuse my claim and withhold the privilege purchased for them by my children's forefathers and cast me and them . . . upon the unfriendly stranger what am I to expect but misery worse than death."[33]

The town fathers made an important distinction between petitioners who came to Charleston merely to benefit from the generosity of its citizens, which included those who migrated from the rural areas as well as immigrants, and those who were natives. Mary Ann Ferenbach was mindful of this distinction when she appealed to the commissioners to take one of her sons whom she could not control. An immigrant from Germany, abandoned by her debt-plagued husband, she explained that she was asking the town for nothing for herself, only for her six children. When the board of the Orphan House decided that assuming care for one son from a family fulfilled their obligation, she wrote an impassioned reply begging them to relieve her of a "burden she could not bear": "My children are yours, They are natives, they are Southerners, and though their Father has forgotten himself, and deserted them, this is their country. And though poor and friendless, shall my son not be heard because a Mother's tongue alone urges his claim. . . . Oh, save him from being a curse to the soil that gave him birth, and spare the Mother from the anguish which this Mother must endure at the mere debasement of her child."[34] Fearful that she had injured her case by violating the traditional deferential mode of address of applicants for the city's charity she added: "Be not offended by my language, I am filled with anxiety." As in the case of Margaret Boggs, the commissioners did not grant Ferenbach's petition until a respectable man from her neighborhood wrote on her behalf.[35]

Through the agency of the Charleston Orphan House, thousands of the city's immigrant and poor white children developed ties to the community, learned to view the city elite as benevolent patriarchs, and studied the lessons of the Protestant faith in Sunday school and chapel services. Since that institution could house only about 350 children annually, in 1854 the town fathers established free schools to bring a greater percentage of the city's 4,000 youth in harmony with the white community and as a means of eventually improving the status of the South's white working class. William Henry Trescott shared the concern of many southern leaders that there was a need to maintain the distinctions between the "lowest and humblest of white laborers and the highest development of black" through education.[36]

After the mechanism for the schools was in place and properly funded, there remained the task of inducing the poor to send their children. Sporadically, the commissioners of the poor made rules, then usually failed to enforce them, tying the receipt of free rations by outpensioners living in the city to the school attendance of their children. In 1860 schoolteachers were given the names of all children whose parents, usually just a mother, were dependent upon the charity of the city. Strict records of attendance were kept and excuses for absences demanded. Even with the threat of losing their allowance of bread and beef, attendance remained spotty, for mothers resented this intrusion upon their families and especially disliked having their children singled out for ridicule. Most of the excuses were likely artifice—"mother's finger sore," "mother sick"—and others admitted they had no shoes to wear. Unwilling to account to the city for the whereabouts of her child, the mother of C. M. Neal returned her ration book and kept her son at home.[37]

Mrs. Neal's small mutiny illustrates an important point about the relationship between the recipients of public largesse and the men who dispensed it. There seems to be a certain point at which the poor would close their lives to intervention by the city fathers and would suffer deprivation if necessary. Women refused rations rather than be cross-examined by the Poor House commissioners about their fitness to receive the city's benevolence or slept under houses to avoid the restrictions and stigma of the Poor House. Women who found it impossible or improvident to steal their children back from the Orphan House devised ways to subvert the commissioners' authority. The uniforms of the orphans, designed to identify them as "children of the public," proved particularly irksome to mothers because they advertised that poverty had severed their bonds with their children. As a remedy, disgruntled mothers began carrying paper bags with old clothes when they picked up their children on visiting day. As soon as they rounded the corner and were out of sight of the Orphan House, the children shed their sartorial stigma and took on the appearance of an ordinary family out on Saturday errands.[38]

What the town fathers understood but historians sometimes forget was that the poor were actors in their own lives. They made decisions regardless of attempts at manipulation by social reformers or urban elite. By withholding their participation in public programs the poor exercised some control over the town governors, who, in Charleston at least, were anxious to bring them into the community of obligation. The Charleston free school system underwent a costly and extensive renovation in 1856 to attract the poor children who had previously eschewed the "pauper academies."[39] The Charleston Orphan House also tried to inculcate the next generation into the deferential society. It was with this object in mind that Poor House Commissioner John Horlbeck urged the board of the children's asylum to accept the son of a woman whose husband was ill and dying because "by receiving him upon the Bounty of that institution you will confer a lasting obligation upon her and the Child." John England, bishop of Charleston, wrote to the Poor House commissioners in 1823 reminding them that a larger number of the Catholic poor who were in desperate need would enter the Alms House if they felt that in doing so they need not give up the practice of their faith; they particularly feared dying without last rites or being buried in unconsecrated ground. England observed that in his experience neither the city nor the church could "force this class of people though we may win them and guide them and lead them."[40]

It is difficult to evaluate the success of the commissioners of Charleston's public charities in winning or leading the poor women of the city. In deriving the equation of "what the social classes owed each other," the urban elite exchanged a subsistence living and the opportunity for the poor womens' children (mostly the boys) to be upwardly mobile for deference to their authority and acceptance of community mores. For some women, this was a good bargain, for others a bitter one. One incident perhaps gives some indication of how thoroughly the patriarchs of Charleston had convinced the poor women that their best interests would be served under the patronage of the elite. In 1863 and 1864 food shortages caused by speculation and poor distribution victimized the poor of the urban South. Women of Savannah, Richmond, and Mobile armed themselves with kitchen knives and hatchets and expressed their anger and sense of betrayal by rioting in the commercial districts. In Charleston, however, because of the long tradition of paternalistic charity and assurances by "a Voluntary Union of Gentlemen" known for their benevolent work that they would maintain food supplies for the poor, no poor woman carried a placard threatening "Bread or Blood."[41]

Notes

I would like to thank David L. Carlton, Deborah Clifford, and David Macey, who read drafts of this essay and made many helpful suggestions.

1. The classic study of the development of northern paternalism is Clifford S. Griffin, *Their Brothers' Keepers: Moral Stewardship in the United States, 1800–1865* (New Brunswick: Rutgers University Press, 1960); also useful is Lois Banner, "Religious Benevolence as Social Control: A Critique of an Interpretation," *Journal of American History* 40 (June 1973): 23–41. The most recent

scholarship on the relationship between the humanitarian and the poor is collected in Frances F. Piven and Richard A. Cloward, *Social Welfare or Social Control? Some Historical Reflections on Regulating the Poor*, ed. Walter I. Trattner (Knoxville: University of Tennessee Press, 1983). Michael P. Johnson, "Planters and Patriarchy: Charleston, 1800–1860," *Journal of Southern History* 46 (February 1980): 45–72, is an excellent discussion of the patriarchs' perception of their role in urban society. Anne C. Loveland, *Southern Evangelicals and the Social Order, 1800–1860* (Baton Rouge: Louisiana State University Press, 1980), especially pp. 159–85, considers the desire among the evangelicals to "uplift" the urban poor through temperance and other moral reforms.

2. Reverend Thomas McGruder, *Report Presented to the Female Domestic Missionary Society of Charleston, South Carolina* (Charleston: Observer Office Press, 1837), p. 8; E. W. Edgerton to commissioners of the Orphan House, December 27, 1855, application file, Charleston Orphan House Papers, City of Charleston Archive (hereafter OH Papers). I do not use [sic] with quotations from the correspondence of the Orphan House or the Poor House.

3. For a discussion of the colonial vestry's approach to the urban poor see Barbara Bellows Ulmer, "Benevolence in Colonial Charleston," *South Carolina Historical Association Proceedings* (1980), pp. 1–6. Robert M. Weir describes the unique nature of colonial South Carolina politics and the development of ideological consensus in " 'The Harmony We Were Famous For': An Interpretation of Pre-Revolutionary South Carolina Politics," *William and Mary Quarterly*, 3d ser., 26 (1969): 473–501.

4. Robert Mills, *Statistics of South Carolina* (Charleston: Hurlbut and Lloyd, 1826), p. 428. In 1822, 938 people were relieved by the Poor House, either by admission or by grants of free rations at a cost to the city of almost $17,000. One guide to the wages of domestic servants may be the $6 monthly salary paid to the nurses, maids, and "drudges" of the Poor House and Orphan House, which probably included meals and perhaps a room; the average salary for women working in Charleston's bakeries was $6.90 a month (Charleston County, Manufacturing Census, 1850). Wages for women were notoriously low in all southern cities. The *Richmond Daily Dispatch* (February 9, 1857) remarked: "If a lady has a job by which she can earn 50 cents to 60 cents a day, she is considered to be entirely independent. Many, however, have to support themselves and children on much less sums and we know more than one who are actually making up shirts and drawers for six and one-quarter cents each."

5. Michael P. Johnson, "Wealth and Class in Charleston in 1860," in Walter J. Fraser, Jr., and Winfred B. Moore, Jr., eds., *From the Old South to the New: Essays on the Transitional South* (Westport, Conn.: Greenwood Press, 1981), p. 69.

6. Johnson, "Planters and Patriarchy," pp. 46–48; Overseers of the Poor, Richmond, Virginia, Minute Book, 1818–28, June 5, 1820, Virginia State Archives, Richmond.

7. A thorough account of the continuous struggle by city fathers to reform the denizens of the city to fit the middle-class mold may be found in Paul Boyer,

Urban Masses and Moral Order in America, 1820–1920 (Cambridge, Mass.: Harvard University Press, 1978). Christopher Silver, "A New Look at Old South Urbanization: The Irish Worker in Charleston, S.C., 1840–1860," *South Atlantic Urban Studies* 3 (1978): 141–71, describes the fear that the white working class was falling out of sympathy with the institution of slavery and with slaveholders.

8. "Yellow Fever in Charleston," *Southern Quarterly Review* 7 (1853): 144. See also Ira Berlin and Herbert Gutman, "Natives and Immigrants, Free Men and Slaves," *American Historical Review* (December 1983): 1176–2000.

9. Johnson, "Wealth and Class in Charleston," p. 73. Whenever the commissioners of the Orphan House discovered white children of the lower class being cared for in the homes of Negroes, they promptly committed them to the city orphan asylum, which only accepted white children. Even when it was decided that free blacks who had paid taxes had a claim to the charity of the city in their old age, the stipulation was made that they be kept separate from the white poor because "the distinction of castes must be strictly and broadly preserved in slave holding communities" (*Proceedings of the Commissioners of the Poor of the City of Charleston* [Charleston: N.p., 1842]), p. 4, Berlin and Gutman, "Natives and Immigrants," p. 1179.

10. William H. Gilliland, Account Book, September 26, November 15, 1860, Perkins Library, Duke University.

11. Application file, February 24, 1825, OH Papers.

12. *Southern Episcopalian* 7 (February 1860): 585–88.

13. *Charleston Courier*, March 25, 1848.

14. A. Toomer Porter, *Led On! Step by Step* (1896; rpt. New York: Arno Press, 1967), pp. 98–100.

15. *Constitution and Bylaws of the Female Humane Association of the City of Richmond, Adopted 1833* (Richmond: Shepherd and Colin, 1843).

16. This figure, based upon the United States manuscript census of the city of Charleston for 1860, is lower than the 9.5 percent found to be employed in Petersburg, Virginia, by Susan Lebsock, *The Free Women of Petersburg* (New York: Norton, 1983), and the 8.9 percent at work in Mobile in 1860 in Alan Smith Thompson, "Mobile, Alabama, 1850–1861: Economic, Political, Physical, and Population Characteristics" (Ph.D. dissertation, University of Alabama, 1979), pp. 255–56. The probable explanation is that the lower four wards of Charleston were compared with the records of the Charleston Poor House, which admitted only the residents of the lower wards until 1854. The upper wards and the Charleston Neck had large working-class populations, so it is possible that counting all the wards would raise the percentage. Also, Charleston lacked the opportunities for factory work that were available to the women of Petersburg and Richmond. Among the women of Charleston's lower wards, 10 percent were milliners and 11 percent were seamstresses, but this likely means they were skilled as opposed to those who took in sewing to supplement husbands' incomes or subsidies from public or private charity; 44 percent worked as domestic servants, housekeepers, or washerwomen.

17. McGruder, *Report Presented to the Female Domestic Missionary Society,* p. 8. The best information on the outpensioners of the Charleston Poor House is for the years 1817–25; other information is less complete and often the total numbers receiving aid are not broken down by sex. In 1820, 94 percent (176 versus 186) of the outpensioners were women, 60 percent of whom were widowed, 51 percent lived alone and supported children, 13 percent lived alone, 11 percent were married but received the rations in their name, and 23 percent were old or sick. Based upon the proportion of women among the outpensioners in several years, one may calculate that the number of women receiving rations would be for 1830, 212; 1840, 117; 1850, 186; 1860, 328 (Thomas Stien to commissioners of the Orphan House, November 25, 1852, application file, OH Papers).

18. William Bell, "Report of the Committee on Discipline," ca. 1855, Commissioners' File, OH Papers.

19. Lydia Crafts to commissioners of the Orphan House, June 14, 1833, application file, OH Papers.

20. Caroline M. Street to commissioners of the Orphan House, August 19, 1852, inmates file, OH Papers.

21. Visiting Commissioners' Report, March 2, 1863, application file, OH Papers.

22. Caroline Taylors to commissioners of the Orphan House, March 30, 1831, application file, OH Papers.

23. Mary Kains Spearing to commissioners of the Orphan House, June 23, 1870, Commissioner's Report, n.d.; commissioners' file, OH Papers.

24. Ibid.

25. Orphan House Minutes, March 2, 1848; Susan Ridley to commissioners of the Orphan House, April 20, 1826; Mrs. Carson to commissioners of the Orphan House, February 2, 1854, indenture file, OH Papers. From 1830 to 1839, for example, 260 children were admitted to the Orphan House; 51 girls and 92 boys were committed by a parent. Ten percent were reclaimed by their mothers, 5 percent went to other relatives, and only one boy was removed from the asylum by his father (indenture files, OH Papers).

26. Ann Kimmy to commissioners of the Orphan House, December 22, 1842, rejected indenture file; Catherine E. Biggs to commissioners of the Orphan House, application file, November 9, 1831, OH Papers.

27. For an excellent discussion of this important member of Charleston's intellectual and reform community, see Adrienne Koch, "Two Charlestonians in Pursuit of Truth: The Grimké Brothers," *South Carolina Historical Magazine* 69 (1968): 159–70.

28. Thomas Grimké, "Report on Sunday Schools," April 1825, Commissioners' file, OH Papers.

29. Margaret Boggs to commissioners of the Orphan House, April 17, 28, 1827, indenture file, OH Papers.

30. Ibid.

31. George Jacoby to commissioners of the Orphan House, April 8, 1830, application file, OH Papers; commissioners of the Charleston Poor House, Minute Book, January 20, 1841, Poor House Papers, City of Charleston Archives (hereafter PH Papers).

32. Henry A. Desaussure, Report on John Smythe, December 23, 1852, Commissioners' file, OH Papers.

33. Elizabeth H. Whitney to commissioners of the Orphan House, October 27, 1863, application file, OH Papers.

34. Mary Ann Ferenbach to commissioners of the Orphan House, ca. November 1844, application file, OH Papers.

35. Ibid.; John Phillips to commissioners of the Orphan House, November 5, 1844, application file, OH Papers.

36. William Henry Trescott quoted in "The Free Schools of Charleston," *Southern Quarterly,* n.s., 2 (November 1856): 150.

37. Commissioners of the Charleston Poor House, December 12, 1860, March 20, 1861, Minute Book, PH Papers.

38. Commissioners of the Orphan House, October 27, 1845, March 2, 1848, OH Papers.

39. Laylon Wayne Jordan, "Education for Community: C. G. Memminger and the Origination of Common Schools in Antebellum Charleston," *South Carolina Historical Magazine* 80 (1981): 99–115, presents a thoughtful discussion of Charleston's antebellum school reform.

40. John England to commissioners of the Poor House, September 22, 1838, Minute Book, PH Papers; John Horlbeck to commissioners of the Orphan House, September 16, 1824, Commissioners' file, OH Papers.

41. "An Ordinance to provide for the Removal of Negroes and Other Property from the Portions of the State which may be Invaded by the Enemy," in Yates Snowden, "Charleston in Wartime," *Yearbook of the City of Charleston* (Charleston: Walker, Evans, 1908), p. 53.

The Perrys of Greenville:
A Nineteenth-Century Marriage

Carol K. Bleser

When Benjamin Perry died in 1886, his grieving widow noted with deep satisfaction that her husband's last words to her were that he loved her even more at that moment than on their wedding day fifty years before. In the little time remaining to Elizabeth Perry, she set about with the aid of her family to gather together for publication her husband's letters, speeches, editorials, and historical sketches. Love for her husband, she wrote, dictated her course, which was to reveal to the world the "noble character" and great "Patriot" her husband had been, having "labored for 30 years to *preserve* the Union," yet having been treated after the Civil War "as those were who labored to *destroy* it." The more she read his writings and copied portions of his journal, the more she loved him. While seeking to memorialize the Unionist politician and lawyer from the up-country of South Carolina, Elizabeth Perry seemed also to be inviting the reader into the private world of their marriage.[1]

Benjamin Franklin Perry, born in Pendleton District, South Carolina, on November 20, 1805, was the third of the four children of Benjamin and Anna Foster Perry. His mother, the daughter of a Virginian, and his father, an immigrant from Massachusetts, met in the remote, picturesque backcountry of what is now Oconee County. When they married in 1798, the senior Benjamin Perry was thirty-eight years old and his bride twenty-one. Anna and Benjamin, with the labor of three sons and twelve to fifteen slaves, led a reasonably comfortable life on their frontier farm of seven to eight hundred acres. Young Benjamin, an obsessive reader from his early teens, hated the farm and wrote that he felt "like a bird in a cage." He vowed he would not be a farmer. Fortunately for him, his

72

mother's brother, Robert Foster, a well-to-do merchant in Greenville, offered to advance him the money for a formal education, which his parents were unable to provide.[2]

Benjamin entered Asheville Academy in 1821 when he was sixteen
years old. Two years later he moved to the village of Greenville, which in
1823 had a population of about five hundred, and attended Greenville
Academy. His ambition was to enter the junior class of South Carolina
College in 1824, but he decided the expense would be too great and
began reading law in the office of a local attorney. Admitted to the bar in
1827, the young lawyer and aspiring politician came of age at the incep-
tion of the nullification crisis in South Carolina. Throughout his career,
Perry stated that the *Federalist Papers* and George Washington's *Farewell
Address* provided the foundation for his political ideology. From the very
beginning of his political life he was a Unionist and opposed the popular
clamor for states rights. He wrote that he was sustained in these beliefs at
first by "Mr. Calhoun, Governor McDuffie, Judge Butler . . . and Governor Hamilton. But a sudden change came over the state and all of these
gentlemen acquiesced in the change"—all, that is, except Perry, who "remained steadfast in the faith" of his youth. In 1830 he became the editor
of the *Greenville Mountaineer,* and in its columns he challenged the views
of the champions of nullification, even fighting a duel in 1832 with
Turner Bynum, editor of the *Greenville Southern Sentinel.* At the nullification convention in 1832, Perry, a delegate from Greenville, refused
to join the other Unionist representatives in signing the ordinance that
declared the tariffs of 1828 and 1832 null and void. After the crisis with
the federal government was resolved, at least temporarily, in 1833, Perry
ran for a seat in the United States Congress in 1834 and again in 1835
but was defeated both times by nullifiers.[3]

Perry was elected in 1836 to the state legislature from Greenville District, a Unionist stronghold. He served for more than twenty-five years
with the exception of the term 1842–44, when he withdrew from politics, and 1848, when he ran again for a seat in Congress. Throughout his
tenure he was a leader of a minority in the state legislature, waging battle
against the dominant states-rights party. In the same year that he won
election to the legislature, the thirty-year-old Perry wrote in his journal
that he was lonely and depressed. He observed, "Every man ought to get
married if possible—man must have something to have and to take care
of—I feel the want of this something."[4]

Elizabeth Frances McCall, the daughter of Susan Branford Hayne and
Hext McCall, was born in Charleston, October 28, 1818. Her mother
was the sister of Robert Young Hayne of the Webster-Hayne debate, who

was governor at the height of the nullification crisis. Hext McCall, a law partner of Robert Hayne, died suddenly in 1821, leaving his widow with five young children to raise. Mrs. McCall never remarried, but she lived until 1875. Elizabeth, called "Lizzie," or "Liz," grew up with her brother and three sisters among the members of her mother's affluent planter family. When Liz was ten years old, her mother moved to New Haven, Connecticut, to further the education of her children. Liz's brother William entered Yale, his father's alma mater, and she and her three sisters attended Miss Peter's Academy in New Haven to gain, in her mother's words, "the advantage of thorough educations." The two eldest sons of Robert Hayne were also at Yale while the McCalls were in New Haven, and they visited their aunt often. The youngest McCall child, Martha, died of scarlet fever during their stay in Connecticut, and when William became ill, Mrs. McCall returned with her family to Charleston, where William died in 1833 soon after their arrival. Liz's formal education ended when she and her family returned to Charleston. She was fourteen years old.[5]

In the summer of 1836 seventeen-year-old Elizabeth was staying with her mother and two sisters, Susan and Anne, at the Mansion House, a fashionable summer resort in Greenville, where Perry boarded year-round. He sought an introduction to the McCall women "and was particularly pleased with" Mrs. McCall's youngest daughter, Liz. Perry described the blue-eyed blonde as "slender and sylph-like . . . with a beautiful complexion and wearing her hair short and in curls. Her voice was sweet. She was amiable, and I thought beautiful and intelligent . . . I walked to the Falls with her one moonlight night and began to feel an interest in her."[6] Liz later claimed that he fell in love with her the first night they met.

No fortune hunter, Perry was not diverted when, in the midst of his whirlwind courtship of Liz, Ann Pamela Cunningham arrived with her parents. Perry recorded in his autobiography that he had thought "something of Miss Pamela, and had been frequently at her father's house [and plantation, Rosemont] and was a great favorite with him and Mrs. Cunningham, but," he insisted, "I had never said one word of love to her." He added that Miss Pamela was pretty, very intellectual, accomplished, and rich, whereas, Liz's mother was "in very moderate circumstances." By late 1836, after Perry had ridden two legal circuits and returned to Liz at the Mansion House, he knew he "was in love, deep and determined."[7]

Elizabeth recorded that her love for Benjamin developed more gradually: "I was so young; I did not at once realize the character of the noble man who had given his great heart into my keeping." He pressed her for an answer. She wondered aloud why he was so drawn to her and delayed her reply. She probably was attracted to his maturity and to his promise of becoming a leading attorney and politician, as well as to his good looks. He described himself about that time as being "six feet two and one-half inches tall, slender and erect, a manly but not handsome face, hazel eyes, long nose, high forehead . . . and a good chin." When he asked again if she would marry him she sent him to her mother. Mrs. McCall suggested that he visit them at home after the adjournment of the legislature, at which time a wedding date might be set. Considering himself conditionally engaged, he gave Liz his miniature and a gold watch and chain.[8]

Perry hastened to Charleston after the close of the legislative session in late December and spent two weeks in the company of Liz and her family. He recalled that every evening after tea "the old lady and her other two daughters retired and left Lizzie and myself to enjoy the remainder of the evening alone." He wrote, "In this way my time passed most blissfully." When he left for Greenville, the wedding date had been set.[9] On April 27, 1837, Perry, then thirty-one years old and an ardent Unionist of up-country South Carolina, married the eighteen-year-old niece of the prince of nullifiers, Robert Young Hayne. Perry was not the only up-country lawyer in South Carolina to marry into a distinguished family from the low country. The most famous to do so were John C. Calhoun, James Henry Hammond, and James L. Petigru. Unlike Hammond, Perry was cordially received into his wife's planter family despite "the knowledge of your opinions and your cause," as Liz's aunt wrote to him in the midst of the secessionist crisis in 1851.[10]

It was to be a marriage of affection and cooperation; some historians refer to such liaisons as companionate marriages. Perry wrote Liz before their wedding that he was disposed to follow the maxim he had read in the Bible that "after marriage the husband should neither go to war nor engage in business for one year, but stay at home and comfort his wife." He inquired, "What say you? For in this matter I am very much inclined to consult your pleasure."[11] A man of his word, during the first year of their marriage he helped fix up their new house in Greenville. While she made the carpets and curtains, he built shelves in the kitchen and benches and shelves in the basement, helped her tack down the carpets and hang curtains, planted trees, roses, strawberries, and raspberries, and even helped her make strawberry preserves.[12] Several years later he recorded their domesticity in his journal: "I get up in the morning at five o'clock. Liz rises at the same time. We finish dressing at the same time. She in her curtained room, I in the open chamber . . . I see nothing of her until I see her dressed. She then dresses our little Will and the maid servant makes up the bed and arranges the room. I go down stairs and walk to the stables, see the cows, hogs and horses fed; look at the garden and return."[13]

He would read until breakfast, either to Elizabeth, if she was not occupied with household affairs, or to himself. They ate breakfast at seven o'clock. He then went to his law office, which was in the center of town near the courthouse and only one town lot away from his house. He returned home "a couple of times a day" to see Liz, the children, and the garden and to eat a midday dinner. He never returned to the office after supper unless there was urgent business. The evenings were spent at home, in the early years reading to Liz and, after the children came along, talking and playing with them.[14]

Distressed that Liz's formal education had ended when she was fourteen, Perry sought to become her tutor, "cultivating with care and assiduity" her taste for reading. At first, he attempted to read to her all that he had read, and his journal entries record that he read her "a portion of Virgil, Milton's works, Pope's *Rape of the Lock, An Essay on Man, Conversations of Lady Blessington with Lord Byron,* Lockhart's *Life of Scott,* and Plutarch's *Lives.*" As time passed, however, he purchased for her "a complete set of Bulwer's novels for the female library in 20 volumes" and contemporary books of advice such as William A. Alcott's *The Young Wife: Or, Duties of Woman in the Marriage Relation.* Nowhere does he list purchasing Alcott's *The Young Husband: Or, Duties of Man in the Marriage.*[15]

Despite their marital affection, Perry fully subscribed to the doctrine of two spheres, an ideology held by many American nineteenth-century husbands and wives, who thought that nature dictated sharply differentiated roles for each sex. The usual assumption was that the sphere of the man consisted of activities outside the home, business, politics, and the world in general, whereas the sphere of the woman included the emotional and physical maintenance of the home, the care of the children, the nurturing of the husband, and serving as the ethical and spiritual guardian of the family.[16] In 1879, after forty-two years of married life, Perry addressed the students at Walhalla Female College on women's place in marriage. He stated emphatically that "the Almighty created man for one purpose and woman for another, and gave them different properties and qualities suitable to the purposes for which he created them. He gave the man strength and courage; and to the woman he gave grace, modesty, timidity, and physical weakness. The man was to provide for and defend the woman. She on her part was to depend on him and confide in him." Perry was unwilling to see women "pass out of their proper sphere and invade the domain of men by becoming legislators, military commanders, lawyers, judges, doctors, and ministers of the gospel." Women, he believed, should marry and support their husbands' endeavors in these fields and "nurse the children, superintend . . . household affairs, make the home pleasant and agreeable and enjoy themselves in ease and quiet."[17] In private he gave his daughter Fannie the same advice that he gave to the women at Walhalla Academy, even though he acknowledged the intellectual superiority of his daughter over his five sons, writing in his autobiography in 1874 that "she would have been a distinguished man."[18]

Perry was a good provider. In the spring of 1838 the couple moved into a larger, newly built house. They lived there for more than thirty-three years. As his family increased and his book collection grew to more than eight hundred law books and seventeen hundred miscellaneous volumes, Perry added a library and another bedroom. In 1844 he bought a two-hundred-acre farm a few miles out of town, on which he raised thoroughbred Berkshire pigs and planted some crops. His income from his law practice grew as his reputation spread beyond the circuit, and his services were sought for important cases around the state. The year he married he earned $2,800; twenty years later, in 1857, his professional income was $7,000 or $8,000, and in 1860 his annual income reached $10,000. By 1843, he was out of debt and owned $17,420 worth of property. In 1856, Perry estimated that his property was worth $54,640, of which $12,750 was invested in twenty slaves.[19]

While Benjamin's income was growing, Liz was almost always pregnant. In the first ten years of marriage, she gave birth to four children, had two stillborn daughters, and suffered four miscarriages. Perry complained about his wife's fertility, as though he himself had nothing to do with it, but consoled himself with the Victorian cant that "all women are anxious to have children and none are happy who are married without them." This condition, he wrote, was natural. "It is a feeling of nature planted in the bosom of women . . . their happiness through life depends on it. They must have something to nurse, love, and pet, something to hope for in the future." The healthy, energetic, and lucky Liz Perry had at least thirteen pregnancies. She raised seven children to young adulthood: William Hayne born in 1839, Anna born in 1841, Benjamin Franklin in 1843, Elizabeth Frances in 1847, Hext McCall in 1851, Robert Hayne in 1854, and Arthur Hayne in 1856. Three of these children, Anna, Benjamin, and Robert, died of tuberculosis in 1859, 1860, and 1872 respectively, and the accounts of their deaths are heartrending.[20]

Childrearing, both parents agreed, was the primary responsibility of the mother. With Benjamin away much of the time every spring and fall at court and at the annual month-long session of the legislature, Elizabeth kept house and raised the children with the help of a growing number of domestic servants. Liz was frequently annoyed by the behavior of the slaves and complained to Benjamin in many of her letters of their "idleness and impudence." Before the children started attending a local school at the age of five or six, Liz taught them their letters and some spelling. Perry, more indulgent with the children than was Liz, thought she whipped them too much, and, she, in turn, wrote that it was easier to manage the children alone because when he was home they fled to him to avoid punishment. She wrote, "If we can agree in our system of bringing up our children, we will be an assistance to each other, though the responsibility during their years of infancy rests upon me, the Mother who am constantly with them." Perry, an extraordinarily attentive parent, who frequently walked the floor at night with his colicky children and took them off, each in turn, to ride the circuit with him or to attend an annual session of the legislature, readily agreed to her prerogatives in this sphere and seldom thereafter interfered with the day-to-day responsibility of child care.[21]

By the early 1840s, as a family man, Perry was at the center of a growing circle of people who were devoted to him. In 1841, Liz's mother, who considered him a son, moved to Greenville to be near Elizabeth and her family. Benjamin mused in 1843 on the perfection of his marital state: "What a pleasure to return to one's wife and children, it is like returning to oneself. I love [and] need to be happy with my wife and children. There is no fault to find with them." He noted, "My dear Lizzie is the most affectionate of wives. Little Will is very handsome, intelligent, good disposed and promising. Little Anna will make a charming woman, and is now the most interesting little creature of her age in the world."[22] Will was almost four and Anna was seventeen months old.

Benjamin Perry's biographer, Lillian Kibler, was convinced that the Perrys' married life of fifty years was one of uninterrupted domestic tranquillity and marital bliss, and so it was presented in autobiographies Perry wrote in 1849 and 1874, in the journal he kept between 1832 and 1863, in the "Extracts from Governor Perry's Journal" with comments and explanations made by his wife in 1888, in the "Sketch of the Life of Governor B. F. Perry Written by His Wife" in 1889, as well as in the 207 letters of Perry to his wife, which after his death in December 1886 were carefully selected and published, in one volume by their son Hext in 1889 and in another by Liz in 1890. The picture presented, however, was more than that of a successful, happy marriage, which their union certainly was. It was, in addition, a portrait of an ideal domestic concord fitting every conventional form prescribed for the middle-class Victorian marriage. Perry, a lifelong maverick in politics, presented his domestic life and his wife as the very models of unquestioned conventionality. In this telling he was abetted by both his wife and his son.

Fortunately, as has been noted by Hugh Thomas, the golden age of letter writing ran from the invention of the railroad to the invention of the telephone. The post office was so efficient that husband and wife, when apart, could carry on an almost daily exchange of letters. Thus this period provides for the historian a rare opportunity to analyze the inner workings, the private rather than the public aspects of many marriages. Libraries now hold extensive collections of family papers, many of which are rich with the correspondence exchanged between husbands and wives, providing a treasure trove of simple, direct, intimate, and unaffected letters recording the minutiae of family life.

In recent years 540 unpublished letters exchanged between Elizabeth and Benjamin Perry have been found and are now deposited at the South Caroliniana Library of the University of South Carolina. Until these letters were found, there had existed only one extant letter of Mrs. Perry, even though Perry had written his bride-to-be in 1837, "You make a request in your last letter which I can never grant 'that when we meet again our letters are to be exchanged and yours committed to the flames whilst mine are to be handsomely bound.' No, Lizzie, your letters will ever be faithfully preserved whilst it is in the power of man to do so." In this newly discovered collection, Liz Perry is the principal correspondent between 1836 and 1853, and Benjamin's letters make up the bulk of the correspondence between 1854 and 1867.[23] At the very least, these letters enable the historian to reconstruct the Perrys' marital relationship as very different from that depicted by Perry and perpetuated by his heirs. In these letters Mrs. Perry is revealed to be an articulate, pragmatic, assertive woman who wanted fame and fortune for her husband, herself, and their children. Forced to live her life through him, Liz, an independent-minded woman, expressed in her letters to Perry not only her strong views on childrearing, religion, and household arrangements, topics within the sphere of women, but also her well-informed opinions on the important political issues of the day and the means by which her husband could advance his political career. Thus the dark, deep "secret" of their Victorian marriage, carefully closeted away, did not involve sex but rather the feelings of an ambitious, intelligent, and articulate woman.

For more than thirty years the Perrys conducted a lively exchange on political matters. She instructed him that "what is last said [in debate] produces the greatest impression." In another letter she reminded him to "take the part of the *upper country* in debate; *be kind* to your *colleagues; attentive* in sending pamphlets to your constituents." She warned him that if he intended to write articles for the local newspaper he must "take great pains with them; you must be a consistent Politician." His politics had been inconsistent: "You are for Van Buren; yet against the Subtreasury, a Democrat yet making speeches in favor of the Whigs." She advised Perry not to introduce legislation to establish a state penitentiary, a politically unpopular idea in South Carolina; he did, and it was defeated. She opposed the Mexican War and considered that her husband was "too zealous" in his support of it, "particularly as you are a candidate [for Congress]; and it is such an unpopular war."[24] She reached her opinion against the war, she informed him, after reading speeches by supporters and critics.

In 1844 Mrs. Perry worried that her husband's vote against a resolution requesting the governor to expel Judge Samuel Hoar of Massachusetts, who had come to Charleston to institute a test case against the state's black seamen's act of 1822, might be misconstrued as an antislavery stand. Perry had written her, "I stood alone against the whole Senate. . . . This vote has given Colonel Memminger [who dissented in the House] and myself quite a distinction—a minority of one." She replied, "If you are not an *abolitionist* you certainly act as if you were one. I am *surprised* that you should be opposed to the *whole Senate,* you certainly must be the *wrong* one."[25]

Although Mrs. Perry wrote that she knew "men do not like to receive advice from their wives, and naturally go contrary, just to show they are not going to be governed by them," she nevertheless justified her directives to Perry because "the advice comes from a *wise* and *loving* wife, who has her husband's interest at heart, so he must follow it, because it is such wholesome good advice." She continued, "You know I am very *generous* to you in furnishing a constant supply *free of charge.* I do not wish you, to be in debt to me, as you certainly would, if I charged." On another occasion, she boasted, "Never was a husband blessed with *so wise a wife* . . . I have more wisdom in affairs generally, than most of the female sex. I must be more than ordinary for *you* to be satisfied with me."[26]

To this steady and generous supply of advice, Perry responded on one occasion, "I have much respect for your opinions and counsel; but you need not be uneasy as to the influence which they may have on my political action. I always reflect when I differ with you in opinion that it is because you are not so well acquainted with the subject as I am; that you have not reflected so much about it, or have not seen it in all of its bearings."[27]

Ambition was a powerful force in Elizabeth Perry's life, but she felt its lack in her husband, and that was a "constant source of annoyance to me. You had better," she warned him, "for *my sake* be elected to some [higher] office; until you are I will give you no peace." Again, she wrote, "I believe I would be happier if you were a stupid ignorant man, for then I would expect nothing for you . . . but as it is, my opinion of you is so *exalted*, my expectations for you are *great*, and as they are not *realized*, I am unhappy." Over the years Elizabeth pressed Perry to become a United States congressman, a judge, a state senator, and the governor of the state. In 1846 she wrote, "I am more anxious than ever that you should represent the people at Washington. . . . You can then become a *great-man*, or at least be *known* as a great-man; for you have all the ingredients of one already." Several times she threatened Benjamin that "the next time you go to Columbia, unless it is as Senator, I'll not write at all." Elizabeth thought that "to be *Senator's Wife* is good, *Wife of* [the] *President of the Senate, still better*."[28] On other occasions she informed him that "Judge Perry sounds remarkably well; but Judge Perry's wife and children sound better. I assure you when I married you, I had a distant thought of being a Judge's lady . . . it is such a respectable office . . . for the sake of your wife and children you must think of it."[29]

In 1841 Perry wrote Elizabeth that he intended to leave the legislature at the end of the next session because "home has more attractions than any other place, and more pleasures and happiness. I could spend every day and hour of my life at home without a wish or inclination to go anywhere. I am tired too of legislation, it is hard work and I do not take the same interest in it that I used to do. I do not expect to be a candidate again." Elizabeth responded, "I can *never consent* to your leaving the Legislature . . . the two reasons you give for wishing to leave, namely, love of home, and finding Legislation hard, I cannot admit of, the first is effeminate, the second selfish." Perry insisted, "I know more about these matters than you do" and refused to stand for reelection.[30]

Although Perry enjoyed his absence from politics, to Elizabeth it meant that "their" life was over. "It disturbs me," she wrote him, "that already your career in public life is run, and that you have quietly resigned all pretension to fame, honour, and distinction among your fellow man; and that for the remainder of your life, you are to pass only as a *plodding Greenville Attorney*." She told him, "I would willingly give up several hundred dollars to see your name mentioned in the paper with honour and distinction as I used to."[31]

81

Perry acceded to his wife's wishes and returned to the legislature in 1844 and ran for Congress in 1848. Liz wrote him early in his congressional campaign that he must hold on to his Whig support if he hoped to win a seat in the House. When his opponent, James L. Orr, announced for Zachary Taylor in the presidential election, she feared that Perry would act "imprudently . . . just to show your *independence*" and come out boldly for Lewis Cass, which would lose him the votes of most of the Whigs and many of the Democrats repulsed by Cass's doctrine of popular sovereignty. "Merit," she warned him, "does not always bring its reward, art, intrigue, vanity, and deceit, oftener triumph, thus it behooves you to do all that is *honorable* to ensure success." Though Perry knew his wife's advice was sound, he felt he had no choice but to adhere to the Democratic party and support Cass's candidacy for president. He lost the 1848 election primarily because he lost the support of the Whigs. Undaunted, Liz wrote Perry that he should "run again and beat the *drunken demagogue* . . . he is not fit to black your boots."[32] In 1852, when Perry declined to run for governor, she wrote in frustration, "Now what can you attain to, *nothing at all;* and you will be never more than a Member of the Legislature and a Village Lawyer toiling for meat and clothes for his family." In her opinion, "Somehow a mistake has been made, and you have not fulfilled your destiny."[33]

It is clear from Benjamin's comments that he was perfectly content as a village lawyer. During his two years away from the legislature, he wrote in his journal that his life was "spent very pleasantly in my office with my books and in my home with my wife and children. I am almost out of debt and have a good practice. I am really as happy as a man need wish to be."[34]

By the time of the secession crisis in South Carolina in 1850–52, Mrs. Perry had become a staunch Unionist. They named a son born to them in June 1851 Hext McCall after his maternal grandfather and dedicated the infant to the Union in the pages of the *Southern Patriot,* a newspaper edited by Perry. No one is more zealous than the recent convert, and Liz Perry chided her husband in 1850 for being too soft on South Carolina disunionists—secessionists and cooperationists alike. Where, she asked, was the northern aggression Perry spoke of? She listed for him numerous examples of "Southern aggression" which she believed had led to the current crisis, including the war with Mexico, Calhoun's "Address of the Southern Delegates," southern congressmen delaying for more than two years the passage of the bill creating the Oregon territory, and the Nashville Convention. Two days later she added, "If the South is so oppressed, why do not the other Southern states *feel it besides* South Carolina?" She concluded this exchange a few days later in a letter in which she stated, "The North ought to *make* South Carolina *leave* the Union and be glad to get rid of her, important as she thinks herself." Soon after, she consoled him, "It is hard that those in the minority who dare to express their opinions are branded as Traitor."[35]

On other issues before the state legislature her voice was equally strong. In 1851, when Perry's bill to have the state voters elect presidential electors failed to pass, she persuaded him to continue to present reform legislation: "You know nothing is to be expected from the *present Legislature,* they were elected before the people were *enlightened* . . . the *next Legislature* will be different. . . . You are now rowing *against* the *current* next session the current will *go along with* you." She wrote, "I will always go down with you" and begged him not to be discouraged. Perry persistently introduced bills for the popular election of presidential electors and governors of the state, but his efforts were in vain, and the legislature continued to elect nearly all the state officials until after the Civil War.[36] Her final words on the secession crisis were uttered in April 1852. She wrote her husband that if South Carolina seceded from the Union it would be no loss "but a *good riddance,* She and her *selfish vainglorious* Sons. The Union can go on prosperously without her; and she has abused it, so long, it is time now she should leave it."[37]

Letters from Mrs. Perry end in 1853, but her husband's letters to her written between 1854 and 1867 indicate that she corresponded with him regularly. His letters to her reflect her continuing keen interest in political life and his appreciation of her advice and support in the late 1850s in the face of the growing spirit of disunionism which he sought to counter. Nevertheless, when the war came, Perry went with his state and continued to serve in the legislature.

From the statehouse in December 1862, Perry wrote Liz that he was glad to hear from her, "but you are foolish about my not being elected Speaker [of the House], do, my dear wife, never mention to me again about any office. I would not have foregone the pleasure of making my Speech for the speaker's chair." Four days later he wrote tenderly, "One of my chief pleasures when absent from you is writing to you and receiving letters from you. How different from some of the members who seldom write to their wives or receive letters from them." Perry wondered if they loved their wives as he did her, or if their wives loved them: "I suppose the truth is that most people after being married for a long time forget all about love. They think of each other just as they do of their houses or their horses or cattle or fields."[38]

At the end of the war, President Andrew Johnson appointed Perry the provisional governor of South Carolina—his reward for having tried for more than thirty years to keep the Palmetto State from seceding. Elected to the United States Senate in the fall of 1865, he wrote to Liz in November that "I hope now, my dear wife, you will love me the more for my success and feel proud that your husband is both governor and United States Senator at the same time." He thought these dual honors vindicated his "uncompromising and principled course of action" in the antebellum years, and he looked forward to receiving "one of the prettiest more affectionate letters you have ever written."[39]

Denied, he thought only temporarily, his seat in the Senate by the first postwar Congress, Perry wrote his wife that he was glad he could come directly home from Columbia after being relieved of his duties as provisional governor. "The truth is," he wrote, "I had rather be with you and the children than to be in Washington with all the great men of the country." The response he provoked must have been vintage Liz Perry for he replied caustically, "How apt you are to make mistakes. It seems you always construe everything of a public nature wrong." In that same letter he remarked to Liz that former Governor Francis Pickens kept annoying him by writing him long letters asking for help in securing his presidential pardon and that Pickens kept reminding Andrew Johnson of his case. "Pickens," wrote Perry, "may as a result have done something that will not be to his liking. He is very much like you—you are some kin I believe."[40] When the postponement of his Senate seat became permanent, Perry returned home, and his letters to his wife ended.

The personal correspondence between Elizabeth and Benjamin Perry, which the family sought to conceal, is one-half of an interlocking puzzle, the other half being the records they presented for posterity. When both halves are joined together, a comprehensive account emerges of the intimate life of a nineteenth-century southern upper-middle-class couple—possibly the most thoroughly documented record of a middle-class marriage in the entire South. Although one case study cannot perfectly mirror a society, it may provide us with a clue to the culture of which it was a part.

The Perry marriage was based on romantic love, although it crossed Perry's mind that if had thought of marrying for a fortune, it was not likely that he could, in his "poverty and obscurity have won the hand of an heiress."[41] When put to the test, he chose Elizabeth McCall over Ann Pamela Cunningham, preferring the woman who swept him off his feet to one who stood to inherit a large fortune. During the courtship he saw Liz on numerous occasions in her Charleston home without the presence of either a chaperon or a slave, something we have been told did not occur among the southern elite—which certainly Liz was, though he was not. The bride-to-be admitted her love for him developed more gradually than his love for her. Mrs. McCall's ready consent to the marriage is surprising given the prestigiousness of the Hext-McCall-Hayne family connections and the lack of such connections on the part of the husband-to-be.

Once the couple was married, the union was a companionate one in keeping with recent findings on Victorian marriage, but a companionate marriage should not be equated with an equalitarian union.[42] Most nineteenth-century marriages studied so far have subscribed to the doctrine of two separate spheres in which the primacy of the husband's role was at the very least an unspoken assumption. Frequent separations were part of the Perry relationship, but unlike many plantation mistresses, who lived in isolated areas and were lonely for their absent spouses, Liz lived on Main Street in Greenville and never complained of missing her husband. Rather, in almost every letter Benjamin wrote of missing home and family.

Especially striking about the Perry relationship is Mrs. Perry's keen interest in politics. In her letters to her husband she discussed many other subjects. Having had at least thirteen pregnancies in nineteen years, seven children to raise, a large household to oversee, a mother and two sisters residing close by, friends and neighbors to call upon and to receive at home, and flocks of friends and relatives from Charleston staying over with her at the beginning and end of each summer as they passed through Greenville going to and returning from the mountains, her life was very busy. Although she touched upon some of these topics in her letters to him, wrote forthrightly of her love for him, and noted after almost fifteen years of marriage, that "our love increases, instead of diminishing," and of how "essential you are to my happiness,"[43] politics dominated her letters. From the time of her marriage to him in 1837, when she was only eighteen years old, until his retirement from politics in 1867, when she was forty-eight, Liz Perry showed an abiding interest in the political questions of the day, continuously encouraged her husband in his political career, carried on a lively and perceptive discussion of these matters with him, and forcefully expressed political opinions even if they were contrary to his.[44]

Having stood virtually alone in politics for more than thirty years, Perry appreciated the stability, affection, and support of his wife, whose judgment he respected and whose support was therefore very meaningful to him. To keep up appearances in a society that frowned upon independent-minded and ambitious wives, he suppressed all evidence of her personality. In public Perry spoke condescendingly of women's place in marriage, but in private he acknowledged Liz to be his principal adviser and confidant. Without the fortuitous preservation of more than five hundred of their letters we would never have known that Elizabeth Perry was a talented woman of wit and intelligence and that the marriage was one of give and take, almost equalitarian in tone. In the search for a clearer understanding of marital relationships and intrafamily dynamics in the mid-nineteenth-century South, case studies such as that of the Perrys of Greenville can make a most significant contribution.

Notes

1. "Sketch of the Life of Governor B. F. Perry written by his wife, August 8, 1889–September 20, 1889," pp. 117, 127, 130–31. On September 23, 1889, Mrs. Perry began another "Sketch" of Perry, which was to be 292 pages long; the sketch completed on September 20 is 132 pages long. Both bound volumes are on deposit in the Benjamin F. Perry Papers, South Caroliniana Library, University of South Carolina. Unless otherwise indicated, all correspondence and unpublished manuscripts cited are from the Benjamin F. Perry Collection at the South Caroliniana Library, Columbia.

2. "Sketch of the Life of Benjamin F. Perry," pp. 21–22; Lillian A. Kibler, *Benjamin F. Perry: South Carolina Unionist* (Durham: Duke University Press, 1946), pp. 3–33.

3. "Sketch of the Life of Benjamin F. Perry," pp. 21–46; Kibler, *Benjamin F. Perry,* pp. 34–64, 87–176; Benjamin F. Perry Journal, 1832–63, 2 vols., vol. 1, November 1832–December 1835, Southern Historical Collection, University of North Carolina, Chapel Hill (hereafter SHC); Benjamin F. Perry Autobiography, 1874, MS., pp. 63–64, 139, 151–60.

4. Journal, vol. 1, May 6, 1836, SHC.

5. Elizabeth McCall to Hext M. Perry, March 27, 1889; "Sketch of the Life of Benjamin F. Perry," pp. 49–50; Theodore Jervey, "The Hayne Family," *South Carolina Historical Magazine* 5 (July 1904): 168–88.

6. Journal, vol. 1, September 30, 1836, SHC; Autobiography, 1874, p. 167.

7. Autobiography, 1874, pp. 167–68; Journal, vol. 1, November 7, 1836, SHC; "Sketch of the Life of Benjamin F. Perry," pp. 50–53.

8. Autobiography, 1874, pp. 168–70; "Sketch of the Life of Benjamin F. Perry," pp. 50–53; Journal, vol. 1, July 9, 1837, SHC.

9. Autobiography, 1874, p. 170.

10. Eliza B. Hayne to Benjamin F. Perry, March 28, 1851, Benjamin F. Perry Papers, Alabama Department of Archives and History, Montgomery. Statistical studies of upper-class southern women in the early nineteenth century are not in agreement on the average age at first marriage. Ann Williams Boucher in "Wealthy Planter Families in Nineteenth Century Alabama" (Ph.D. dissertation, University of Connecticut, 1978), pp. 41–42, stated that in Alabama the average age of marriage was 18.5, whereas, in the Southeast, according to Jane

Turner Censer's findings in *North Carolina Planters and Their Children, 1800–1860* (Baton Rouge: Louisiana State University Press, 1984), pp. 91–92, the average age at first marriage was twenty. Catherine Clinton's findings in *The Plantation Mistress: Women's World in the Old South* (New York: Pantheon, 1982), pp. 60, 233, are in agreement with those of Censer. Men in professions usually did not marry until their late twenties. Perry was thirty-one when he took for his bride a woman thirteen years his junior. The discrepancy in their ages, although great, was not unusual in the antebellum South (Bertram Wyatt-Brown, *Southern Honor: Ethics and Behavior in the Old South* [New York: Oxford University Press, 1982], p. 204). Despite the age difference, their relationship did not develop into a paternalistic one.

11. Benjamin F. Perry to Elizabeth McCall, February 15, 1837, in Hext McCall Perry, ed., *Letters of My Father to My Mother, Beginning with Those Written during Their Engagement with Extracts from His Journals* (Philadelphia: Avil, 1889), p. 37.

12. Journal, vol. 1, January 31, June 14, 1838, SHC.

13. Ibid., May 31, 1841.

14. Ibid.; Autobiography, 1874, p. 188.

15. Journal, vol. 1, July 5, 12, 1837, January 31, May 15, July 19, December 7, 1838, and March 5, 1843; Benjamin F. Perry to Elizabeth McCall Perry, December 7, 1838, and n.d., in Perry, ed., *Letters of My Father*, pp. 78–80, 100–103. Alcott published *The Young Wife* in Boston in 1837 and *The Young Husband* in 1841.

16. Russell L. Blake, "Ties of Intimacy: Social Values and Personal Relationships of Antebellum Slaveholders" (Ph.D. dissertation, University of Michigan, 1978), pp. 81–85; Carl Degler, *At Odds: Women and the Family in America from the Revolution to the Present* (New York: Oxford University Press, 1980), pp. 26–28; Barbara Welter, "The Cult of True Womanhood, 1820–1860," *American Quarterly* 18 (1966): 151–74. For a brilliant historiographical essay on this subject see Linda Kerber's "Separate Spheres, Female Worlds, Woman's Place: The Rhetoric of Women's History," paper presented at the Annual Meeting of the Organization of American Historians, April 1984.

17. "Address of the Honorable Benjamin F. Perry before the Philophrenian Society of Walhalla Female College, June 24, 1879," pp. 465–81, in Stephen Meats and Edwin Arnold, eds., *The Writings of Benjamin F. Perry*, 3 vols. (Spartanburg, S.C.: Reprint Company, 1980), 1:471–73.

18. Autobiography, 1874, p. 174.

19. Journal, vol. 1, February 22, 1839, May 9, 1840, September 5, 1841, February 29, 1852, January 1856, April 17, 1858; Benjamin F. Perry to Elizabeth McCall Perry, March 9, 1861; Kibler, *Benjamin F. Perry*, pp. 183–85, 196–98, 202–3, 313. Despite the war and Reconstruction, which Perry claimed ruined "his worldly Estate," he left at his death on December 3, 1886, more than $42,000 in real estate, a library valued at $8,000, farm equipment, and a stock of horses, mules, and pigs to be divided as he stipulated among his four surviving children. To his wife, Elizabeth F. Perry, "who has a handsome

property of her own," he bequeathed his notes, bonds, railroad stock, horse and carriage, and all of his personal property not otherwise disposed of. The "handsome property" of his wife came from three legacies: at her mother's death in June 1875, she received $5,000 and one-half interest in her parents' house; in 1872, and in 1873, Liz benefited from the inheritances of two aged aunts, sisters of her father, who left their niece approximately $7,000, for a total inheritance from these three sources of $12,000 in cash, plus half-interest in a house. At Elizabeth's death on September 24, 1891, her estate was divided among her four children (will of Benjamin F. Perry, Estate Papers, Greenville County, Apt. 50, File 22; wills of Martha McCall, Apt. 33, File 33, Sarah Mathew, Apt. 36, File 10, and Elizabeth F. Perry, Apt. 56, File 22, South Carolina Department of Archives and History, Columbia). See also Beverly T. Whitmore, ed., *The Presence of the Past: Epitaphs of 18th and 19th Century Pioneers in Greenville County, South Carolina and Their Descendants* (Baltimore: Gateway Press, 1976), pp. 34–38; Works Progress Administration, South Carolina Statewide Historical Project, Christ Episcopal Churchyard, Epitaphs, Greenville County.

20. "Sketch of the Life of Benjamin F. Perry," pp. 1–131, passim; Autobiography, 1874, p. 174; Journal, vol. 1, July 13, October 6, 1839, April 27, 1847, and vol. 2, February 10, 1861, SHC.

21. Elizabeth McCall Perry to Benjamin F. Perry, November 29, 1841, December 8, 1844; Benjamin F. Perry to Elizabeth McCall Perry, July 13, 1846, in Elizabeth M. Perry, ed., *Letters of Governor Benjamin F. Perry to His Wife* (Greenville: Shannon and Co., 1890), pp. 101–3.

22. Journal, vol. 1, March 5, 1843, SHC.

23. Benjamin F. Perry to Elizabeth McCall, March 4, 1837, in Perry, ed., *Letters of My Father*, p. 41. All but 71 of these 540 letters were found packed away in a carton in a closet of a Greenville law firm in 1980. The South Caroliniana Library purchased the smaller collection of 71 letters in 1962 from Schindler's Antique Shop in Charleston, and the larger collection was a donation to the library in 1981.

24. Elizabeth McCall Perry to Benjamin F. Perry, November 22, 28, December 6, 1840, May 20, 1844, December 6, 1847; Kibler, *Benjamin F. Perry*, pp. 230–31.

25. Benjamin F. Perry to Elizabeth McCall Perry, Friday night [December 1844], Perry, ed., *Letters of Governor Benjamin F. Perry*, pp. 47–48; Elizabeth McCall Perry to Benjamin F. Perry, December 8, 1844. Perry was as thoroughly committed to slavery as he was to the Union. He believed the strongest protection slavery could have was in the "Union of these States," which provided constitutional guarantees for the institution that could be lost if the Union were dissolved (John Barnwell, *Love of Order: South Carolina's First Secession Crisis* [Chapel Hill: University of North Carolina Press, 1982], pp. 189–90; Kibler, *Benjamin F. Perry*, pp. 237–38, 314–46).

26. Elizabeth McCall Perry to Benjamin F. Perry, March 28, 1848, December 5, 7, 1851.

27. Sunday morning [1840], in Perry, ed., *Letters of My Father,* p. 106.

28. Elizabeth McCall Perry to Benjamin F. Perry, April 27, November 27, December 3, 1844, July 20, 1846, December 3, 1848, November 27, 1851, and December 2, 1852.

29. Elizabeth McCall Perry to Benjamin F. Perry, December 7, 1843, October 31, 1846.

30. Benjamin F. Perry to Elizabeth McCall Perry, Friday morning [November 1841], Friday morning [December 1841], in Perry, ed., *Letters of My Father,* pp. 114, 117–18, 122; Elizabeth McCall Perry to Benjamin F. Perry, December 6, 1841.

31. Elizabeth McCall Perry to Benjamin F. Perry, December 4, 1842.

32. Elizabeth McCall Perry to Benjamin F. Perry, November 26, 1847, June 20, June 30, October 10, 22, 1848; Kibler, *Benjamin F. Perry,* pp. 222–25.

33. Elizabeth McCall Perry to Benjamin F. Perry, December 7, 1852.

34. Journal, vol. 1, July 16, 1843, SHC.

35. Ibid., vol. 2, July 11, 1851; Elizabeth McCall Perry to Benjamin F. Perry, December 3, 5, 7, 15, 1850.

36. Elizabeth McCall Perry to Benjamin F. Perry, December 5, 7, 11, 1851; Kibler, *Benjamin F. Perry,* pp. 227–28, 303–4.

37. Elizabeth McCall Perry to Benjamin F. Perry, April 27, 1852.

38. Benjamin F. Perry to Elizabeth McCall Perry, December 3, 7, 1862.

39. Benjamin F. Perry to Elizabeth McCall Perry, November 2, 6, 1865.

40. Benjamin F. Perry to Elizabeth McCall Perry, December 5, 14, 15, 1865. See also Francis W. Pickens to Benjamin F. Perry, September 7, October 6, November 23, 30, 1865, Benjamin F. Perry Papers, SHC.

41. Autobiography, 1874, p. 165.

42. Robert L. Griswold in his excellent book *Family and Divorce in California, 1850–1890: Victorian Illusions and Everyday Realities* (Albany: State University of New York Press, 1982), pp. 4–16, comes close to asserting just that.

43. Elizabeth McCall Perry to Benjamin F. Perry, July 29, 1846, December 6, 1851.

44. Benjamin Perry, as has been noted throughout this essay, also did not confine himself to "his" sphere. Instead, he partook with great zest in the rearing of his children and in being a central figure in the domestic scene. Unlike their treatment of Liz's participation in the political sphere, neither Benjamin in the writing of his journal and two autobiographies nor his family in the publication of his correspondence following his death felt it necessary to cover up his active participation in household matters. The ease with which the Perrys crossed the boundaries of each other's sphere is of especial interest in light of the recent publications of Catherine Clinton and Bertram Wyatt-Brown, who have depicted the sex roles of men and women to have been particularly confining in the antebellum South. One case study of a couple's willingness to bend convention to suit their temperaments does not of course prove or disprove a general proposition.

The Not-So-Cloistered Academy: Elite Women's Education and Family Feeling in the Old South

Steven M. Stowe

The story of women's education in pre–Civil War America often has been presented as a bleak study of intellectual bondage, emphasizing the values that segregated women and held them down rather than the social conditions women shaped to their advantage. What we know best about women's education between 1825 and 1860 is derived from studies of institutions and doctrine, largely centered in the North, which bolstered the rising middle class. My aim in this essay is to shift attention to the propertied class of the South and to suggest a more inclusive perspective on women's education, which links women's intellectual lives to their perception of family and family feeling.[1]

The growth of women's academies and their ideology of domestic, sentimental womanhood has been well established historically. What is needed is an understanding of how a girl's schooling was only a part of her education to womanhood. Schooling came at a certain time in a young woman's life and was only one of several related experiences that shaped her childhood to the role that was both proper and possible for a mature woman. The focus of this essay is, first, to describe the relations between the wider social purpose of schooling and the personal sense a woman had of learning something important. This relationship was not always smooth, as the lives of planter-class women aged fourteen to eighteen in Virginia, the Carolinas, and Georgia reveal. Looking at schooling in this way involves not only an appreciation of academic standards and organization but also a willingness to listen to the young women themselves as they parsed out the meaning of intellect, femininity, and, perhaps most important, family expectations. Second, if we see education as more than schooling, the experience of these women immediately after graduation takes on a new importance. Becoming a woman meant more than mastering lessons. It meant keeping ties with women friends, meeting marriageable men, and confronting the changed conditions of her family life as she contemplated beginning a new family.[2]

For most women this passage from schooling through courtship was education broadly conceived, an exciting, memorable, sometimes harrowing time. Fortunately for historians, it was marked by an extraordinary amount of writing, mostly letters, which women relied upon to chart the passage and clarify their choices. Letters to parents, friends, and lovers are a particularly valuable text on the experience of women not simply because of the information they contain but because letter-writing itself was a formal act of schooling and courtship. Learning and lovemaking would have been unthinkable without letters, and the blend of literary convention and personal voice in correspondence is an especially good measure of what it meant to come of age. Letters thus provide a transcript of women thinking about womanhood. In considering the meaning of schooling and courtship, therefore, I will give special attention to the role of written expression: the forms, themes, and usages that channeled the passage into the woman's sphere.[3]

Education, one popular mentor wrote in 1839, provided that women "may be fitted to fulfill with honour to themselves, and with happiness to others, the duties of a station for which God created woman, and to which so large a proportion of our sex is called." Both southern and northern women heard such elevated characterizations of their schooling, but southerners were given additional conditions for female accomplishment. The young southern woman was told in various ways that all eyes were upon her and that a certain "deleterious influence" in southern society made true womanhood particularly crucial to the harmony of social relations. Women's education in the South also accented the beauty and peace of rural life, where "breathing space is given for the young pulsations of the opening feelings," as one moral writer expressed it. Southern country life would singularly settle the female mind and affections.[4]

Along with the allusions to slavery and the praises of rural life southerners placed a value on education as a way of strengthening family ties.

To be sure, individual achievement was held to be important, and women were expected to undertake work in "training the body to healthful exercises, and elegant accomplishments, in cultivating and developing the mental powers, in regulating the passions." But these attainments were firmly linked to family life and through it to the social order. One planter-educator typically described the teacher as one "called to bind and interlock one generation with the other by the transmission of truth and wisdom, and to evoke noble, pure, patriotic, righteous and benevolent feelings in the breasts of the young." Texts on moral philosophy popular in the South, such as the one by Jasper Adams, extolled the family as the fulcrum of social order and the focus of all education. A young woman was not merely a future lady and wife but a daughter who must continue to share in her family's reciprocal duties, which "occur every day, and almost every hour of every day," and were essential to the "quietness" Adams and others hoped to discover at the core of family relations.[5]

These broad but nevertheless highly charged values began to assume a new institutional shape after 1825 in the form of regional academies. The reasons for academies' increasing popularity among the families who could afford them were many and can only be noted in passing. Some institutions were arms of evangelical Christianity; others were founded by particularly successful itinerant teachers. Although a few larger schools took in students from around the South, many of the smaller academies were supported by local planter families who felt a need, especially by the 1840s, for the "Southron" education of both girls and boys. As academies became widespread, other reasons emerged for sending daughters to them which did not reflect well on home education. Few educators criticized home lessons outright, but they recommended academies as organized alternatives that would "distribute in their just proportions, the *useful* and the *ornamental*" in a girl's lessons and would counteract (in the words of a postbellum observer) the plantation's "occasions for despondency, discouragement, and all the temptations that besiege the home of a more favored class." In sum, these academies were intended to bring groups of girls into a safe, social, and intellectually appropriate world which they would share while becoming women.[6]

Inside academy walls, the daily routine both supported and counterpointed the general values attributed to women's education. A girl's developing sense of her sex and social place was subtly woven into the routine and rules of academy life. Significantly, family rhetoric abounded in academy literature and practice. "My Dear Child," began a typical letter addressed to new students: "You have left your home, your brothers and sisters, and your parents," but she and other students would learn the satisfactions of "this large family of which you have become a sister." Headmistresses such as Charleston's Madame Ann Marsan Talvande mothered their students by setting strict rules and then indulging certain lapses. As in most academies, for example, visitors to Talvande's in the 1830s were allowed only one or two afternoons a week, girls wore uniforms to make them equal as individuals and distinctive as a group, packages and sometimes even letters were inspected, and pocket money was controlled. Even so, the chief cook, Maum Jute, slipped up to the dormitory each night with pastry or cake, and although Madame could be fierce about laziness or tale-telling, she let her girls see her at her ease, running about in the mornings, hair down, in backless slippers. Although they had time to play, young women were required to make fine distinctions in matters of their appearance as ladies. "[H]eads up—chins down—shoulders back—backs in—elbows close—toes out," commanded a teacher in one account of academy life. "In moving your elbows, avoid making a sharp angle, but form the curved line of grace in every motion." With an attention most girls probably would not have received at home, teachers made every personal detail, from tone of voice to shape of fingernail, a matter of instruction and display.[7]

Although obviously meant to fit young women for a future as ladies and wives, academy routine was neither bloodless in its formality nor strictly forward-looking. The all-female world in most instances powerfully joined the authority of instruction to the immediate intimacy of shared womanhood. The academy created a safe, often delightful world. Most women's letters and later memoirs noted the pleasure of outings and soirées and the plain, happily predictable rhythm of days. At special celebrations, as on the Fourth of July or Christmas, girls were taken to a ball or to a boys' academy to see the cadets drill and then to a picnic afterward. Dressed alike, walking in order of height or beauty, young women told of the satisfactions of being female together and of being seen in the atmosphere of femininity which enclosed all academy girls. Days were spent with other "blooming girls . . . buoyant as skylarks, frolicsome as young colts," as one teacher wrote. Young Mary Ferrand told her grandmother, "We have a great many little girls to play with and we all agree very well together." And Charlotte Daly contentedly described "the never ending routine of St. Mary's, and how hour crowds upon hour and bell echoes bell, ever compelling us to part from our own private plans." The sleeping alcoves, decorated with personal belongings, were favorite places. Although mentor literature warned teachers against taking pets and grimly instructed students not to overdo "confidential discourse," most academies at least tacitly fostered emotional closeness. Girls routinely slept two to a bed, and as one women recalled, "We two girls could snuggle up together in each other's arms, and sleep the sleep that only the young can ever know and enjoy." At Madame Talvande's, wrote a former student, "We secured a modicum of privacy by bed curtains formed of our frocks and petticoats. . . . Twelve young barbarians coupled in this room and never under one ceiling rioted a lighter hearted more joyous band."[8]

Academies thus created a family ideal, which consisted of stern parenting and close control on the one hand and a routine that encouraged safe, loving intimacy between women on the other. But although the effectiveness of this balance in rearing girls seems clear, the possibility for a distinct tension also existed. At the same time that academies created a sisterhood they ostensibly were training women to take their places in the heterosexual, risky world beyond the academy walls. From an educator's point of view, sisterhood among students might keep loneliness at bay in the short run and might stifle precocious thoughts of men, but it had little direct bearing on a grown woman's duties. After all, the true purpose of schooling was not to encourage a world of sisters.

Academies seem to have acknowledged this tension by formally structuring a young woman's obligation to her parents, thus attempting to balance sisterhood with a compelling bond to the world outside the school. The schools did this primarily by insisting on the duty of writing letters home. As will be seen, letters between students and their parents often embodied rather than solving the tension in family ideals. But first, understanding this tension means appreciating the emphasis schools placed on a wide range of correct self-expression. Two aspects of language were accepted as epistemological truths. The first was that writing or speech, because of its social character, was the unifying factor of all knowledge. Second, language drew a clear line between the sexes. Unlike many other academic subjects, English composition held that each sex had its own linguistic terrain and that instruction in usage was instruction in gender ideals. It was axiomatic, for example, that "a lady neither writes nor speaks to a gentleman as she would to one of her own sex, and a gentleman addresses a lady in a style of more courteousness and respect than he does a male correspondent." Women were told that they were particularly susceptible to language, almost to the point of having a preternatural affinity for words. This characteristic could cause difficulties. Women were criticized for their "voluminous correspondence" on light topics and yet praised for their inventiveness; they were pounced upon for trivial chatter but discouraged from political or theoretical discussion. Teachers often seemed confused about just what sort of letter a young woman should write to her parents, or to anyone for that matter. Some tried to simplify the endeavor. "A correspondence between two persons, is simply a conversation reduced to writing," one text began confidently, recommending "an artless arrangement of obvious sentiments." Lydia Sigourney even suggested that intuition should be a guide: "We learn to talk without rules," she wrote, "and letter-writing is but talk upon paper." But to most educators this view was dangerously antinomian. "False grammar, in good society, is not tolerated, even *en famille*," one teacher wrote. "Neither can it be in a letter. In the most familiar epistle, we should recollect what we owe to our language, to our correspondent, and to ourselves."[9]

The importance attributed to this curriculum is further seen in the way that parents' letters bolstered the meaning of correspondence as the sign of both academic progress and filial duty. Parents referred regularly to the act of writing, and letters to their daughters became, in effect, vessels of definite capacity and form relied upon to hold family feeling. This is not to say that mothers and fathers ignored a girl's other studies or devalued her learning of geography or needlework. Parents did indeed pay attention to intellectual growth as well as ladylike attainments. But the most often repeated theme in parents' letters, and the one most historically consistent, was the concern for receiving letters that displayed both a daughter's love and her learning. Some parents made this connection simply but repeatedly, as did the North Carolina mother who wrote her daughter in 1844, "Your letter was a real pleasure to us, we hope to see an improvement very often." Other parents, including John C. Calhoun, formally called upon their daughters to provide such pleasure and to display improvement in language which echoed advice literature. As he wrote to his daughter in 1831, "I do not know a more desirable aquirement (I mean of the literary kind) in a lady, than that of writing a good letter." Comment on letter-writing became the standard way for parents to express satisfaction or disapproval regarding their daughter's "*refinement* of the mind and the *improvement* of the person." A balky correspondent, in the words of William Gaston to his laconic daughter, created "that lethargy of soul which I so dread and abhor—which paralyzes all energies of intellect and ultimately blasts the best affections of the heart." Daughters who compressed their love, imagination, and duty into a well-written letter, however, typically were praised in such elevated terms that the importance of letters can scarcely be overlooked. "Highly gratified by the assurance of your affection," a planter wrote to his daughter in 1805," I cannot forbear to express the pleasure your conduct has given me, and in turn I shall endeavor to do you justice as a correspondent." Forty years later, just as typically, another father wrote his daughter that he had received her "sweet affectionate letter" and that he valued her words highly and looked forward to "your ever welcome letters as proofs of affection." Even allowing for some studied self-consciousness, it is clear that the overriding theme in parents' letters was the bond of family love and its proof in writing, which tied generations of daughters ever more firmly to family and home. There is comparatively little in parents' letters to suggest that daughters would ever love or owe more to anyone else, and mention of specific plans after the academy appears only infrequently. The new sisterhood and the future aside, daughters were supposed to keep family bonds tight.[10]

It is not surprising in view of the combined efforts of teachers, authors, and parents that most young women responded with professions of love and duty. Students' earliest letters home usually conjured up family memories, and later letters mirrored many of their parents' expressions of the respect and affection found in correspondence. Too, girls began to write of studies, sometimes going beyond the simplest responses to engage their parents intellectually. Nevertheless, and in spite of curriculum and parents' efforts, the dominant theme that emerges in young women's letters was neither family obligation nor intellectual leanings but contentment and delight with the sisterhood. Stories of games, mutual activities, and rivalries filled girls' letters and provided a counterpoint to—a tension with—parents' exhortations. It was not that daughters ignored parental concerns but that they overwhelmed them with their own motif of sisterhood's intimacy. One girl wrote, typically, of days spent with friends tucked away from the outside world, of confidential early morning walks, of joining a "working society" for missionaries in Greece, and of "nipping about over the yard . . . like so many mountain Tomboys." Another girl, lately named the academy's "Sprout," told her mother of happy days spent with a schoolmate "for whom I have formed a very strong attachment." Others wrote about feeling safe in group excursions to town, walking "two by two, eight under each teacher with Mr. Smedes at the head," and about much-loved teachers, who, like the one at a North Carolina academy, "lets me lay my head on her shoulder and cry whenever I want to." Such frequent, plain expressions of delight in the female world were not necessarily at odds with parents' urgings to family loyalty, and certainly only a few parents saw them as such. Even so, young women's letters reveal that the most important things they were learning concerned life within the sisterhood apart from both childhood and future home.[11]

The tension in this correspondence was broken by the end of schooling and the scattering of classmates. But it was not resolved. After two to four years together, women felt a sharp loss when the time came to leave their world. Just as their end-of-the-year oratory and poignant tableaux at graduation traced figures of love and loss, so did women's letters to one another. "Yes Elizabeth," Louisa Lenoir wrote her friend, "you are still dear to me as ever; but . . . is it possible that Lizzy no longer loves me? can she prove false?" Telling her absent friend about a new acquaintance, Charlotte Daly wrote, "I am sure she would win all your heart away from me. . . . She would love you, I know, and I am equally certain that she would completely *enchant* you, for she is one of the loveliest beings." No matter the self-indulgence or adolescent self-pity, these words were lovers' words and a measure of real loss. For most young women, schooling was followed by a return to parents and home, and even for the most mature of them it was a trying time. Away from friends, perhaps not yet courted by a man nor wishing to be, women felt filled with hopes raised by the academy, hopes for beauty, intellectual purpose, usefulness, now cut adrift from the community that had nurtured them. Like the longing for friends, the power of daydreaming became a clear theme in women's letters. Bessie Lacy spent whole days "behaving all the time" back in her father's house, yet "while I am sitting up straight and knitting my thoughts take long jaunts in dreamland." The return to her childhood home muted a woman's satisfaction at graduation. "I suppose, Kate, you are beginning to feel at home," a young woman wrote to a friend recently returned to her father's plantation. "And are in some measure quietly realizing that you are, *almost*, a young lady. Do you not feel some tender regrets at throwing off your school-girl character. . . ? With all the bright promise of the future . . . there is still much to chasten our burning aspirations . . . [in] the breaking up of so many very happy associations." Some women, like Bessie Lacy, envisioned themselves putting their womanly talents to work in their fathers' homes. Bessie promised her father that she would be "a good economist and a good housekeeper" and told him, "I will make your coffee just as strong, your tea just as sweet as you like. I will bathe your head when it aches and comb your hair as long as you like." But other young women, like Penelope Skinner, resented the closeness of home after the peopled world of the school. "I am heartily sick & tired of the life I lead," she wrote her brother from the plantation. "It is too dull and melancholy." But whether they eagerly took on the duties of a lady or felt restricted by them, women just out of school responded to isolation from friends and a chance for something new. These realities made the plight of being unmarried but educated a pressing one. A woman was simply "marriageable" and outside the sphere of either child or wife.[12]

The beginning of a woman's courtship, then, often was inextricable from her strongest family feeling, now renewed with considerable force in the absence of loved friends. Following so soon upon her academy days, a woman's courtship must be seen as a part of her education to womanhood. In many ways it was a kind of final examination in which she mastered a ritual meant to invest marriage with family feeling and tie sexuality to the social order. Compared as a ritual to schooling, courtship was compressed and swift yet not so thoroughly conceptualized. A textual map of courtship ritual remains available to us, however, in three literary sources found in academies and used by mentor and student alike to characterize what love (and men) were supposed to mean. The first of these were books of moral advice, the considerable number and worried logic of which implied doubt about women's "natural" affinity with virtue. Becoming smaller in size as the decades passed from 1800 (intended for pockets rather than libraries), these books also shifted in literary style and authorial voice. The assured authority of a Hannah More early in the century was joined, though not entirely replaced, by various benign "aunts" who, instead of presenting reasoned arguments, depended on evangelical passion or romantic confidence. Chapters became "letters," and essays became "lessons," as this literature moved ever closer to the heart of personal sentiment. In addition to moral advisers were the guides to letter-writing style, which were comparatively utilitarian and less darkly phrased. These guides, too, changed in form and content in the antebellum years, from compendia of weather forecasts, famous letters, and home remedies to systematic collections of model letters, in which courtship correspondence outnumbered all other kinds. Ribald stories gave way to predicaments of romantic love solved by the right exchange of letters. Novels were the third textual source of courtship ritual, arguably the one most relied upon by young women themselves. Changing from cautious tales early in the century to complicated epics, women's novels perhaps best trace the emerging importance of feeling and form when a woman fell in love.[13]

These three literary texts of courtship did not, of course, form a seamless ritual; moralists warned against novel-reading, letter-writing guides parodied the moralists, and novels tried to swallow and digest both. Taken together, however, these three sources of courtship ritual show two striking similarities of theme and purpose which cannot be ignored in assessing the formal meaning of the ritual in a woman's coming of age. First, all three acknowledged the significance of outward appearance or form in meetings between the sexes. As in academic training, the nuance and timing of appropriate language were crucial. It was imperative in the view of the moralists, for example, for a woman in love to be able to "distinguish the effects of real esteem from idle gallantry and unmeaning fine speeches" in her courtship. Letter-writing guides were premised on the power of lovers' correspondence and the sorrow that followed mis-used words. Most novels contained scenes in drawingrooms and ball-rooms (those most formal of meeting places), which turned on the con-trast between linguistic artifice and true expression, false wit and true love. Along with the emphasis on form was the danger of passion. Letter-writing guides stressed both form and passion, as if for choice or balance; one popular sequence of model letters showed courtship as a formal agreement while another was essentially a short work of fiction ending with a couple's passionate joy. And although moralist literature decried the transports of passion which most novels indulged, both texts were in striking accord on how passion was to be described. Thus the Methodist Margaret Coxe warned a young woman against "yielding herself pas-sively to the indulgence of precipitate or inordinate affection," and the popular novelist Emma Southworth has a heroine boldly celebrate her "vast capacity for, and propensity to, *inordinate* affection. . . . There is . . . a *great void* unfilled—a *vast want* unsatisfied."[14]

Painstaking attention to form—gazing, so to say, on one's own courtship—was thus counterpointed by the chance for a passion unlike anything else. And in this wordy ritual, the disturbing passion regarding men often was balanced by the safe familiarity of kin. So unpredictable, even alien, were men that many female moralists only alluded to meeting them instead of giving a clear set of instructions. Letter-writing guides reinforced this idea by including scores of taut and guarded letters to suitors. And the twists and plunges of fictional plots involving inscrut-able, cold, or silent men are well known. But if men were to be encoun-tered with extraordinary care, a woman's family was her refuge, or at least a known territory. Moral advisers uniformly praised the loving guidance of parents in the maze of lovemaking, and letter-writing guides, though depicting family strife, also provided a sampler of respect and love between children and parents. Novels were more complicated, often peopled with evil stepmothers, conniving cousins, and weak fathers. Yet even in these ruinous relations, the shadow of the ideal family was a backdrop to the heroine's romantic adventure.

The dual theme of men's strangeness and the family's haven shows up clearly in actual courtships, though with more variation. Even before a formal courtship began, women were busy imagining what the other sex was really like. In looking at women's letters to one another, the conclusion is inescapable that most women on the verge of courtship had had as little contact with men as academy life implied and frequently evaluated them in terms of female culture. In speculating about courtship, therefore, women speculated first about themselves: how lovely they were, whether vanity would overwhelm character, whether this or that friend had a better chance of being "caressed by the beauxs [sic]." Men were referred to collectively as possessing qualities good or bad. Mary Townes grew so frustrated with the men she saw that she wrote her brother for advice on "how to dispose of the troublesome cattle for the better kind." Even when expressing approval, women frequently drew upon the images of fiction and morality, language that reveals how men at a distance were not so much individuals as representatives of manliness. Young Mary Moragne, for example, described men in her diary in words fresh from novels and the academy: "the stately, storming vivacious Burt . . . that pretty smiling Adonis—Wardlow." And another woman, judging a man recently met, noted with regret that although he was "so pure, so warm-hearted, so pious" it was "a pity that his manners are not prepossessing to strangers and that his voice is defective." Piety and warmth, perhaps especially in the South, could not make up for a lack of manly display.[15]

It is striking how often the first letters of actual courtship also reflected the conventions of courtship form, especially those that stressed the alienation between the sexes. As the literature proposed, women took extraordinary care with the appearance of their letters, using the finest pen nibs and paper and often drafting letters more than once. And, as letter-writing guides suggested, regular correspondence was the most tangible token of regard. If a woman accepted a correspondence with a man, she was accepting more than a casual, picnic-and-outing acquaintance, and if she called a halt to the letters, courtship was considered to be at an end. The first letters of a courtship also relied upon exact usages, which enhanced the exciting strangeness of men. As in fiction, moral advice, and letter-writing guides, women frequently held men at bay by using the third-person address, and both sexes kept watch over every new turn in salutation or signature (such as dropping "Miss" or "Mr." and using the first names or, even more intimately, omitting signatures). And as in the academy, letters did both social and personal work. Women encouraged men's elaborate (not to say verbose) epistolary performances, in which pun and poem combined to amuse and inspire reflection. Though obviously intended for one's sweetheart, letters nevertheless were social benchmarks. Elizabeth McCall admired her suitor's love letters precisely because he adhered so closely to form that they "*could* be read with *interest* by others*.*" Sometimes men, in writing these letters, worried that theirs would not measure up to ones women read in novels or imagined receiving.[16]

But as the formality of early letters gave way to longer, less reserved correspondence, women translated the distance between the sexes into a language of passion and ideal. Some attempted to tell their lovers something about themselves, of "what strange visions come to me, and pictures; and what music sometimes whirls and rushes through my brain." Other women closed the distance between themselves and their men by declaring a new identity, "to become all that you believe and wish me to be." Women, cautiously telling more about themselves as the courtship continued and slowly lifting demands on a man's time and invention, thus moved into a phase of the ritual when the relationship stood or fell. It was at this point, when a courtship became less formal but still remained bound to certain conventions, that the social, and especially the familial, nature of courtship emerged.[17]

A true courtship was expected by everyone to lead to a marriage and a new family, and regardless of her idiosyncrasies or convenience, a woman in love received the full attention of family and friends. The advice, support, and even direct interference of kin and confidants in a romance seems to have been much more obvious in the planter class than in the northern middle class. Moralists' warnings about meddling friends went unheeded by most southern women, who anxiously sought advice and rumor from female confidants. But close family involvement was more pervasive, for even as a courtship aimed at establishing a new family, the woman's parents and other kin involved themselves in ways calculated to keep her firmly tied to them. As a courtship became well known, for example, lovers were flooded with the most elevated pronouncements from kin, casting their courtship in terms of social obligation and even timeless values. Of one woman, as of many others, it was said that her courtship "will stimulate [her lover] to 'deeds of noble daring' " and that after she became his wife she would be sure to "operate powerfully and beneficially upon him." Young lovers heard that courtship would truly bring them from "the shores of celibacy & [launch] your bark upon a tide of matrimony" and that marriage was "a *duty you owe yourself*—your *family & Society* at large." Parents combined such rhetoric with more worldly advice. One prospective bride was praised for being a Methodist, having a "pretty face & figure," and being "worth morally 100000000 &

pecuniarily 7 or 8 thousand." Kin also judged a daughter's courtship in terms of family loyalty, many agreeing with the Georgia planter, who upon hearing that his sister was "a little taken" with a certain man, noted, "She ought not to think of anybody that we don't know." William Gaston, like many fathers, praised his daughter Susan for her "candor" in telling him of a marriage proposal and applauded her sense of family feeling. And sometimes the courtship of a woman seemed as much a family matter as one of individual preference. Noting that his brother was disinclined to marry soon, a North Carolina man wrote of the woman concerned, "I am more & more pleased with Miss Carrie & think we must have her in the family in some way."[18]

The thorough, often intense involvement of family in a woman's courtship, with its constant reminder that even in this most intimate matter her desires did not reach beyond her family, is also apparent in the conflicts that arose. Most women seem to have consulted parents out of a combination of duty and love. One North Carolina woman told her lover that they must inform her father of their correspondence for "I am beginning to have in my heart the deep, true love and a sincere respect that a child ought always to have for a parent." But other women clashed with parents over a certain man or over parental power. A young sweetheart of Joseph Bryan was "shocked at the indelicate position" in which she found herself when her father ended her correspondence with Bryan. Anna White haplessly opened a letter from her secret sweetheart in her family's presence, was compelled to read it aloud, and saw her father return it and other letters to the young man. Thomas Lenoir determined of his daughter Laura's courtship that she should "come to the conclusion that it would be best for [her] to defer this matter for awhile or forever." Penelope Skinner complained to her brother that "Father is so strict & particular that the young men will I fear soon begin not to come here at all." Elopement, always rare, was met with parental shock and anger. In sum, entering further into womanhood through courtship did not free a woman from old family bonds of the most intimate and demanding sort. Though historians have lately depicted nineteenth-century marriage as "affectionate" to distinguish it from an earlier materialist, father-dominated style, it seems that fathers were able to assert themselves in a daughter's affair by using family affection. The rise of affection as a basis for marriage, in the planter class at least, cannot therefore be seen as a simple advance in women's autonomous choice of lover or mate. Parents stood close by to influence as best they could a new family relation in the image of the old.[19]

Much remains to be unearthed about exactly how planter-class women and men perceived their growing up and how these perceptions and their social circumstances changed over time. In the antebellum period, however, it seems clear that certain tensions among different kinds of families were essential to a woman's coming of age and provide one threshold for our historical understanding. Such conflict may have influenced both sexes throughout their life cycles; the complications of family life never have been remote in southern studies. But in the youth of a planter-class woman the tensions were particularly sharp. Living through them, she construed the crucial changes in her life as changes in family ties, shifting from her childhood family to the sisterhood of the academy and then into the courtship that promised yet another family bond. This was less a transition from one sheltered existence to another than a rough dialectic of feminine worldliness. She left her parents but continued to find them in both her lessons and her love. Loving a man, she did not forget the intimacy with her sisters. It was in this often intense autobiographical excursion through prior and alternative visions of family that a woman became educated: she discovered the emotions, obligations, and ideals with which to create the particulars of womanhood for herself.

Notes

1. For a sample of recent work on education of upper-class women see Phillida Bunkle, "Sentimental Womanhood and Domestic Education, 1830–1870," *History of Education Quarterly* 14 (Spring 1974): 13–30; Ann D. Gordon, "The Philadelphia Young Ladies Academy," in Carol Berkin and Mary Beth Norton, eds., *Women of America: A History* (Boston: Little, Brown, 1979). Also useful are Eleanor Thompson, *Education for Ladies, 1830–1860* (New York: King's Crown Press, 1947); Edgar Knight, *The Academy Movement in the South* (Chapel Hill: University of North Carolina Press, 1920); and Florence Davis, "The Education of Southern Girls from 1750 to 1860" (Ph.D. dissertation, University of Chicago, 1951).

2. Two recent studies that place education in a broad family context in the South are Jane Turner Censer, *North Carolina Planters and Their Children, 1800–1860* (Baton Rouge: Louisiana State University Press, 1984); and Jan Lewis, *The Pursuit of Happiness: Family and Values in Jefferson's Virginia* (New York: Cambridge University Press, 1983).

3. Personal letters as a literary genre with social implications are given sophisticated treatment in Elizabeth Hampsten, *Read This Only to Yourself: The Private Writings of Midwestern Women, 1880–1910* (Bloomington: Indiana University Press, 1982); and Marilyn Motz, *True Sisterhood: Michigan Women and Their Kin, 1820–1920* (Albany: State University of New York Press, 1983).

4. Margaret Coxe, *The Young Lady's Companion in a Series of Letters* (Co-

lumbus, Ohio: I. Nap Whiting, 1839), p. 69; Virginia Cary, *Letters on Female Character* (Richmond, Va.: A. Works, 1828), p. 135; Caroline Gilman, *Recollections of a Southern Matron* (New York, 1838), p. 57. See also James M. Garnett, *Lectures on Female Education* (Richmond, Va.: T. W. White, 1825).

5. Almira Phelps, *The Female Student, or Lectures to Young Ladies on Female Education* (New York: Leavitt, Lord and Co., 1836), p. 29; Francis Lieber to "a committee of the Euphradian Society," November 22, 1848 (MS copy in Lieber's hand), Francis Lieber Papers, South Caroliniana Library, University of South Carolina, Columbia, S.C. (hereafter SCL); Jasper Adams, *Elements of Moral Philosophy* (Cambridge, Mass.: Folsom, Wells, and Thurston, 1837), pp. 143, 146.

6. St. Mary's Hall, *An Appeal to Parents for Female Education on Christian Principles* . . . (Burlington, N.J.: J. L. Powell, 1837), pp. 16–17; Amory Dwight Mayo, *Southern Women in the Recent Educational Movement in the South* (1892; rpt. Baton Rouge: Louisiana State University Press, 1978), p. 134. On the founding and ideology of academies see John S. Ezell, "A Southern Education for Southrons," *Journal of Southern History* 17 (August 1951): 303–27; Ralph M. Lyon, "The Early Years of Livingston Female Academy," *Alabama Historical Quarterly* 37 (1975): 3–28. For antebellum opinion on the importance of "Southron" education, see *Southern Literary Messenger* 18 (February 1852): 116–22 and *Southern Quarterly Review*, n.s., 5 (April 1852): 507–35.

7. Katherine Batts Salley, ed., *Life at St. Mary's* (Chapel Hill: University of North Carolina Press, 1942), pp. 16–17; for Talvande's see Mary Boykin Chesnut, "A Boarding School Fifty Years Ago," pp. 305–7, Williams-Chesnut-Manning Papers, SCL; Caroline Lee Hentz, *Eoline, or Magnolia Vale* (Philadelphia: A. Hart, 1854), p. 39.

8. Hentz, *Eoline*, p. 33; Mary Ferrand to Mary Steele, July 15, 1831, John Steele Papers, Southern Historical Collection, University of North Carolina, Chapel Hill (hereafter SHC); Charlotte Daly to Katherine DeRosset, February 10, 1847, DeRosset Papers, SHC; Coxe, *Young Lady's Companion*, p. 71; Salley, *Life at St. Mary's*, p. 22; Chesnut, "Boarding School," p. 275.

9. *The New Universal Letter-Writer* (Philadelphia: D. Hogan, 1850), pp. 11, 15, 21; Charles Butler, *The American Lady* (Philadelphia: Hogan and Thompson, 1836), p. 152; Lydia Sigourney, *Letters to Mothers* (Hartford, Conn.: Hudson and Skinner, 1838), pp. 163–64.

10. Eliza DeRosset to Katherine DeRosset, December 14, 1844, DeRosset Papers; John C. Calhoun to Anna Calhoun, December 30, [1831], in Clyde N. Wilson, ed., *Papers of John C. Calhoun*, 14 vols. (Columbia: University of South Carolina Press, 1978), 2: 531–32; John P. Richardson to Elizabeth Richardson, April 11, 1805, Richardson Papers, SCL; William Gaston to Hannah Gaston, July 7, 1828, Gaston Papers, SHC; Armand DeRosset to Katherine DeRosset, July 18, 1847, DeRosset Papers.

11. Mary Ann Lenoir to Selina Lenoir, June 13, October 5, 1835, Lenoir

Papers, SHC; Katherine DeRosset to Armand DeRosset, December 1, 1844, DeRosset Papers; Bessie Lacy to Drury Lacy, January 27, 1848, Lacy Papers, SHC.

12. Louisa Lenoir to "Elizabeth," 1819, Lenoir Papers (letterbook); Charlotte Daly to Katherine DeRosset, November 4, 1848, DeRosset Papers; Bessie Lacy to Thomas Dewey, May 10, 1852, Lacy Papers; Charlotte Daly to Katherine DeRosset, February 10, 1847, DeRosset Papers; Bessie Lacy to Drury Lacy, January 27, 1848, Lacy Papers; Penelope Skinner to Tristram Skinner, February 26, 1840, Skinner Papers, SHC.

13. For changes in moralist literature, compare Hannah More, *The Works of Hannah More*, 2 vols. (New York: Harper and Brothers, 1846–47), and Cary, *Letters on Female Character;* for letter-writing guides, see *The American Academy of Compliments; or, the Complete American Secretary . . .* (Philadelphia: Deshong and Folwell, 1796), and R. Turner, *The Parlour Letter-Writer and Secretary's Assistant* (Philadelphia: Thomas, Cowperthwait and Co., 1845); for contrast in novels popular with southern women, see Gilman, *Recollections of a Southern Matron*, and Emma Southworth, *Love's Labor Won* (Philadelphia: T. B. Peterson and Brothers, 1862). For the intellectual context of women's fiction, see Nina Baym, *Woman's Fiction: A Guide to Novels by and about Women in America, 1820–1870* (Ithaca: Cornell University Press, 1978), and Mary Kelley, *Private Woman, Public Stage: Literary Domesticity in Nineteenth Century America* (New York: Oxford University Press, 1984). On courtship see Guion G. Johnson, "Courtship and Marriage Customs in Ante-Bellum North Carolina," *North Carolina Historical Review* 8 (October 1931): 384–402; Ellen K. Rothman, "Sex and Self-Control: Middle-Class Courtship in America, 1770–1870," *Journal of Social History* 15 (Spring 1982): 409–25; Steven M. Stowe, " 'The *Thing* Not Its Vision': A Woman's Courtship and Sphere in the Southern Planter Class," *Feminist Studies* 9 (Spring 1983): 113–30.

14. Hester Chapone, *Letters on the Improvement of the Mind: Addressed to a Lady* (Boston: James B. Dow, 1834), pp. 22–23; Coxe, *Young Lady's Companion,* p. 192; Emma Southworth, *Retribution; or, the Vale of Shadows: A Tale of Passion* (New York: Harper and Brothers, 1849), p. 14.

15. Mary Townes to William A. Townes, September 17, 1837, Townes Papers, SCL; Mary Moragne diary, February 20, 1837, in Delle Mullen Craven, ed., *The Neglected Thread: A Journal from the Calhoun Community, 1836–1842* (Columbia: University of South Carolina Press, 1951), p. 25; Julia [Pickens] to Eliza Lenoir, May 15, 1834, Lenoir Papers.

16. Elizabeth McCall to Benjamin Perry, February 21, 1837, Mrs. Benjamin F. Perry Papers, SCL.

17. Bessie Lacy to Thomas Dewey, May 7, 1852, Lacy Papers; Emmie Roberts to Robert Sams, February 16, 1864, Sams Family Papers, SCL.

18. Henry Townes to George Townes, January 16, 1834, Townes Papers; J. A. Graves to William Augustus Townes, June 28, 1837, Townes Papers;

Henry Cumming to Julia Cumming, October 4, 1828, Hammond-Bryan-Cumming Papers, SCL; William Gaston to Susan Gaston, October 2, 1826, Gaston Papers; Henry Townes to William Augustus Townes, February 8, 1846, Townes Papers.

19. Bessie Lacy to Thomas Dewey, June 30, 1852, Lacy Papers; Maria Bryan to Julia Cumming, August 14, 1839, Hammond-Bryan-Cumming Papers; Augustin Taveau to Rosalie Simons, March 1846, Taveau Papers, Perkins Library, Duke University, Durham, N.C.; Thomas Lenoir to Selina Lenoir, December 26, 1835, Lenoir Papers; Penelope Skinner to Tristram Skinner, November 5, 1838, Skinner Papers. Two studies arguing that the affectionate nature of marriage in this class was primary are Daniel Blake Smith, *Inside the Great House* (Ithaca: Cornell University Press, 1980), and Censer, *North Carolina Planters.*

Antebellum College Life and the Relations between Fathers and Sons

Jon L. Wakelyn

Antebellum college life has been viewed as a microcosm of southern life in general. If so, its reflection of relations between fathers and sons should reveal information about that aspect of life in the region's society. On one level, the father-son relationship was the key to the transmission of values and of material and political power from one generation to another. On another level, the relationship is informative about the structure of the southern family. If one is to understand how college life related to that society, the fathers' influence on their sons at college and the sons' family values as reflected in their behavior as students require study.

Few of the works on higher education in the Old South address either relationships between fathers and sons or student life. Many of them are narrowly focused institutional studies, usually commissioned by the colleges to show how they survived the past. Some of the best of them made excellent contributions to our understanding of how colleges were founded and conducted administratively. There are a few fine studies of faculty and curricula. The best, such as those of the state colleges of Georgia, Alabama, North Carolina, and Virginia, contain information about student life. Although they describe many student diversions, such as life in the surrounding community and the debate societies, they mainly focus on violence and order.

Some of the most suggestive work on college life has come from recent studies which are not primarily concerned with colleges. In a study of southern intellectuals, many of whom taught in colleges, Drew Gilpin Faust discussed a paradox between colleges that supposedly provided "rigorous intellectual training for an elite" but many of whose students "were not merely ignorant, but entirely uncontrollable." College professors were "prisoners of the often arrogant and fractious sons of the gentry who paid the instruction fees." Those young elite "gentlemen" were poorly prepared, quick to take offense, and just like their dominant fathers. In Faust's view, the colleges educated an elite exactly as the fathers wished.[1]

In his article "The Ideal Typology and Antebellum Southern History," Bertram Wyatt-Brown discusses college life as an extension of the father-son relationship. Wyatt-Brown maintains that northerners surrendered family control over children to religion and education but that antebellum southern patriarchs did not. The southern tradition of passing values and simple agricultural career choices occurred within the household. In *Southern Honor,* Wyatt-Brown further suggests that even when planters sent their sons to college, the colleges simply "catered to the raw planter mentality." Colleges stressed what the dominant fathers wanted, and the cult of "manliness" often resisted scholarly learning. Wyatt-Brown does maintain, however, that because the sons were separated from the fathers, college threatened "the patriarch's authority." Tantalizingly, he states that southern college students had "sacred obligations to one's peers, against the world if need be."[2] But neither Wyatt-Brown nor Faust studied actual college life, so they were unable to verify their brilliant assertions.

A number of recent studies which concentrate on family life offer somewhat different views of college in the context of father-son relations. In *North Carolina Planters and Their Children,* Jane Turner Censer suggests that fathers inculcated values of industry, hard work, and individual choice to their sons at an early age. Most fathers supported school rules, and "by college age, sons were exhorted to provide their own discipline." Sons were to attend college to develop their own career goals, and study was stressed by fathers who "touted success in school as an important goal."[3] In her most recent work Drew Faust says that college life was for the ambitious young. In the case of James Henry Hammond, his fellow students believed that "position and preference were granted on the basis of ability."[4] Censer provides a view of an entirely different world than does Wyatt-Brown, but she also makes little analysis of life at college. Faust seems to have changed her views, but Hammond is the only student whose life she examines in any detail. Only by turning to the institution itself is it possible to test the prevailing views of what fathers expected from sons and how college life affected their relationship.

It is important at the outset to get a feeling for current expectations regarding the father-son relationship and why fathers wanted their sons to go to college. The literature of family life, that era's equivalent of books on how to raise children, shows much interest in father-son relations. Almost all of the writers maintained that fathers were the sources of power and the keepers of law and order. In this role, the father had a duty to his family to subdue the sons and to channel their energies into useful endeavor. Since the sons also harbored the desire to rule their fathers, some form of accommodation as well as some outside institutional support were needed to keep the sons in line. After all, the contemporary authors maintained, the sons were the future leaders of the society, and their training was important to all.

Many of those writers were clergymen, and some, such as the Baptist John L. Dagg, served as college presidents. Obviously, they would choose college as the institutional apparatus to harness the sons' desires and energy. These authors maintained that fathers owed their sons a college education. Dagg suggested that the father's own personal usefulness and happiness required him to educate his son, especially since "the education of children should be adapted to the business which they are expected to pursue." Another writer insisted that the "instruction of the school, should be fully sustained by the parents." Only the most able and most ambitious sons should be sent to college, and fathers were expected to continue to care for them there.[5]

College professors also discussed why planters sent their sons to college. The University of Nashville's president Philip Lindsley described college as useful to the business of the local community. He believed that prudent fathers would give their sons an education because "every son of Tennessee will look up with deference to the better class of citizens for models for imitation." Thomas R. Dew of William and Mary insisted that slaveholders should send their sons to college to learn leadership skills. James H. Thornwell of the College of South Carolina regarded college as an instrument of the existing order. More to the point, Henry St. George Tucker proclaimed that education should "keep our sons from losing caste, and sinking in society below the grade we occupy ourselves." But Henry Ruffner of Washington College bitterly condemned wealthy planters who insisted that their sons go to college, not for education but to "acquire some smattering of knowledge befitting a gentleman who was above the necessity of professional labor, or any other sort of labor."[6]

Fathers gave their own reasons for educating their sons. Some of them regarded college as a means for their sons to rise in life. J. Marion Sims's father insisted that even though it was expensive, college was the only way for a person of his son's means to attain a suitable career. The ambitious mother of Robert L. Dabney sent him to college to restore the status of his fatherless family. Sterling Ruffin suggested that at Princeton his son Thomas could cultivate friendships with his wealthier cousins and thus preserve the family position. Although the elder Ruffin always spoke with paternal affection, there was an expression of urgency in the words of this marginal planter, who often told Thomas that college was a way to get ahead. The itinerant North Carolina schoolteacher John Dickson, who constantly reminded his son of his wealthy cousins, sent him to college to "develop worthwhile friendships" and ordered him to show deference to his peers and to cultivate a "likeable personality."[7]

Not all planters were so ambitious for their sons. The Episcopal minister Charles Pettigrew sent his sons to the University of North Carolina to shape their Federalist principles. Also aware that college polished rough rural youths and prepared them to assume their rightful leadership rank, the elder Pettigrew told his sons that they would emerge from college better prepared for life in their aristocratic plantation world of North Carolina. The patriarch of the Deveaux family of low-country South Carolina wanted his son to attend the University of Virginia to be with neighboring planters' sons. Governor Isaac Shelby of Kentucky sent his son to college because that was what his fellow southwestern elites did. He also expected his son to receive the training that would enable him to take advantage of changes in business practice in that rapidly growing region.[8]

Letters from fathers who did not believe in higher education for their sons are in short supply. Those who sent sons to college described their reasons to the youths, who seemed to offer few ideas of their own. The more aspiring lesser aristocrats saw opportunities for their sons, and the more powerful sought means to perpetuate their good names, status, and fortune. Surely Censer's view is buttressed by the opinion of Jabez L. M. Curry, who wrote of college as a place for sheer intellectual pleasure.[9] But sons' freedom of choice seems nonexistent because many fathers decided which colleges the boys would attend. Other fathers, who sent sons to be with their friends, seemed to be little concerned about learning, as Wyatt-Brown and Faust suggest.

The reasons given for sending sons to college indicate much interest in higher education. Yet Wyatt-Brown is surely correct when he maintains that a number of planters, especially those who rose out of the middling classes in the antebellum period, resisted college as insignificant. Still, colleges were founded throughout the antebellum period, and the student population grew and diversified. My own study of more than 600 Confederate leaders, not all of whom came from the established planter wealth, reveals that more than 400 had attended college. Ralph Wooster has shown that most of the delegates to the southern secession conventions had attended college. In a random sample of 180 southern congressmen, some of whom came from middle-class families, 95 had attended college and 67 took degrees. From her group of North Carolina's large planters, Jane Censer found that two-thirds sent at least one son to college and at least half that group sent two or more. In his discussion of 440 South Carolina planters, Chalmers G. Davidson found that two-thirds had attended college. If less than 3 percent of all antebellum southern males went to college, most probably over 40 percent of the future planters, professionals, and politicians spent a part of their adolescent life in college.[10]

Given their motivations for sending their sons to college, fathers surely wanted some control over their lives while there. One way fathers could exert influence was by governing the institution, either as members of the boards of trustees or through friends who were trustees. During most of the antebellum period, the trustees exercised much authority over colleges through gifts of land, fund-raising, and personal bequests. In addition, trustees often hired faculty and presidents, chose textbooks, made decisions about student admissions and promotions, and set the rules for student deportment, which gave them authority to expel students.[11] Fathers certainly felt secure in asking their friends for special favors and considerations.

Such institutional influence naturally affected the faculty and the president. Fathers wrote school authorities describing their sons' characteristics and weaknesses and asking them to keep an eye on the boys. Faculty also had a policy of informing fathers about student behavior, class attendance, and class work. Many faculty members believed, or said they did, that fathers should influence their sons' activities at school. In an address to students, Thomas R. Dew advised sons never to forget why their fathers had sent them to college. The fathers had a right to expect hard work, decent behavior, and deference from their sons. William Hooper rationalized paternal power, claiming that if fathers did not accept the way their sons were treated, they would remove them and thus destroy the college. William R. Davie of the University of North Carolina best captured faculty deference in a letter to trustee John Haywood, insisting that the "principles of parental Government are the true models for that of literary Institutions."[12] But Davie told Haywood that he expected fathers to leave discipline to the faculty, who no doubt felt they could use the threat of paternal power to maintain order among the students.

Students, too, came to understand that a father's influence over the institution could be a source for their own gain. Many knew that if they did not succeed at one college, father could get them into another. Faculty deference to the fathers, one supposes, was not entirely lost on the sons. Thus the sons could also use their fathers, as young Thomas Law confided to his diary concerning the results of the Citadel student riots of 1858. Law described how his father visited at the son's request and straightened out the situation. Other sons used their fathers' pride to protect them from dismissal and even to request that certain faculty members be fired.[13] This action, of course, may be seen as both the sons' dependency and a shrewd use of fatherly power.

In addition to learning directly from the institution, fathers expected their sons to keep them informed of life at college. The style and content of those letters and messages reveal much about father-son relations. Some sons believed that their fathers had the right to be informed, and they deferred to their fathers' wishes for information; others seemed to resist by their silence. The sons as snitches contributed to their own power and importance as well as to their fathers' interest in what happened to their lives away from home.

In their letters fathers showed much interest in what their sons learned at college. Sterling Ruffin was pleased that his son Thomas had achieved first place in his class. He wrote, "It gives eclat to a young man which goes with him into the World, and he commences business under every advantage which talents can bestow." John Dickson insisted that his son read the classics thoughtfully and industriously, for they helped in retention of memory, and "all our distinguished lawyers and scholars . . . have the best memories." Stephen Deveaux, obviously unsettled over faculty reports of his son's efforts, tried to control the number of classes the boy took and the subjects he chose. He insisted that a future leader had to study moral philosophy seriously. "I hope," he exclaimed, "therefore you will be particularly attentive to it as it is a science which teaches men their duty and the reasons for it."[14]

The younger Deveaux resisted his father's admonitions and stated that his father had little understanding of the requirements. He suggested that good friends and professors were better guides. He also resented his father's use of faculty reports to try to control his activities. Still, he promised that if forced he would follow his worthy father's advice, and he signed his letters, "accept the best from your dutiful son." Young John Pettigrew seemed delighted to inform his father that he was forced to read Thomas Paine and that the faculty believed in Paine's teachings. Young Thomas Law criticized his French instructor as "being quite worrying and unpleasant." Few fathers offered resistance when sons wanted to change direction in their studies. Even the ambitious Sterling Ruffin sided with his son against President Samuel Stanhope Smith's harsh treatment of students.[15]

The fathers also exercised control of sons' financial expenditures. The poor but proud John Dickson insisted that his son watch every penny. He advised him to "let nobody get you to buy what you do not need or cannot afford." But Dickson also wanted him to dress respectably to conform to social pressures. Still, he resented his son's wealthy South Carolina friends at Yale and warned, "Don't calculate on the friendship of any youth pampered by the indolence and indulgence of a slaveholding region." More typical were Rev. Charles Pettigrew's admonitions to his sons for their tavern expenses; he suggested that only disreputable young men habituated such places. Poorer students such as young Dickson and Ruffin had no choice but to obey their fathers. But even Dickson never let his father forget the connection between status and allowance. More typical of the planter class were the actions of Ralph Elliott, who avoided his father's scorn by writing his mother for cash but always ended his letters, "Tell Papa the money is required." Robert Deveaux summed up the plight of the rich when he haughtily told his father how expensive it was for the upper classes to live well in Charlottesville.[16]

Student deportment was the principal reason for exchange of correspondence. Fathers seemed to fear that college posed a threat to the social order as they understood it, and they worried that their advice might be powerless against peer pressures. William Elliott told his son that he trusted him to leave home without "being led into irregularities—that might have the most fateful effect on your prosperity in life." He warned him to stay away from those who game and smoke and admonished him to be worthy of his name and connections. Rev. Charles Pettigrew expected his upper-class sons to set examples for their fellow students. He also cautioned them, "Don't disgrace your father." Stephen Deveaux once accused his son of inciting a school riot. But most fathers reacted as did John Dickson, who expected his son to avoid other southern boys who might get him into trouble but supported his son's defense of his rights against slights from other students and faculty.[17]

Sons in turn told their fathers how they responded to campus disorder. John Pettigrew took delight in informing his father about undisciplined fellow students. Thomas Law deplored duels and other dangers of student life, and his major complaint against his fellows was that their rioting hurt the college's reputation among the citizenry of Charleston. Other sons insisted that campus riots were mere pranks and resented being lumped with their violent fellow students. On one occasion Robert De-veaux sharply denied his father's accusation that he had participated in campus riots. After a faculty report was sent home, he confessed that he had participated in a harmless disturbance when students blew horns late at night. With clear understanding of his father's ambivalence over vio-lence on campus, he stated, "I hope that you will believe that your son has sense enough to keep a straight forward course and not engage in any thing that will bring disgrace . . . and mortification to his parents and friends."[18]

Fathers clearly maintained a close interest in their sons at college. Their connections with the colleges gave them access to their sons' doings, and college policies were to inform fathers about their sons. That the fathers controlled finances and the length of time their sons could stay at college put them in a position of power. Fathers who perhaps expected sons to behave in their own image seemed to deplore excesses of disorder. Among families that should have conformed to the behavior pattern of Censer's independent and academically ambitious sons, there is some suggestion that many students and their fathers took school seriously. But the sons were not as independent or as well-trained as her argument sug-gests. In their interactions fathers were torn between the desire to control and the hope for mature and independent behavior from their sons. Sons in turn were dependent upon their fathers but also used their fathers' influence for their own advantage.

A demonstration of this counterpoint with poignant overtones may be seen in an exchange between Governor Henry A. Wise of Virginia and his son Richard on the eve of secession. His father thought Richard loved the College of William and Mary and his fellow students for the wrong rea-sons. Henry wanted the boy to remain in school, especially as secession tension rose in the state. Richard joined the faculty military company against his father's wishes but told him that if fighting occurred he was "going home and go with you." What proof of paternal influence: the son would defy college authorities to assist his father. But that was not what Henry had wanted. Not only had the college supported fealty to the fa-ther but it had created a spirit of independence that gave Richard the nerve to inform his father just what action he would take.[19]

Fathers' comments to their sons reveal tension concerning behavior, study, and seriousness of intent. They particularly discussed the effects of college on their plans for their sons' careers. The elder Deveaux was in-censed that his supposedly dutiful son trafficked with student nullifiers. He told Robert that by leaving college to go to Charleston to join a radi-cal political movement he had ruined his chances for law school. J. Marion Sims, too, fell out with his middle-class father, who had had high hopes for his success. The elder Sims had wanted the boy to study law, but instead he had developed an interest in medicine while in college. His father claimed that if he had known his son had wanted to study medicine, he would never have sent him to college. An example of a father who spitefully questioned why college life had diminished his influence over his son was James Henry Hammond. Carol Bleser suggests that Hammond viewed his family as an extension of himself and was "determined to train his sons to become masters themselves on his landed estates." But his eldest son, Harry, went to medical school and then, instead of taking over a family plantation, spent a year at Harvard to prepare for a teaching post. To his brother Marcus, Hammond poured out what many a planter surely felt: "All hope of establishing a rich, educated, well-bred and predominant family . . . is over with me though it has been all I have devoted my life to." He felt as though Harry "had died," for he was "not the son I loved and hoped for in old age."[20]

Clearly there were influences at college that subverted fatherly control, as demonstrated in the sons' independence and the fathers' recognition of it. At college sons developed relationships separate from the family, although no doubt their earlier experiences influenced their college friendships. Sons saw constant reminders of their fathers in the college planter community, but they also had the opportunity to observe how other fathers functioned. Many sons had had experience with deferential and at times brutal teachers in their preparatory school days, but their relations with college instructors were entirely different. In addition, relations with college peers were numerous and more intense than those with young playmates. One must therefore examine the student alone with his peers as he negotiated for leadership, peer ranking, and friendships because sons had to get along with their fellow future planters, businessmen, and political leaders in ways that they did not have to get along with their fathers.

An important aspect of college life was the experience of separation from the family. Some students did not see their fathers for as long as two years, although the average was more like nine or ten months. The average student remained at college no more than eighteen months, so the changing population meant constant turnover in friendships. The average age of the college student was either fourteen to sixteen or eighteen to twenty, revealing different levels of maturity. Although there is little information about the age at which puberty was experienced or about its intensity, these boys were thrown together during that most trying time. Because there were different age groups, physical size was also important in a place where strength and prowess were important. Admissions policies were uneven, and, according to faculty complaints, the quality of preparation made for great discrepancies in intellectual talents. Boys usually attended college in their home state, although some fathers sent sons out of state. Different accents, different climates, and sectional loyalties thus affected student relationships. Furthermore, class distinctions were reflected in student friendships and groupings. In sum, age, distance from home, loneliness, class, and levels of preparation threw an uneven group of youths together to work out ways of mutual accommodation.

Perhaps one of the most sensitive of college instructors to the potential results of loneliness among the students was President Frederick A. P. Barnard of the University of Alabama and later of the University of Mississippi. Barnard wanted to end the dormitory system because he believed that much of the nurturing of the students took place in the surrounding community, especially among the prominent families. He wanted the students to board with local families so those families would gain an understanding of the college and the students would be exposed to local businessmen and planters who would stimulate their ambitions and encourage them to do their school work. Barnard hoped that a boarding arrangement would recreate the home family setting and thus give the students guidelines to a civilized life in polite company.[21]

Not all students took advantage of the community as Barnard wished. Many isolated themselves from a society they found "uncultivated and uninviting." Town or countryside–gown relations were often strained. Students fought with local toughs, created disturbances in the neighborhood, frequented local taverns and houses of ill repute, and generally were too boisterous for the community to tolerate. Local leaders sometimes wished that they could avoid contact with their friends' children. By 1859 the strain between town and students at the University of Alabama reached open warfare. The *Tuscaloosa Monitor* reported that the college was isolated from the community and therefore "more or less antagonistic to it." The paper lamented that students were deprived of contacts with these families and especially the refinement of the opposite sex.[22]

Many students, however, profited from contacts with local families. Jefferson Davis became close friends with Henry Clay, Jr., and was often invited to Ashland. Thomas Law made friends among the Charleston medical students and was a guest in their homes while he attended the Citadel. In his diary he described the many kindnesses paid him by leading citizens. Apparently he was virtually adopted by two local ministers, who took him to church and no doubt influenced his decision to pursue ministerial studies. Charles Hardee of Georgia remembered that "socially, I had a very nice time during the whole four years I was at college. I was 'persona grata' at the houses of the best families in Athens and was always invited to all the parties given by the young ladies." For some students, such parties provided nearly the only female contact they had at college. Jabez L. M. Curry's father had sent his son to Athens not only because he had relatives there but also because the surrounding community had "attracted a class of citizens for the most part educated and refined." Young Curry, who was a classmate of Linton Stephens, often dined with Alexander Stephens and his younger brother when the congressman visited Athens.[23]

Young Robert Deveaux's experiences in Charlottesville society summed up the advantages and learning experience of the student among the local gentry. Robert had been sent to the University of Virginia because local friends from South Carolina were also attending. When such wealthy families as the Singletons visited the community, Robert was often invited to the homes of the local planters. Because Robert did not go home for more than two years, he spent holidays and vacations with those families. He developed a close relationship with the planter John Brockenbrough, who took him to Washington and introduced him to leading political figures. Brockenbrough also discussed business and career possibilities with young Deveaux. But Robert learned the differences between up-country Virginia gentry and his wealthy low-country South Carolina family. In a letter to his father Robert exclaimed that Virginians were much too lax with their slaves, who consequently were surly and lazy.[24]

Faculty members also took students into their homes and exposed them to the polite company of wives and children. The ever-critical Robert L. Dabney pithily remarked that the local planters near Lexington, Virginia, were poor and uneducated. But the lonely young man remembered the kindness of Mrs. John Holt Rice, who took him in as a boarder. Young faculty members included among their duties civilizing their charges, and their homes were open for conversation and student parties. Faculty wives often became the confidants of the students. In one community, however, a horrible story circulated that students had abused these friendships by taking advantage of a professor's female house slave.[25]

Although faculty-student relations were often adversarial to the point of armed violence, the faculty became the most important substitutes for the sons' fathers. Despite faculty deference to fathers and trustees, throughout the antebellum period they struggled for the right to govern and control student behavior. One professor suggested that future leaders could be trained only if they were separated from societal and parental influence. Archibald D. Murphy's report of 1817 on student riots blamed the unrest in part on fathers' upbringing of sons and continued interference in college disciplinary matters. The experience of governing and educating students thus forced faculty to attempt to wrest control of the students from the fathers. In his *Letters on College Government*, Barnard offered the professor as a substitute for the father but cautioned that college governance should perform like family governance.[26]

Of course the faculty had the unique advantage of being where the fathers were not. The moment boys arrived on campus, a faculty member greeted them, tested them for class placement, and introduced them to the rules and regulations of dormitory life and classroom decorum. Faculty also determined the course of study. They controlled class rank and decided whether the lazy would stay in school. Some faculty members believed that they reinforced their roles through their teaching; a few professors insisted that their lectures allowed them to influence students' beliefs and behavior. John N. Waddell realized his importance to the wealthy southern families: "He who gains the ears and the hearts of the young men of this age is thus furnished with vantage ground for affecting great good to the world."[27] It is doubtful that much from those lectures affected the students. Frederick A. P. Barnard was more realistic about persuasion and faculty power, insisting that certain subjects, if properly taught, influenced how students learned.[28]

Barnard also suggested that the personal relationship between students and faculty was more important than what went on in the classroom: "It would be well, both for students and professors, if there were somewhat more intercourse between them at times when the artificial relations of instructor and pupil might be forgotten, or at least kept out of sight. The consequences would be the forming of personal ties and growth of mutual understanding which would contribute . . . to the harmony and happiness of the college community."[29] In his *Character of the Gentleman*, Professor Francis Lieber wrote of the importance of friendship between teacher and student: "No better opportunity to practice this moral rule is given" than the pupil's relation to his teachers. [30] Many faculty members became confidants of their students.

Yet despite the influence of local elites and faculty, relations with their peers may have been the dominant force in students' lives on campus. Upon arrival at college, most students met competition among faculty and fellow students in matters of education and social life. Their peers advised new students about their classmates and their instructors. Most students were immediately rushed into the debating societies. Young Law recalled that the pressures to join such a society were strong. The membership of these societies reflected the students' home regions and elite groups, usually based on their fathers' social position. For example, up-country Carolinians appeared self-conscious and jealous of students from the low country.[31] Sons thus early confronted one another on the basis of status and geographical identity. Although aspects of their home lives were also reinforced this way, the sons were placed immediately in both union and competition with their peer group.

Peer pressures also caused lasting animosities against other student groups and individuals. Thomas Law bitterly resented his classmates' loose behavior. Less socially precocious than his peers, he despised the lax moral code, which allowed students to bring young women into their dormitory rooms. Thomas also deplored the competition for top places in the class. Robert Deveaux was jealous of his glib-tongued classmates, whom he regarded as more brilliant than he. He therefore kept close to his fellow wealthy Carolinians because he placed much emphasis on social status. Robert L. Dabney had no respect for his spoiled upper-class peers. A loner, supersensitive to slights, he called his classmates' dress extravagant. He thought that they had too much money to spend and that they lorded it over their poorer classmates. Students at the University of Alabama quarreled over the treatment of campus slaves. Some believed that they could deal with the slaves at college just as they had with their own slaves at home; they expected deference and obedience from the slaves as well as from their less well-to-do peers. One observant but bitter young man at that frontier college suggested that elites postured because they were insecure in their family's new wealth.[32]

Yet peer groups and social bonds were often established based on region, age, wealth, talent, and the need for mutual protection. The individual code of not wanting to "appear before my comrades as if I were afraid of anything or anybody" required collective support. That these alliances often turned violent is evident from the number of students who were expelled for fighting and dueling. The threat of violence, whether a fistfight, the semicivilized code of the duel, or a brawl, whether individual outbursts against authority or mass student uprisings, marked the course of student life. Perhaps experiencing violence at such an impressionable age of mutual needs and feelings between boyhood and manhood brought students closer together. Not only did many take solace in forming protective support groups, but the evidence suggests that most of them refused to inform on one another, despite fatherly and faculty pressures. A glaring example of this cohesion occurred when students at the

University of Virginia accepted mass expulsion rather than accede to faculty demands that they report infractions of dormitory rules.[33]

Students thus united against a common enemy—the administration. Barnard commented on the stupidity of faculty attempts to keep order by visiting rooms and establishing rigid honor codes. He regarded students as honor bound to one another and thus willing to obey rules as long as they were not forced to inform on each other. "Students," he claimed, "associated together in the same class, or in the same college, occupy to each other not only the relation of subjects to a common government, but that, to a certain extent, of members of the same family." The Reverend R. S. Gladney observed that student resentment of faculty authority had made self-government vital to their college existence and that such government bound them together.[34]

Perhaps the major influence on student relations was the college debate society. Scholars who have commented on those societies regard them as central to the students' educational experience and personal growth. Debate was the one area faculty did not rule. The societies operated as self-governing bodies, which forced students to learn about their peers' personalities and points of view. They had rigorous rules for members' deportment, which the students took seriously. Those who ran the societies were brutal in dismissing members for rule infractions and tactless in refusing to accept some students as members. Students purchased their society's furniture and books and kept records pertaining to its activities. Honorary memberships for leading political and cultural figures were hotly discussed with students dividing over party loyalty and which public man could best help them in their future plans. Even social events were planned around the society. An example of the tensions of leadership can be seen in the contest over debate schedules and topics at the College of Charleston, in which the pushy but poor James D. B. DeBow lost to the aristocratic William H. Trescott. The brilliant and gifted James Henry Hammond overcame his middle-class background as he schemed successfully to attain the presidency of his debate society.[35] Their conduct of the society's affairs prepared students for future political leadership, business practice, and social class pecking order, sometimes based on talent as well as status.

The societies' principal tasks, however, were debate and other forms of oral discourse, for which students often did more preparation than for their classes. After all, many of them would someday make their living in the verbal presentation of self. Many of the students believed that the techniques of public debate were useful for political life and for status relations in their home communities. College student status was in part based on powers of persuasiveness. J. Marion Sims claimed that there was little class ordering in such gatherings, and he relished a system that allowed the poor James H. Thornwell to become a class leader because of his oratorical skills.[36] The societies' minutes contain rigorous and sharp commentary on individual performance. Since students also had to write their speeches they developed written skills. Although the topics chosen certainly educated students in contemporary affairs, more important was the ability to persuade one's fellows of the merits of one's position. From encounters over governance of debating societies, working to develop skills, and making personal judgments of abilities many students formed intimate and lasting alliances.

Those close confidences among students were revealed in their solicitations of advice and approval for their career choices from their peers. They discussed their hopes and fears for the future in ways they could not with their fathers. Jokingly a classmate told William P. Miles, "I believe I'll study divinity, since preachers always get the prettiest and richest girls." William Garnett confided to Thomas Ruffin that he would study law rather than follow his father as a planter because of "the great aversion which I have to the manner of cultivating our lands in Virginia by slaves." Another student wrote to a friend that whether he wanted to or not he must become a planter because "the great fortunes are made in this country by farming and planting." A friend told Thomas Ruffin that he expected Ruffin would be surprised that he wanted "to become a person of business." James Henry Hammond and a classmate exchanged fears about their choices to become lawyers in wealthy South Carolina and contemplated moving to the Southwest for greater opportunities. Good friends Benjamin Harrison, Jr., and Alfred Shelby worried about matching their fathers' success. Young Harrison proclaimed: "Let us show our country that their sons will be the first to follow their examples."[37]

Although literary conventions in letters of that romantic age required that social relations be described in superlative and flowery terms, the many shared experiences of students indeed revealed bonds of togetherness. An acquaintance of Jabez Curry's described the close relationship of the students in a poignant account of a classmate's death from pneumonia. He regarded his friend as a beloved and promising boy and exclaimed, "I mourn for him as if he were my own." Jefferson Davis used ecstatic terms to describe how his college friendship with Henry Clay, Jr., assisted in "building his career." Roberts P. Johnson, who was in charge of giving demerits to younger students, wrote to William P. Miles that he was "unwilling that the feelings of those who had not acquitted themselves with credit, should be hurt by *me*." After William Garnett had left Princeton, he asked his old friend Thomas Ruffin to inquire about slights against his character so that Ruffin could defend his honor. He commiserated with Ruffin over the humiliation of being thrown out of a debate society. Robert Deveaux became close to his fellow Carolinian Robert Singleton, whose sister he married. Young Deveaux and a friend exchanged sorrows over leaving Charlottesville. His friend declared that he "had formed many and very strong attachments among my fellow students, ties of friendship, created by congeniality of sentiment, and cemented by habit and mutual obligations."[38]

To what extent, then, did college life reflect either the notion of the dominant, aristocratic, planter father or the more open and seemingly middle-class nineteenth-century father-son relationship? There are patterns in the college experience that indicate the presence of both strains. On the one hand, if some paternalistic fathers complained about their sons' independence and questioning of paternal powers, student experiences nevertheless reinforced many of the parental values. Elite class bonding and violent exercise of student authority over their peers prepared many to pattern themselves after their dominant fathers. On the other hand, if the fathers wanted within reason for their sons to build their own values, the fatherly influence was close enough to observe and to help out if necessary. Fathers who were less paternal perhaps took delight in the ways college life, especially in peer relations, made independent sons who learned to compete in both agribusiness and the growing professional world of the Old South.

One would expect these results from college life, for it could hardly be more than an extension of southern life in general. Perhaps more detailed knowledge of the class and professional background of college students' families which then compares student behavior among those different groups will refine the arguments over the shape and the influence of family life on sons. One should also consider that colleges differed in their professed mission, academic activities, and student composition. College life, better defined and classified, should reveal much about the complexity of an evolving economic and political system and the family experience that was both influenced by and influenced that change.

Notes

1. Drew Gilpin Faust, *A Sacred Circle: The Dilemma of the Intellectual in the Old South, 1840–1860* (Baltimore: Johns Hopkins University Press, 1977), pp. 8–9.

2. Bertram Wyatt-Brown, "The Ideal Typology and Antebellum Southern History," *Societas* 5 (Winter 1975): 5–28; Wyatt-Brown, *Southern Honor* (New York: Oxford University Press, 1982), pp. 97–98, 57.

3. Jane Turner Censer, *North Carolina Planters and Their Children, 1800–1860* (Baton Rouge: Louisiana State University Press, 1984), pp. 51, 43–58; see also Russell Lindley Blake, "Ties of Intimacy: Social Values and Personal Relationships of Antebellum Slaveholders" (Ph.D. dissertation, University of Michigan, 1978); Steven M. Stowe, "All the Relations of Life: A Study in Sexuality, Family, and Social Values in the Southern Planter Class" (Ph.D. dissertation, State University of New York at Stony Brook, 1979).

4. Drew Gilpin Faust, *James Henry Hammond and the Old South* (Baton Rouge: Louisiana State University Press, 1982), p. 20.

5. Rufus William Bailey, *Family Preacher* (New York: J. S. Taylor, 1837), pp. 7, 34, 82; John Leadley Dagg, *The Elements of Moral Science* (New York: Sheldon and Co., 1860), pp. 171, 257; James Osgood Andrew, *Family Government* (Philadelphia: Sorin and Ball, 1846), pp. 37, 82–87.

6. LeRoy J. Halsey, ed., *The Works of Philip Lindsley*, 3 vols. (Philadelphia: J. B. Lippincott and Co., 1866), 1:210; Thomas R. Dew, "An Address before the Students of William and Mary," *Southern Literary Messenger* 2 (November 1836): 765; James Henley Thornwell, *Letter to Governor Manning* (Charleston: News and Courier Book Presses, 1885), p. 35; Henry St. George Tucker, *Lectures on Natural Law* (Charlottesville, Va.: J. Alexander, 1844), p. 104; Henry Ruffner, "Early History of Washington College," in *Washington and Lee University Historical Papers,* no. 1 (Baltimore: John Murphy and Co., 1890), pp. 98–99.

7. J. Marion Sims, *The Story of My Life* (New York: D. Appleton and Co., 1884), p. 72; Thomas Cary Johnson, *The Life and Letters of Robert Lewis Dabney* (Edinburgh: Banner of Truth Trust, 1977), pp. 54–55; Sterling Ruffin to Thomas Ruffin, February 3, 1804, in James G. de Roulhac Hamilton, ed., *Papers of Thomas Ruffin,* 4 vols. (Raleigh: Edwards and Broughton, 1918–20), 1:50; John Dickson to John A. Dickson, August 10, 1843, John A. Dickson Papers, Southern Historical Collection, University of North Carolina (hereafter SHC).

8. Charles Pettigrew to John and Ebenezer Pettigrew, September 19, 1795, Pettigrew Papers, SHC; Stephen Deveaux to Robert M. Deveaux, August 9, 1831, Singleton Family Papers, Library of Congress (hereafter LC); Isaac Shelby to Alfred Shelby, April 27, 1819, Papers of the Shelby Family, LC.

9. Autobiography, pp. 28, 38–41, in Jabez L. M. Curry Papers, LC; Jesse Pearl Rice, *J. L. M. Curry* (New York: King's Crown Press, 1949), p. 17.

10. Jon L. Wakelyn, *Biographical Dictionary of the Confederacy* (Westport, Conn.: Greenwood Press, 1977), pp. 17–18; Ralph Wooster, *Secession Conventions of the South* (Princeton: Princeton University Press, 1962), p. 196; Chalmers G. Davidson, *The Last Foray* (Columbia: University of South Carolina Press, 1971), pp. 18–53; Colin B. Burke, *American Collegiate Populations*

(New York: New York University Press, 1982); Censer, *North Carolina Planters,* p. 43.

11. Leonidas Polk, "Biography of William Polk" (1859), E. Mitchell to Col. William Polk, August 15, 1821, Papers of the Polk Family of North Carolina, LC; *Extracts from the Report of President Finley* (Charleston: Miller and Brown, 1847), pp. 7–8; R. W. Gibbes to Lewis R. Gibbes, May 20, 1838, Papers of Lewis R. Gibbes, LC; A. W. Smith to William Elliott, May 5, 1835, Elliott-Gonzales Papers, SHC; Journal of the Proceedings of the Faculty of the College of Charleston, College of Charleston Library.

12. Dew, "Address," pp. 766–67; William R. Davie to John Haywood, September 22, 1805, in James G. de Roulhac Hamilton, ed., *Letters of William Richardson* (Chapel Hill: North Carolina Department of Archives and History, 1907), p. 61.

13. Thomas Hart Law, *Citadel Cadets* (Clinton, S.C.: P. C. Press, 1971), p. 194; John Dickson to John A. Dickson, April 4, 1844, Dickson Papers.

14. Sterling Ruffin to Thomas Ruffin, September 8, 1803, in Hamilton, ed., *Papers of Thomas Ruffin,* 1:46, 60; John Dickson to John A. Dickson, October 2, 1843, Dickson Papers; Stephen Deveaux to Robert M. Deveaux, August 9, 1831, Singleton Family Papers; William Elliott to Ralph Elliott, September 22, Elliott-Gonzales Papers.

15. University of Virginia Report to Stephen Deveaux, October 1, December 1, 1829, Robert M. Deveaux to Stephen Deveaux, June 2, 1830, Singleton Family Papers; John Pettigrew to Charles Pettigrew, October 3, 1795, April 12, 1796, in Sarah McCulloh Lemon, ed., *The Pettigrew Papers* (Raleigh: North Carolina Department of Archives and History, 1971), pp. 169, 183; Law, *Citadel Cadets,* pp. 29, 57, 132.

16. John Dickson to John A. Dickson, March 30, August 30, November 4, 1844, Dickson Papers; Charles Pettigrew to Dr. Andrew Knox, August 20, 1799, in Lemon, ed., *Pettigrew Papers,* pp. 238–39; Ralph E. Elliott to Mother, March 10, 1851, Elliott-Gonzales Papers.

17. William Elliott to Ralph Elliott, September 1851, Elliott-Gonzales Papers; Charles Pettigrew to John and Ebenezer Pettigrew, September 19, 1795, in Lemon, ed., *Pettigrew Papers,* p. 166; Robert M. Deveaux to Stephen Deveaux, June 27, 1831, Singleton Family Papers; John Dickson to John A. Dickson, April 4, 1844, Dickson Papers.

18. Robert M. Deveaux to Stephen Deveaux, October 13, 1830, Singleton Family Papers; see also Law, *Citadel Cadets,* p. 132; John Pettigrew to Charles Pettigrew, October 3, 1795, in Lemon, ed ., Pettigrew Papers, p. 169.

19. Richard A. Wise to Henry A. Wise, March 20, 1860, January 9, 1861, in *William and Mary Quarterly,* 2d ser., 18 (1938): 196–97.

20. Stephen Deveaux to Robert M. Deveaux, August 9, September 26, 1831, John W. Stephenson to Robert M. Deveaux, February 8, 1832, Singleton Family Papers; Sims, *Story of My Life,* p. 116; Carol Bleser, *The Hammonds of Redcliffe* (New York: Oxford University Press, 1981), pp. 16, 58.

21. Frederick A. P. Barnard, *Letters on College Government* (New York: D. Appleton and Co., 1855), pp. 71–100.

22. James Benson Sellers, *History of the University of Alabama* (University, Ala.: University of Alabama Press, 1963), pp. 252–56.

23. Margaret Newnan Wagers, *The Education of a Gentleman: Jefferson Davis at Transylvania* (Lexington, Ky.: Buckley and Reading, 1943), p. 15; Law, *Citadel Cadets*, p. 304; Margaret Gallaudet Waring, ed., "Reminiscences of Charles Seton Henry Hardee," *Georgia Historical Quarterly* 12 (June 1928): 175; Curry, Autobiography, p. 29, Curry Papers.

24. Robert M. Deveaux to Stephen Deveaux, September 12, 1829, October 4, December 31, 1830, Singleton Family Papers.

25. Johnson, *Life and Letters of Dabney*, p. 84; Basil Manley diary cited in Sellers, *History of the University of Alabama* , p. 236.

26. Thornwell, *Letter to Governor Manning*, p. 15; "Thornwell on Moral Philosophy," *Southern Presbyterian Review* 9 (July 1855): 125; John N. Waddell, *Memorials of Academic Life* (Richmond: Presbyterian Committee of Publications, 1891), pp. 162–63; Edgar Wallace Knight, ed., *Documentary History of Education in the South before 1860,* 5 vols. (Chapel Hill: University of North Carolina Press, 1949–53), 2:578; Barnard, *Letters on College Government,* pp. 37–50.

27. Thornwell, *Letter to Governor Manning*, pp. 45–46; Henry St. George Tucker, *Lectures on Government* (Charlottesville, Va., 1844), p. 208; John N. Waddell, "The Lecture System—Its Influence upon Young Men," *Southern Presbyterian Review* 12 (July 1859): 282.

28. Frederick A. P. Barnard, *Report on a Proposition to Modify the Plan of Instruction in the University of Alabama* (New York: Appleton, 1855), pp. 51–55.

29. John Fulton, *Memoirs of Frederick A. P. Barnard* (New York: Macmillan, 1896), p. 155.

30. Francis Lieber, *The Character of the Gentleman* (Cincinnati: J. A. James, 1846), p. 28.

31. Law, *Citadel Cadets*, p. 6.

32. Ibid., pp. 287, 159; Robert M. Deveaux to Stephen Deveaux, July 11, 1830, Singleton Family Papers; Johnson, *Life and Letters of Dabney*, pp. 54–55; Sellers, *University of Alabama*, pp. 233–36, 226.

33. Charles Coleman Wall, Jr., "Student Life at the University of Virginia, 1825 to 1861" (Ph.D. dissertation, University of Virginia, 1978); "Generations," *Daedalus* 107 (Fall 1978): 124–27.

34. Barnard, *Letters on College Government*, p. 22; R. S. Gladney, "Thornwell on Moral Philosophy," *Southern Presbyterian Review* 9 July 1855): 123–28.

35. William H. Trescott to William P. Miles, August 21, 1840, Miles Papers, SHC; Faust, *Hammond*, pp. 19–21.

36. Sims, *Story of My Life*, pp. 106–9; "Minute Book, Chrestomathic Society," pp. 5–94, College of Charleston Library.

37. Henry Laurens Pinckney, Jr., to William P. Miles, July 19, 1841, Miles Papers; William Garnett to Thomas Ruffin, July 12, 1805, George Hairston to Ruffin, February 2, 1806, in Hamilton, ed., *Papers of Thomas Ruffin*, 1:80–81, 97; Thomas H. Edward to James Henry Hammond, March 19, 1826, James Henry Hammond Papers, LC; William Henry Harrison, Jr., to Alfred Shelby, June 6, 1821, Papers of the Shelby Family, LC.

38. Jabez L. M. Curry to his brother, January 26, 1853, Curry Papers; Wagers, *Education of a Gentleman*, pp. 31, 34; Roberts P. Johnson to William P. Miles, July 30, 1840, Miles Papers; see also Samuel Jones to William P. Miles, September 1, 1840, Miles Papers; William Garnett to Thomas Ruffin, September 24, December 3, 1804, in Hamilton, ed., *Papers of Thomas Ruffin*, 1:56, 61; L. Randolph to Robert Deveaux, December 4, 1832, Singleton Family Papers.

Higher Education in the South since the Civil War: Historiographical Issues and Trends

Thomas G. Dyer

S cholars have zealously studied virtually every aspect of southern history. Thus when a topic seems underexploited or, in the parlance of contemporary politics, underdeveloped, it should come as something of a surprise to those who study the region. Such is true of the history of higher education in the South. Although much has been written about episodes and cases, the field has not been assiduously studied, that is, scholars have not focused their energies on attempting to understand this complex and important aspect of the region's past.

Until very recently, only a handful of professionally trained historians have dealt with educational topics, at least partially in reaction to the dominance of the field by professors of education. Historians have generally held schools of education and their scholarly activities in mild contempt and have questioned whether many studies of the educational past have not been tied to the need to justify contemporary educational practices. In addition, historians have long looked with suspicion at the unidimensional character of much educational history, wondering whether superficial research and absence of context do not render it suspect at the very least.

The much-vaunted calls by Bernard Bailyn and Lawrence Cremin to put educational history on a more solid footing are often noted by those who work in the field, but there is little evidence to suggest that either Bailyn, who called for more attention to context in the researching of educational history, or Cremin, who adjured scholars to move away from the adulatory recountings of the history of public education of such scholars as Elwood Patterson Cubberly, have had much effect.[1]

Within the past fifteen years, some worthy attempts have been made to list the historiography dealing with American education, but scholars have not sought to bring order to the articles, monographs, and books that constitute it. Jurgen Herbst's bibliography of American educational history published in 1973 is the most extensive listing dealing with the entire field, and Mark Beach's *A Bibliographic Guide to American Colleges and Universities: From Colonial Times to the Present,* though serviceable, is organized by states and thus excludes a significant amount of literature that does not fall within arbitrary geographic boundaries. Neither of these two works annotates entries, and thus the reader is left without guidance in making judgments not only concerning the quality of the source but very often its contents as well.[2] There has not been, to my knowledge, any attempt to bring bibliographic order to the subfield of the history of southern education generally or the history of southern higher education. In fact, very little has been written concerning the field of southern education as a whole. Wayne Urban's suggestive essay in the *History of Education Quarterly* points to several topics that require examination, but these are largely in areas outside higher education. In addition, a recent edited volume, *Education and the Rise of the New South,* contains several useful essays but gives little emphasis to higher education either in the articles or in the minimally useful historiographical essay that concludes the volume.[3] Therefore, in this chapter I seek to bring into focus some of the more important sources dealing with the history of southern colleges and universities in the post–Civil War period and to suggest potential areas for future scholarly inquiry.

Writing on southern higher education, like that on American higher education generally, has been afflicted with an overwhelming dominance by a particular genre—the institutional history. Often written by retired faculty members at the behest or at the direction of a college or university administration, the institutional history typically reveals the college allegedly under study to have moved from its founding by a group of demigods through trials and tribulations (invariably brought on by sources outside the college) to emerge in the very recent past (normally at a time curiously coincident with the beginning of the administration that commissioned the book) to its full glory as the alma mater of distinguished alumni who were serious but wholesomely rambunctious students.

Such books are usually organized by presidential administrations, the better to illuminate fully the glorious accomplishments of each president, and they overflow with anecdotes and biographical sketches of eccentric but endearing professors. Copious appendixes accompany such books and include a litany of presidents, enrollment figures, trustees, and annual appropriations. The titles of these tomes often capture wonderfully the spirit in which the book was written and the predilections of the author as well. Stars are a particularly attractive metaphor to those who title institutional histories. *Like Stars Shining Brightly: The Story of Abilene Christian College* is only one example of a title that reaches to the galaxies to underscore the brilliance of the institution studied. Other titles suggestive of the genre include *A Burning Torch and a Flaming Fire: The Story of Centenary College of Louisiana; Famous Are Thy Halls: Hardin-Simmons University as I Have Known It;* "Recollections of a Magic Decade at Clark"; *With Optimism for the Morrow: A History of the University of Oklahoma;* "Let a Hundred Antiochs Bloom"; and *God Bless Our Queer Old Dean.*[4]

The most common failing of the institutional history has been its inability to place the institution under study into social, political, cultural, and historiographical contexts. In fact, it is a rare institutional history that takes into account anything that happened outside the college. Similarly, there is a perhaps understandable aversion to discussions of controversy or anything that smacks of impropriety.

Only the very best of the institutional histories attempt to relate the importance of the college to its surrounding or sponsoring society. Even fewer address the major questions of interpretation that occupy historians of the South. The best institutional history produced in recent times deals with a midwestern university, the University of Kansas. Written by an able historian, C. S. Griffin, it provides a model that could be profitably emulated by southern historians. A forthcoming study of Vanderbilt University by Paul Conkin will likely set a new standard for the study of an individual university.

Within recent years institutional histories of several southern colleges and universities have appeared, including Washington and Lee, Virginia Polytechnic Institute and State University, Converse College, Southern Methodist University, Transylvania University, the University of Miami, Furman University, Fisk University, the University of Virginia, Rice University, Elon College, and the University of Tennessee. These twelve books join an already formidable number of histories of individual southern colleges published over the last one hundred years.[5] In addition to book-length studies, there are scores of articles that speak to the general history of a single institution and do not offer specific themes or conclusions.[6]

The institutional history will doubtless remain the dominant art form in the telling of southern higher education. The history of an individual college is relatively easily researched because most institutions maintain archives. For large universities the documentary sources are legion. The most informative and the most useful of the institutional histories, however, will continue to be those that move beyond the confines of college walls and take into account relationships with the larger society—an exercise that necessarily places institutional history within a broad historiographical context.

Despite the preoccupation of the field with the institutional format, many areas of importance in the history of southern higher education cannot be successfully understood by adopting this approach. Many of these areas have already undergone some scrutiny by historians; others have been largely overlooked. A few good biographies of figures prominent in and important to southern higher education do exist. Willard Gatewood's biography of Eugene Clyde Brooks and biographies of Charles D. McIver, John Carlisle Kilgo, and James H. Kirkland are among the better volumes. Biographies of George Foster Peabody, John Hope, and J. L. M. Curry are also available.[7]

The three decades after the Civil War should be one of the most fertile periods for the study of southern higher education. Although virtually every nuance of this era has been unearthed and subjected to interpretation and reinterpretation, practically no research has concentrated on the effects of Reconstruction, Redemption, and the New South on southern colleges and universities. The recovery of southern colleges after the war is not well understood, but it appears that for a few years at least, some of the state universities and denominational institutions flourished because they were patronized by a significant number of veterans. In addition, prewar plans for the modernization of the state universities, debated hotly in the final days before the outbreak of hostilities, resurfaced, and for a time some of the state colleges became more multifaceted, resembling the emergent state universities of the Middle West. The conventional wisdom might suggest that economic distress foiled these Reconstruction-era plans, but it appears, at least in Georgia, that a reassertion of conservative values after the redeemers reclaimed the state ended plans for modernization. Similar efforts appear to have been more successful at the University of North Carolina, where a concerted effort occurred in the decade after the war to redefine the institution and to determine what form an American state university should take.[8]

The dynamics of Reconstruction and Redemption as they affected the colleges are not well understood, and the impact of New South values has been misunderstood. It has generally been argued that education was only a minor portion of the New South creed. Studies of several southern colleges and universities during this period suggest, however, that the values of the New South were taken very seriously within the institutions as they scrambled to adopt technological, scientific, and agricultural emphases that would keep them in step with the emergent mania for industrialization. The establishment in rapid succession of several institutions with engineering emphases during this period supports the belief that primary leaders of the New South movement believed in the need for that specialty if the region were to improve economically. James Brittain and Robert McMath have demonstrated the impact of New South ideology on the founding and development of the Georgia Institute of Technology. Numerous institutional histories also suggest the pervasiveness of this phenomenon.[9]

A substantial body of historiography focuses on black higher education and the roles that blacks have played in that field. Indeed, some of the better institutional histories relate the development of individual black colleges. Joe M. Richardson's recent history of Fisk University provides a solid account of the development of the Nashville institution, and Clarence Bacote's history of Atlanta University, written nearly twenty years ago, remains an extremely valuable source as a survey of the growth of black higher education in Georgia. Like most of the institutional histories, however, those of black institutions vary greatly in quality.[10]

A relatively rich body of scholarly articles dealing with black higher education has appeared in recent years. Scholars have begun to look at the roles of the black colleges and their faculty and students in a number of different subject areas and chronological periods. Although there has been considerable discussion of the impact and influence of the northern missionary societies in the establishment and early growth of the black colleges in the late nineteenth century, the need remains for a fuller understanding of the complex, often stormy relationships between such groups as the American Missionary Association and the American Baptist Home Missionary Society and the emerging black colleges. In addition to studying these groups, scholars could profit by use of the extensive collections of the General Education Board in seeking to comprehend the dynamics of the influence of the Rockefeller Foundation and similar groups upon black colleges. Larger questions concerning the politics of philanthropy in relationship to the management of the colleges also need investigation.[11]

Recent scholarship has also dealt with the emergence of normal education for blacks and has focused on some aspects of student life, in particular the rising student assertiveness of the 1920s and the student strikes that occurred at several black colleges throughout the South during that time. Little is known, however, concerning other aspects of student life in the black colleges and how shifts in student behavior may have been related to what was transpiring in black society. Significant research has recently appeared concerning the early years of the development of black higher education in Tennessee which adds measurably to our understanding of how various black colleges competed and coexisted during the late nineteenth century. In addition, a recent article has examined the politics of distribution of land-grant funds in Tennessee in the wake of the Morrill Act of 1890 showing how white politicians, with the acquiescence of a compliant federal government, managed to evade the intent of the law to distribute land-grant funds equally with black agricultural and mechanical colleges.[12]

Comparatively little has been written on the development of black agricultural colleges in the rural areas of the South although recent articles and a dissertation shed light on the founder of Fort Valley State College and the development of Albany State College in Georgia. Research is also under way concerning the evolution of black medical education. An article by Darlene Clark Hine chronicles the influence of black nursing leaders upon the rise of collegiate nursing schools, and Todd Savitt's forthcoming study of black medical schools in the South will add a much needed dimension to our understanding both of the evolution of professional training in the black colleges and universities and of the influence of black culture on medical education.[13]

The desegregation of southern colleges and universities affords many opportunities for research. Studies have begun to appear which move beyond the often superficial, journalistic accounts of desegregation toward a fuller comprehension of this complex dynamic in southern history. Articles dealing with the desegregation of the University of Oklahoma, the University of Maryland, the University of Texas, and Paducah Junior College in Kentucky have appeared as has a particularly valuable study of the state of North Carolina's policies with respect to graduate education for blacks during the period 1930–51. Marcia Synnott's forthcoming study of the desegregation of five Deep South state universities promises to increase our understanding of the end to legalized segregation on campuses. My own account of the desegregation of the University of Georgia emphasizes the long and arduous bureaucratic path that black applicants had to follow before the judicial desegregation of the institution in

1961.[14] The twenty years since desegregation should provide a fertile field for study of the effectiveness of integration. The persistence of all-white and all-black institutions raises important questions for the historian as well as for the politician. Similarly, the extent to which black students have become a part of institutional life should be studied.

If a relatively large amount of attention has fallen on the role of blacks in southern higher education, the same cannot be said for the fate of women. The coming of coeducation to southern institutions has been only partially studied and then within narrow institutional confines. A variety of southern colleges and universities have been coeducating the sexes since before the Civil War. The progress of coeducation would be the basis for a useful study. Numerous other subjects relative to women and southern higher education could be studied, including a comparison of the social composition of the student bodies in women's liberal arts colleges and in the normal and industrial schools established in most southern states in the late nineteenth and early twentieth centuries.[15]

The dominant values of southern progressivism also found their way onto the campuses. Probably no more direct connection can be made with the progressive ethos than the project undertaken by Chancellor Walter B. Hill of the University of Georgia to transport more than one hundred Georgians by train to the University of Wisconsin for a firsthand view of that university's wide-ranging program of public services for the state. The resultant conversion of the University of Georgia from a backward classical college into a nascent, multifaceted state university may have been a major factor in the introduction of a limited number of progressive reforms into the state. Southern colleges experienced curricular readjustment, the introduction of modern bureaucratic methods, coeducation, the appearance of cooperative extension, the enhanced activities of agricultural experiment stations, the establishment of bureaus for social and business research, and a variety of other phenomena associated with progressive values. These changes have gone largely unstudied.[16]

The Progressive Era also witnessed the beginnings of urban higher education in the South. Characteristically, perhaps, the southern experience in urban higher education set the region apart from much of the rest of the nation. In Atlanta, for example, the presence of a liberal arts college for black women led directly to the establishment of the city's first college for white women. The accompanying fund-raising effort, managed and participated in by the city's leading boosters, had all of the earmarks of Progressive Era fund-raising drives elsewhere except in the blatant appeal that the school be the equal to that already built for black women. Urban boosterism is also evident in the experience of other Atlanta colleges during the period. Emory College moved to Atlanta in the late 1910s as a result of a million-dollar inducement proffered by Coca-Cola magnate Asa G. Candler, and it quickly developed close connections with the city's financial and business establishment. Oglethorpe College, dead since 1870, was resurrected by a consummate educational booster who unsuccessfully sought to emulate Emory. And finally, perhaps in uniquely southern fashion, an academic entrepreneur established a college in the Atlanta area to teach exclusively within the framework of southern values. Lanier University quickly became the official institution of higher learning for the children of Ku Klux Klan members and for a time included on its faculty as professor of Civil War and Reconstruction history William J. Simmons, who was probably better known for his connections with the hooded order than for his academic endeavors.[17]

Throughout the 1920s and 1930s urban junior colleges were established to train secretarial, clerical, and merchandising personnel who would serve the interests of the dominant commercial elites. Branch campuses of public institutions were built in urban areas during this period with primarily the same objectives. The perceptible beginnings of a shift from a rurally located and dominated system of higher education occurred during the 1910s, 1920s, and 1930s but matured with the establishment of numerous urban colleges in the post–World War II period—a phenomenon which, to my knowledge, has been almost totally ignored by historians of the urban South.

Issues of academic freedom have not been confined to the South, of course, but southern colleges and universities appear to have confronted fewer crises over the freedom to teach and inquire than did those in other parts of the nation perhaps because of the minimal respect given academic freedom in southern institutions. Still, there were moments of crisis when academic values collided with major social currents, revealing the special and difficult conditions under which the academic enterprise operated in southern states. Willard Gatewood has shown, for example, how fundamentalist forces collided with college officials in North Carolina over the teaching of the theory of evolution. Other scholars have recounted the recurrent difficulties at the University of Texas when political forces sought to shape the institution and to thwart dissent. Perhaps the most complex and far-reaching confrontation over academic freedom occurred in Georgia in the late 1930s, when Governor Eugene Talmadge began a systematic two-year purge of various colleges within the state system in an effort to rid them, in Talmadge's words, of "reds," "furriners," and "race mongrelizers." Although some scholars have probed the Cocking Affair, as the Georgia incident was called, a fuller study would tell us much more about how these institutions behaved under the severe stress induced by the intrusion of naked political power.[18]

The maintenance of the status quo in southern higher education often meant, of course, the suppression of student and faculty dissent and the careful guarding against invasion by radicals who might infect the minds of southern youth. Incidents at the Georgia State College for Women, Emory University, Mercer University, and the University of Georgia in the 1920s and 1930s showed how threats of radicalism in the colleges were perceived by collegiate and state officials. At the Georgia State College for Women, as William Ivy Hair has shown, college officials had to fight a pitched battle to persuade state officials that the institution had not unwittingly hired communists to teach the daughters of Georgians. At Emory University in the 1930s, a very minor outbreak of student radicalism led to the false imprisonment of a Jewish student thought by Georgia officials to be a communist. In the mid 1920s, students were dismissed from the University of Georgia and publications suppressed after attacks were made upon state officials. At Mercer College, radicalism took a different turn as members of the faculty were accused by student groups (led by the intrepid John Birch) of teaching evolutionary doctrines that contravened scripture. A full-scale heresy trial in 1939 led to the reprimand of several faculty members, who confessed their doctrinal errors, and to the dismissal of a seventy-five-year-old instructor, who did not recant sufficiently.[19]

Southern colleges and universities struggled during the agricultural depression of the 1920s but still participated in the social hijinks and mild student activism that characterized higher education elsewhere. The Great Depression appears to have had both strongly positive and negative effects. Appropriations to state institutions fell dramatically, but enrollments increased just as dramatically, largely offsetting the declines in state revenues. The added infusion of funds as a result of such New Deal programs as the Works Progress Administration, Public Works Administration, and National Youth Administration gave southern institutions a boost they had sorely needed. Federal money, increased enrollments, and modernizing reorganization processes in several states put some southern state universities in a position to participate in the spurt of economic growth that occurred throughout most of the South after World War II.

Such topics need further and regionwide study to clarify the dynamics of southern higher education during the 1920s and 1930s. Each topic, of course, should be considered within the context of the Great Depression and of the collision between southern academic and cultural values.

Numerous other areas could be profitably studied by historians. Both World War II and the appearance of thousands of veterans upon the campuses following the war seem to have had a profound impact upon southern state universities. A phenomenon that has not been investigated adequately on the national or regional level, the influx of veterans wrought profound changes in the concept of *in loco parentis,* induced substantial curricular alterations, and was responsible for the introduction of modern student personnel services in southern institutions.

The role of athletics in southern colleges and universities should be scrutinized, beginning with the appearance of organized collegiate athletics during the early 1880s, continuing through the debate over the appropriateness of intercollegiate athletics, and culminating in the use of intercollegiate athletics during the Progressive Era as a public relations tool. Such research should be conducted with a view to the power of athletics to overturn or at least disrupt traditional academic values. Questionable recruiting practices appeared as early as the 1890s in southern institutions and led very quickly to the establishment of a second college curriculum for recruited athletes. Many questions could be asked concerning the role of athletics, but some of the more germane would concentrate on the profitability of intercollegiate athletics to the larger universities, the role of athletics as a public relations or development tool, and the accommodations required in the colleges to the establishment of programs. Although the marvelous exploits and winning records of southern athletic powerhouses are famous, very little is known about the relationship of those successes to the larger culture and the process that led to what some would see as an inordinate influence of athletics in the region.[20]

Another fruitful subject is the role of religion in southern colleges and universities since the Civil War. Differences in curricula, student life, methods of finance, and the relationships of the denominational colleges with their sponsoring bodies are key topics for study. The responsiveness of the denominational institutions to changing societal and racial mores and to shifts in church doctrine should also be investigated.

All of these topics and more if properly and creatively researched can lead to a much fuller understanding of a woefully neglected area of southern history. Underestimated in its importance and at least partially misunderstood as a social and political phenomenon, southern higher education since the Civil War is an uncharted wasteland, compared with most areas of southern historiography. As scholars become increasingly aware of and interested in the dynamics of social and economic modernization, they may no longer be able to afford to ignore this important topic.

Notes

1. Bernard Bailyn, *Education in the Forming of American Society* (Chapel Hill: University of North Carolina Press, 1960); Lawrence A. Cremin, *The Wonderful World of Ellwood Patterson Cubberley* (New York: Bureau of Publications, Teachers College, Columbia University, 1965). See also the commentary in Laurence Veysey's brief essay on the historiography of American education, "The History of Education," in Stanley I. Kutler and Stanley N. Katz, eds., *The Promise of American History, Progress and Prospects;* special issue, *Reviews in American History* 10 (December 1982): 281–91.

2. Jurgen Herbst, *American Education* (Northbrook, Ill.: AHM, 1973); Mark Beach, *A Bibliographic Guide to American Colleges and Universities: From Colonial Times to the Present* (Westport, Conn.: Greenwood Press, 1974).

3. Wayne J. Urban, "History of Education: A Southern Exposure," *History of Education Quarterly* 21 (Summer 1981): 131–45; Ronald K. Goodenow and Arthur O. White, eds., *Education and the Rise of the New South* (Boston: G. K. Hall, 1981).

4. Don H. Morris and Max Leach, *Like Stars Shining Brightly: The Story of Abilene Christian College* (Abilene, Tex.: Abilene Christian College Press, 1953); William H. Nelson, *A Burning Torch and a Flaming Fire: The Story of Centenary College of Louisiana* (Nashville: Methodist Publishing House, 1931); Rupert N. Richardson, *Famous Are Thy Halls: Hardin-Simmons University as I Have Known It* (Abilene, Tex.: Abilene Printing Co., 1964); Carl A. Murchison, "Recollections of a Magic Decade at Clark," *Journal of General Psychology* 61 (1959): 3–12; Charles F. Long, *With Optimism for the Morrow: A History of the University of Oklahoma,* entire issue of the *Sooner Magazine* 38 (1965); Gerald Grant, "Let a Hundred Antiochs Bloom!" *Change* 4 (September 1972): 47–58; W. Storrs Lee, *God Bless Our Queer Old Dean* (New York: Putnam, 1959).

5. Ollinger Crenshaw, *General Lee's College: The Rise and Growth of Washington and Lee University* (New York: Random House, 1969); Duncan Lyle Kinnear, *The First 100 Years: A History of Virginia Polytechnic Institute and State University* (Blacksburg, Va.: Virginia Polytechnic Institute Education Foundation, 1972); Lillian Adele Kibler, *The History of Converse College, 1889–1971* (Spartanburg, S.C.: Converse College, 1973); Mary Martha Hosford Thomas, *Southern Methodist University: Founding and Early Years* (Dallas: Southern Methodist University Press, 1974); John D. Wright, Jr., *Transylvania: Tutor to the West* (Lexington, Ky.: Transylvania University, 1975); Charlton W. Tebeau, *The University of Miami: A Golden Anniversary History, 1926–1976* (Coral Gables, Fla.: University of Miami Press, 1976); Alfred Sand-

lin Reid, *Furman University: Toward a New Identity, 1925–1975* (Durham: Duke University Press, 1976); Joe M. Richardson, *A History of Fisk University, 1865–1946* (University, Ala.: University of Alabama Press, 1980); Fredericka Meiners, *A History of Rice University: The Institute Years, 1907–1963* (Houston: Rice University Studies, 1982); Durward T. Stokes, *Elon College: Its History and Traditions* (Elon, N.C.: Elon College Alumni Association, 1982); James Riley Montgomery, Stanley J. Folmsbee, and Lee Seifert Greene, *To Foster Knowledge: A History of the University of Tennessee, 1794–1970* (Knoxville: University of Tennessee Press, 1984). For a full listing of institutional histories, see Herbst, *American Education*, and Beach, *Bibliographic Guide to American Colleges and Universities*.

6. Recent additions to the principal articles include the following: Donald S. Armentrout, "The Beginnings of Theological Education at the University of the South: The Role of John Austin Merrick," *Historical Magazine of the Protestant Episcopal Church* 51 (September 1982): 253–67; James Harris Atkinson, "Memories of a University [of Arkansas] Student, 1906–1910," *Arkansas Historical Quarterly* 30 (Autumn 1971): 213–41; Hans W. Baade, "Law at Texas [University]: The [Oran M.] Roberts–[Robert S.] Gould Era (1883–1893)," *Southwestern Historical Quarterly* 86 (October 1982): 161–96; Fred A. Bailey, "Oliver Perry Temple and the Struggle for Tennessee's Agricultural College [1868–87]," *Tennessee Historical Quarterly* 36 (Spring 1977): 44–61; James L. Barnridge, "George Mason Graham [1807–e. 1885]: The Father of Louisiana State University," *Louisiana History* 10 (Summer 1969): 225–40; John K. Bettersworth, " 'The Cow in the Front Yard': How a Land-Grant University Grew in Mississippi," *Agricultural History* 53 (January 1979): 62–70; Alden G. Bigelow, "Student Life at Hampden-Sydney College, 1872–1876: As Reflected in the Letters of Hugh Carrington Grigsby," *Virginia Magazine of History and Biography* 87 (October 1979): 448–54; Anne W. Brown, "The Phoenix: A History of the St. John's College Library," *Maryland Historical Magazine* 65 (Winter 1970): 413–29; Arthur Ben Chitty, "Sewanee: Then and Now," *Tennessee Historical Quarterly* 38 (Winter 1979): 383–400; Eric H. Christianson, "The Conditions for Science in the Academic Department of Transylvania University, 1799–1857," *Register of the Kentucky Historical Society* 79 (Autumn 1981): 305–25; Dick B. Clough, "Teacher Institutes in Tennessee, 1870–1900," *Tennessee Historical Quarterly* 31 (Spring 1972): 61–73; William H. Cobb, "From Utopian Isolation to Radical Activism: Commonwealth College, 1925–1935," *Arkansas Historical Quarterly* 32 (Summer 1973): 132–47; James X. Corgan, "Some Firsts in the Colleges of Tennessee," *Journal of the Tennessee Academy of Science* 55 (July 1980): 86–91; E. Merton Coulter, "A Famous University of Georgia Commencement, 1871," *Georgia Historical Quarterly* 57 (Fall 1973): 347–60; E. Merton Coulter, "The New South: Benjamin H. Hill's Speech before the Alumni of the University of Georgia, 1871," *Georgia Historical Quarterly* 57 (Summer 1973): 179–99; John W. Cresswell, "Character Building at Kingfisher College, 1890–1922," *Chronicles of Oklahoma* 55 (Fall

1977): 266–81; John Crighton, "The Columbia Female Academy: A Pioneer in Education for Women," *Missouri Historical Review* 64 (January 1970): 177–96; Philip C. Davis, "The Modernization of Lindenwood College [St. Charles, Mo.], 1903–1929," *Bulletin of the Missouri Historical Society* 34 (October 1977): 32–44; Calvin Dickinson, "Collegiate Life in Nineteenth Century Texas: A Case Study," *Texana,* Winter 1969, pp. 313–21; Camillus J. Dismukes, "North Georgia College under the Trustees," *Georgia Historical Quarterly* 56 (Spring 1972): 92–100; Charles M. Dye, "Calvin Woodward and the Development of Polytechnic Education at Washington University [1865–96]," *Bulletin of the Missouri Historical Society* 34 (October 1977): 17–31; Harry J. Eisenman, "Origins of Engineering Education in Missouri," *Missouri Historical Review* 63 (July 1969): 451–60; Stanley J. Folmsbee, "Campus Life at the University of Tennessee, 1794–1879," *East Tennessee Historical Society Publications* 45 (1973): 25–50; Carolyn Thomas Foreman, "St. Agnes Academy [in Antlers, Oklahoma] for the Choctaws," *Chronicles of Oklahoma* 48 (Autumn 1970): 323–30; Isabelle Foster, "Washington College and Washington College Academy [Jonesboro, Tennessee]," *Tennessee Historical Quarterly* 30 (Fall 1971): 241–58; Willard B. Gatewood, Jr., "Woodrow Wilson and the University of Arkansas [1884–1885]," *Arkansas Historical Quarterly* 30 (Summer 1971): 83–94; Roger A. Griffin, "To Establish a University of the First Class [University of Texas]," *Southwestern Historical Quarterly* 86 (October 1982): 135–60; Ronald B. Head, "The Declension of George W. Blaettermann [1782–1850]: First Professor of Modern Languages at the University of Virginia," *Virginia Cavalcade* 31 (Spring 1982): 182–91; Jack W. Humphries, "Old Austin College in Huntsville: An Early Chapter in East Texas Educational History," *East Texas Historical Journal* 16 (Spring 1978): 24–33; William P. Jackameit, "The Evolution of Public Higher Education Governance in West Virginia: A Study of Political Influence upon Educational Policy," *West Virginia History* 36 (January 1975): 97–130; William P. Jackameit, "The Sims Higher Education Cases of West Virginia: A Study of Conflict between a State Elected Official and the Governing Boards of Public Higher Education, 1949–1957," *West Virginia History* 37 (October 1975): 1–10; Jesse B. Johnson and Lowell H. Harrison, "Ogden College [Bowling Green, Ky.]: A Brief History [1877–present]," *Register of the Kentucky Historical Society* 68 (July 1970): 189–220; Jack C. Lane, "Liberal Arts on the Florida Frontier: The Founding of Rollins College, 1885–1890," *Florida Historical Quarterly* 59 (October 1980): 144–64; Margaret H. Lokey and Beverly J. Wyatt, "Chickasaw Education and Murray State College," *Chronicles of Oklahoma* 59 (Fall 1981): 335–44; Kenneth M. Ludmerer, "Reform of Medical Education at Washington University," *Journal of the History of Medicine and Allied Sciences* 35 (April 1980): 149–73; Royster Lyle, Jr., and Matthew W. Paxton, Jr., "The VMI Barracks," *Virginia Cavalcade* 23 (Winter 1974): 14–29; G. Ray Mathis, ed., "Correspondence [July–August 1899] Concerning Chancellor [William E.] Boggs' [1838–1920] Decision to Leave the University of Georgia," *Georgia Historical Quarterly* 54 (Fall 1970): 419–27;

Ray Mathis, "Walter B. Hill [1851–1905], a New Chancellor for the University of Georgia," *Georgia Historical Quarterly* 57 (Spring 1973): 76–84; Ray Mathis, "Walter B. Hill [1851–1905] and the Savage Ideal," *Georgia Historical Quarterly* 60 (Fall 1976): 228–38; Robert W. Meriwether, "Galloway College: The Early Years, 1889–1907," *Arkansas Historical Quarterly* 40 (Winter 1981): 291–337; James M. Montgomery, "John R. Neal and the University of Tennessee: A Five-Part Tragedy," *Tennessee Historical Quarterly* 38 (Summer 1979): 214–34; James Tice Moore, "Battle for the Medical College: Physicians, Politicians, and the Courts, 1882–1883," *Virginia Cavalcade* 31 (Winter 1982): 158–67; Cynthia Neverdon-Mortin, "Self-Help Programs as Educative Activities of Black Women in the South, 1895–1925: Focus on Four Key Areas," *Journal of Negro Education* 51 (Summer 1982): 207–21; Neal O'Steen, "The University of Tennessee: Evolution of a Campus," *Tennessee Historical Quarterly* 39 (Fall 1980): 257–81; William A. Owens, "The Golden Age of Texas Scholarship: [Walter Prescott] Webb, [J. Frank] Dobie, [Roy] Bedichek, and [Mody C.] Boatright," *Southwest Review* 60 (Winter 1975): 1–14; Stafford Poole, "The Founding of Missouri's First College: Saint Mary's of the Barrens, 1815–1818," *Missouri Historical Review* 65 (October 1970): 1–22; David F. Prindle, "Oil and the [Texas] Permanent University Fund: The Early Years," *Southwestern Historical Quarterly* 86 (October 1982): 277–98; J. J. Propps, "Memories [1911–1915] of Hendrix College," *Arkansas Historical Quarterly* 28 (Spring 1969): 49–71; Tommy Wayne Rogers, "Oakland College [near Rodney, Miss.], 1830–1871," *Journal of Mississippi History* 36 (May 1974): 143–60; James E. Roper, "Southwestern [University] at Memphis, 1848–1981," *Tennessee Historical Quarterly* 41 (Fall 1982): 207–23; Gary G. Roth, "Wake Forest College and the Rise of Southeastern Baptist Seminary, 1945–1951," *Baptist History and Heritage*, April 1976, pp. 69–79; Thomas Rothrock, "The University of Arkansas's 'Old Main,'" *Arkansas Historical Quarterly* 30 (Spring 1971): 3–52; Catherine M. Rottier, "Ellen Spencer Mussey [1850–1936] and the [founding of] Washington College of Law [1898]," *Maryland Historical Magazine* 69 (Winter 1974): 361–82; Philip R. Rulon, "Angelo Cyrus Scott: Leader in Higher Education, Oklahoma Territory [President, OSU, 1899–1908]," *Chronicles of Oklahoma* 47 (Spring 1969): 494–514; Brent Tarter, "The Making of a University President: John Lloyd Newcomb and the University of Virginia, 1931–1933," *Virginia Magazine of History and Biography* 87 (October 1979): 473–81; Roger D. Tate, Jr., "Franklin L. Riley and the University of Mississippi (1898–1914)," *Journal of Mississippi History* 42 (May 1980): 99–111; James H. Thomas and Jeffry A. Hurt, "Southwestern Normal School: The Founding of an Institution," *Chronicles of Oklahoma* 54 (Winter 1976): 461–67; William P. Vaughn, "'South Carolina University—1876' of Fisk Parsons Brewer [1832–90]," *South Carolina Historical Magazine* 76 (October 1975): 225–31; James Walter Wilson, "Joseph Nash McDowell [1805–1868], M.D.: Part II. The 'McDowell Medical College'—A Fortress Unfinished;

Part III. Conflict and Confrontation." *Register of the Kentucky Historical Society* 68 (October 1970): 341–69.

7. Willard B. Gatewood, *Eugene Clyde Brooks: Educator and Public Servant* (Durham: Duke University Press, 1960); Rose Howell Holder, *McIver of North Carolina*, (Chapel Hill: University of North Carolina Press, 1957); Paul N. Garber, *John Carlisle Kilgo, President of Trinity College, 1894–1910* (Durham: Duke University Press, 1937); Edwin Mims, *Chancellor Kirkland of Vanderbilt* (Nashville: Vanderbilt University Press, 1940); Louise Ware, *George Foster Peabody: Banker, Philanthropist, Publicist* (Athens: University of Georgia Press, 1951); Ridgely Torrence, *The Story of John Hope* (New York: Macmillan, 1948); Edwin A. Alderman and C. Gordon Armistead, *J.L.M. Curry: A Biography* (New York: Macmillan, 1911).

8. Germaine A. Reed, "David Boyd [1834–80], LSU, and Louisiana Reconstruction," *Louisiana Studies* 14 (Fall 1975): 259–76; James Moore, "The University and the Readjusters," *Virginia Magazine of History and Biography* 78 (January 1970): 87–101; Arthur B. Chitty, *Reconstruction at Sewanee: The Founding of the University of the South and Its First Administration, 1857–1872* (Sewanee: The University Press, 1954); Robin Brabham, "Defining the American University: The University of North Carolina, 1865–1875," *North Carolina Historical Review* 57 (October 1980): 427–55; George A. Dillingham, "The University of Nashville, a Northern Educator [William Harold Payne], and a New Mission in the Post-Reconstruction South," *Tennessee Historical Quarterly* 37 (Fall 1978): 329–38; Hal Bridges, "D. H. Hill and Higher Education in the New South," *Arkansas Historical Quarterly* 15 (Summer 1956): 107–24.

9. James E. Brittain and Robert C. McMath, Jr., "Engineers and the New South Creed: The Formation and Early Development of Georgia Tech," *Technology and Culture* 18 (April 1977): 175–201.

10. Joe M. Richardson, *A History of Fisk University, 1865–1946* (University, Ala.: University of Alabama Press, 1980), and Clarence Bacote, *The Story of Atlanta University: A Century of Service, 1865–1965* (Atlanta: Atlanta University Press, 1969).

11. David Wallace Adams, "Education in Hues: Red and Black at Hampton Institute, 1878–1893," *SAQ* 76 (Spring 1977): 159–76; A. Gilbert Belles, "The College Faculty, the Negro Scholar and the Julius Rosenwald Fund," *Journal of Negro History* 54 (October 1969): 383–92; Ann DeRosa Byrne and Dana White, "Atlanta University's 'Northeast Lot': Community Building for Black Atlanta's 'Talented Tenth,' " *Atlanta Historical Journal* 26 (Summer–Fall 1982): 155–76; Clarice T. Campbell, "Exploring the Roots of Tougaloo [Miss.] College," *Journal of Mississippi History* 35 (February 1973): 15–27; Frederick Chambers, "Histories of Black Colleges and Universities," *Journal of Negro History* 57 (July 1972): 270–75; Babalola Cole, "Appropriation Politics and Black Schools: Howard University in the U.S. Congress, 1879–1928," *Journal*

of Negro Education 46 (Winter 1977): 7–23; Walter C. Daniel, "W.E.B. Du-
Bois at Lincoln University: Founders' Day Address, 1941," *Missouri Historical
Review* 74 (April 1980): 243–55; Henry S. Enck, "Tuskegee Institute and
Northern White Philanthropy: A Case Study in Fund Raising, 1900–1915,"
Journal of Negro History 65 (Fall 1980): 336–48; Beverly Guy-Sheftall, "Black
Women and Higher Education; Spelman and Bennett Colleges Revisited,"
Journal of Negro Education 51 (Summer 1982): 278–87; J. John Harris III,
Cleopatra Figgures, and David G. Carter, "A Historical Perspective of the
Emergence of Higher Education in Black Colleges," *Journal of Black Studies* 6
(September 1975): 55–68; Robert A. Holmes, "The University and Politics in
Atlanta: A Case Study of the Atlanta University Center," *Atlanta Historical
Journal* 25 (Spring 1981): 49–66; William P. Jackameit, "A Short History of
Negro Public Higher Education in West Virginia, 1890–1965," *West Virginia
History* 37 (July 1976): 309–24; Allen W. Jones, "The Role of Tuskegee In-
stitute in the Education of Black Farmers," *Journal of Negro History* 60 (April
1975): 252–67; Monroe H. Little, "The Extra-Curricular Activities of Black
College Students, 1868–1940," *Journal of Negro History* 65 (Spring 1980):
135–48; Frenise A. Logan, "The Movement in North Carolina to Establish a
State Supported College for Negroes," *North Carolina Historical Review* 35
(April 1958): 167–80; Rayford W. Logan, "The Evolution of Private Colleges
for Negroes," *Journal of Negro Education* 27 (1958): 213–20; Aldon Morris,
"Black Southern Student Sit-in Movement: An Analysis of Internal Organiza-
tion," *American Sociological Review* 46 (December 1981): 744–67; J. M. Ste-
phen Peeps, "Northern Philanthropy and the Emergence of Black Higher
Education—Do-Gooders, Compromisers, or Co-Conspirators," *Journal of
Negro Education* 50 (Summer 1981): 251–69; B. L. Perry, Jr., "Black Colleges
and Universities in Florida: Past, Present, and Future," *Journal of Black Studies*
6 (September 1975): 69–78; Martha S. Putney, "The Black Colleges in the
Maryland State College System: Quest for Equal Opportunity, 1908–1975,"
Maryland Historical Magazine 75 (December 1980): 335-43; Joe M. Richard-
son, "Fisk University, the First Critical Years," *Tennessee Historical Quarterly*
29 (Spring 1970): 24–41; Thomas Rothrock, "Joseph Carter Corbin [1833–
1911] and Negro Education in the University of Arkansas," *Arkansas Historical
Quarterly* 30 (Winter 1971): 277–314; Donald Spivey, "Crisis on a Black
Campus: Langston University and Its Struggle for Survival," *Chronicles of
Oklahoma* 59 (Winter 1981): 430–47; C. Robert Tifton, "The Fisk Jubilee
Singers," *Tennessee Historical Quarterly* 29 (Spring 1970): 42–48; Charles Vin-
cent, "Laying the Cornerstone at Southern University," *Louisiana History* 17
(Summer 1976): 335–42; Michael R. Winston, "Through the Back Door: Aca-
demic Racism and the Negro Scholar in Historical Perspective," *Daedalus* 100
(Summer 1971): 678–719.

12. Lester C. Lamon, "The Tennessee Agricultural and Industrial Normal
School: Public Higher Education for Black Tennesseans," *Tennessee Historical
Quarterly* 32 (Spring 1973): 42–58; Martha S. Putney, "The Formative Years of

Maryland's First Black Postsecondary School [Bowie Normal School]," *Maryland Historical Magazine* 73 (Summer 1978): 168–79; Elizabeth L. Wheeler, "Isacc Fisher: The Frustrations of a Negro Educator at Branch Normal College, 1902–1911," *Arkansas Historical Quarterly* 41 (Spring 1982): 3–50; Martha S. Putney, "The Baltimore Normal School for the Education of Black Teachers: Its Founders and Its Founding," *Maryland Historical Magazine* 72 (Summer 1977): 238–52; Lester C. Lamon, "The Black Community in Nashville and the Fisk University Student Strike of 1924–1925," *Journal of Southern History* 40 (May 1974): 225–44; Edward K. Graham, "The Hampton Institute Strike of 1927: A Case Study in Student Protest," *American Scholar* 38 (Autumn 1969): 668–83; Herbert Aptheker, "The Negro College Student in the 1920s—Years of Preparation and Protest: An Introduction," *Science and Society,* Spring 1969, pp. 150–67; Eugene TeSelle, "The Nashville Institute and Roger Williams University: Benevolence, Paternalism, and Black Consciousness, 1867–1910," *Tennessee Historical Quarterly* 41 (Winter 1982): 360–79; Cynthia Griggs Fleming, "A Survey of the Beginnings of Tennessee's Black Colleges and Universities, 1865–1920," *Tennessee Historical Quarterly* 39 (Summer 1980): 195–207; Samuel H. Shannon, "Land-Grant College Legislation and Black Tennesseeans: A Case Study in the Politics of Education," *History of Education Quarterly* 22 (Summer 1982): 139–57.

13. Donnie D. Bellamy, "Henry A. Hunt [1866–1938] and Black Agricultural Leadership in the New South," *Journal of Negro History* 60 (October 1975): 464–79; John R. Wennersten and Ruth Ellen Wennersten, "Separate and Unequal: The Evolution of a Black Land Grant College in Maryland, 1890–1930," *Maryland Historical Magazine* 72 (Spring 1977): 110–17; Darlene Clark Hine, "From Hospital to College: Black Nurse Leaders and the Rise of Collegiate Nursing Schools," *Journal of Negro Education* 51 (Summer 1982): 222–37.

14. John T. Hubbell, "The Desegregation of the University of Oklahoma, 1946–1950," *Journal of Negro History* 57 (1972): 370–84; Michelle Celarier, "A Study of Public Opinion on Desegregation in Oklahoma Higher Education," *Chronicles of Oklahoma* 47 (Autumn 1969): 268–81; John T. Hubbell, "Some Reactions to the Desegregation of the University of Oklahoma, 1946–50," *Phylon* 34 (June 1973): 187–96; Edward J. Kuebler, "The Desegregation of the University of Maryland [1896–1952]," *Maryland Historical Magazine* 71 (Spring 1976): 37–49; Glen Murrell, "The Desegregation of Paducah Junior College," *Register of the Kentucky Historical Society* 67 (1969): 63–79; Alton Hornsby, Jr., "The 'Colored Branch University' Issue in Texas—Prelude to *Sweatt* vs *Painter,*" *Journal of Negro History* 61 (January 1976): 51–60; Augustus M. Burns III, "Graduate Education for Blacks in North Carolina, 1930–1951," *Journal of Southern History* 46 (May 1980): 195–218; Charlotte H. Scott, "College Desegregation: Virginia's Sad Experience," *Virginia Quarterly Review* 58 (Spring 1982): 221–35; Michael L. Gillette, "Blacks Challenge the White University [of Texas]," *Southwestern Historical Quarterly* 86 (October

1982): 321–44; Donnie D. Bellamy, "Whites Sue for Desegregation in Georgia: The Fort Valley State College Case," *Journal of Negro History* 64 (Fall 1979): 316–41; Calvin Trillin, *An Education in Georgia: The Integration of Charlayne Hunter and Hamilton Holmes* (New York: Viking Press, 1964); Russell H. Barrett, *Integration at Ole Miss* (Chicago: Quadrangle Books, 1965); John H. Franklin, "Jim Crow Goes to College: The Genesis of Legal Segregation in Southern Schools," *South Atlantic Quarterly* 58 (1959): 225–35; Thomas G. Dyer, *The University of Georgia: A Bicentennial History* (Athens: University of Georgia Press, 1985).

15. Cynthia Horsburgh Requardt, "Alternative Professions for Goucher College Graduates, 1892–1910," *Maryland Historical Magazine* 74 (Fall 1979): 274–81; William E. Stephenson, "The Davises, the Southalls, and the Founding of Wesleyan Female College, 1854–1859," *North Carolina Historical Review* 57 (July 1980): 257–79; Anne H. Freeman, "Mary Munford's Fight for a College for Women Co-ordinate with the University of Virginia," *Virginia Magazine of History and Biography* 78 (October 1970): 481–91; Elizabeth Patton Hollow, "Development of the Brownsville Baptist Female College: An Example of Female Education in the South, 1850–1910," *West Tennessee Historical Society Papers* 32 (Spring 1978): 24–33; Kathryn Babb Vossler, "Women and Education in West Virginia, 1810–1909," *West Virginia History* 36 (July 1975): 271–90; Doak Sheridan Campbell, *A University in Transition: Florida State College for Women and Florida State University, 1941–1957* (Tallahassee: Florida State University, 1964); Brandt Van Blarcom Dixon, *A Brief History of H. Sophie Newcomb Memorial College, 1887–1919* (New Orleans: Hauser, 1928); William George Dodd, *Florida State College for Women: Notes on the Formative Years (1905–1930), with a "Postscript: The Twenties, The Thirties" and "Epilogue: The Forties 1940–1944"* (Tallahassee: N.p., 1958–59); John A. Logan, *Hollins, An Act of Faith for 125 Years* (New York: Newcomer Society in America, 1968); Virginia Terrell Lathrop, *Educate a Woman: Fifty Years of Life at the University of North Carolina* (Chapel Hill: University of North Carolina Press, 1942); Regina B. Fisher, "Coeducation at the University of Virginia, 1920–1940" (Master's thesis, University of Virginia, 1942); Margaret Helen Ingram, "Development of Higher Education for White Women in North Carolina Prior to 1875" (Ph.D. dissertation, University of North Carolina, 1961); William H. Cato, "The Development of Higher Education for Women in Virginia" (Ph.D. dissertation, University of Virginia, 1941); Alden L. Carlson, "A History of Mary Washington College" (Master's thesis, University of Virginia, 1948).

16. Larry D. Hill and Robert A. Calvert, "The University of Texas Extension Services and Progressivism," *Southwestern Historical Quarterly* 86 (October 1983): 231–54; Margaret Ripley Wolfe, "The Agricultural Experiment Station and Food and Drug Control: Another Look at Kentucky Progressivism, 1898–1916," *Filson Club Historical Quarterly* 49 (October 1975): 323–38; also see Dyer, *University of Georgia,* chap. 7.

17. Thomas G. Dyer, "The Klan on Campus: C. Lewis Fowler and Lanier University," *South Atlantic Quarterly* 77 (Autumn 1978): 453–69; Kenneth R. Johnson, "Urban Boosterism and Higher Education in the New South: A Case Study [Florence, Alabama]," *Alabama Historical Quarterly* 42 (Spring and Summer 1980): 40–58.

18. Willard B. Gatewood, *Preachers, Pedagogues and Politicians: The Evolution Controversy in North Carolina, 1920–1927* (Chapel Hill: University of North Carolina Press, 1966); Lewis L. Gould, "The University [of Texas] Becomes Politicized: The War with Jim Ferguson, 1915–1918," *Southwestern Historical Quarterly* 86 (October 1982): 255–76; Alice C. Cox, "The Rainey Affair: A History of the Academic Freedom Controversy at the University of Texas, 1938–1946" (Ph.D. dissertation, University of Denver, 1970); Ronnie Dugger, "The University of Texas: The Politics of Knowledge," *Change* 6 (February 1974): 30–39; B. Carlyle Ramsey, "The University System Controversy Reexamined: The [Eugene] Talmadge–[Joseph W.] Holley Connection," *Georgia Historical Quarterly* 64 (Summer 1980): 190–203; Sue Bailes, "Eugene Talmadge and the Board of Regents Controversy," *Georgia Historical Quarterly* 53 (December 1969): 409–23; James Cook, Jr., "Politics and Education in the Talmadge Era: The Controversy of the University System of Georgia, 1941–42" (Ph.D. dissertation, University of Georgia, 1972); James R. Montgomery and Gerald Gaither, "Evolution and Education in Tennessee: Decisions and Dilemmas," *Tennessee Historical Quarterly* 28 (Summer 1969): 141–55; William E. Ellis, "Frank LeRond McVey: His Defense of Academic Freedom [as President of University of Kentucky, 1917–40]," *Register of the Kentucky Historical Society* 67 (January 1969): 37–54; Earl W. Porter, "The [John Spencer] Bassett Affair [1903]: Something to Remember [academic freedom]," *South Atlantic Quarterly* 72 (Autumn 1973): 451–60; John Spencer Bassett, " 'Stirring Up the Fires of Race Antipathy': The Seventy-Fifth Anniversary of the 'Bassett Affair,' " *South Atlantic Quarterly* 77 (Autumn 1978): 389–98.

19. William I. Hair et al., *A History of Georgia College* (Milledgeville, Ga.: The College, 1979); William F. Mugleston, "The Press and Student Activism at the University of Georgia in the 1920s," *Georgia Historical Quarterly* 64 (Fall 1980): 241–52; also see Dyer, *University of Georgia,* chap. 10.

20. Dyer, *University of Georgia,* chaps. 7 and 8; Mary K. Dains, "University of Missouri Football: The First Decade," *Missouri Historical Review* 70 (October 1975): 20–54; James W. Pohl, "The [Dana] Bible Decade and the Origin of National Athletic Prominence [of Texas University]," *Southwestern Historical Quarterly* 86 (October 1982): 299–320.

Black Schooling during Reconstruction

Bertram Wyatt-Brown

Despite a recent outpouring of books and articles on southern educational history, especially with regard to race relations, most of these works have a narrowly institutional cast. There is nothing wrong with that. Yet the "new social history," although no longer really new, offers an opportunity that educational historians should seize. The purpose for applying cultural approaches would not be to conform to intellectual fashions of the moment. Rather, the prospect would be to grapple with some of the knotty problems in black educational history that institutional studies have not altogether explained.

Chief among these issues is the question of why black Americans so often have failed to reach their intellectual potential. By and large, scholars are agreed that the chief handicap has always been white racism and the consequently meager institutional, financial, and political support given to those involved in black education. Indeed, who would quarrel with so just an assessment? After all, racism not only withered freedmen's hopes 120 or more years ago but continues to poison life in the modern-day ghetto, the rural black community, and wherever poverty and government neglect help to stunt intellectual growth.[1]

The objective of this essay is to combine some traditional findings with ones borrowed from anthropology and sociology, so that we move from the tragically familiar but always significant problems of white class and racial bias to more subtle obstacles lying in the path of the black school-child during Reconstruction and, by implication at least, in our own lifetime. The subject, why blacks learned less than they might have, falls into three interconnected categories: (1) the most visible problems: white sectional and racial arrogance of which both native southerners and Yankee teachers were grievously guilty; material and financial deficiencies; internal bickerings among teachers and administrators; classroom bias affecting teachers' attitudes toward children and parents; (2) methodological and cultural confusions, including the limitations of the white teachers' methods of teaching the three R's; and (3) the unfortunate but all too understandable resistance of the black community to advanced individualistic learning as opposed to forms of group learning to which oral traditions and community life were amenable.

In regard to the first issue, so much historical investigation has appeared in print that only a brief review need be included here to show the interaction with the other two areas.[2] Former rebels were in no welcoming mood when a petticoat invasion began even before the guns fell silent. "It is heaping coals of anguish—to have sent among us a lot of ignorant, narrow-minded, bigoted fanatics," wrote a Norfolk editor in 1866, "just as if we were Feejee Islanders and worshippers of African fetish gods, snakes, toads, and terrapins." In the lower South, the *Tuscaloosa Observer* echoed the unpleasant refrain: "False calves, palpitating bosoms and plimpers are all the rage now in the land of wooden hams among the poor slab sided old maids who are coming South to teach the Negroes to lie and steal." Even that debunker of cherished southern myths, W. J. Cash, could not resist the stereotype of the "Yankee schoolma'am" who, "horsefaced, bespectacled, and spare of frame," seemed to him "at best a comic character, at worst a dangerous fool, playing with explosive forces which she did not understand."[3] Indeed, the female missionaries, like Rachel, stood amid the alien corn and cotton, with little hope of gaining a place on the proverbial southern pedestal reserved for native specimens of the gender.

Nevertheless, by 1870 the Yankee "schoolma'ams" and others had reached a total of 9,503, and more than 200,000 black scholars were enrolled. That figure represented about 12 percent of the 1.7 million black school-age children, a healthy though small beginning for a people barred for centuries from access to education by law and custom. White mission agencies such as the venerable antislavery American Missionary Association (AMA), largest in the field, sustained 1,388 teachers. Other agencies, including the Freedmen's Bureau educational branch, raised the total of Yankee-born instructors to nearly 5,000 during the peak of Radical Reconstruction.[4] Although most attention has focused on their work, one should bear in mind, as James D. Anderson, educational historian, stresses, that freedmen themselves organized and paid for teachers (about 1,000 in 1870) from their own community without outside support. Also, the black churches enrolled 107,109 pupils in 1869, a figure that increased to 200,000 by 1885.[5] These weekly schools undertook basic instruction in reading and writing for religious purposes, thus reinforcing the daily studies at regular schools. Some of the Yankee teachers were themselves black. Especially noteworthy were those trained at antislavery Oberlin College, which supplied a large number of teachers for the evangelical American Missionary Association.

All missionaries, regardless of color, encountered bitter reprisals. A typical example of southern intimidation was the case of the Reverend John Bardwell, who had sought to open a school in Grenada, Mississippi. He and a group of spirited freedmen moved a small cabin from a nearby military camp and placed it in the midst of the black quarter of town. A Colonel Adams, CSA, accused him of "stealing a house," and Bardwell prepared to defend himself before the bench. While conferring with his attorney, he was violently struck down by a drunken town alderman who had rushed into the lawyer's office. "I have received no martyrdom," Bardwell declared while nursing gashes about his head, "but if it comes I shall not shun it, if God grants me the grace sufficient unto the day."[6]

Courageous and dedicated though they were, the missionaries brought some of the antagonisms upon themselves. Many of them had very little appreciation of southern white values and social habits. Certainly the nineteenth century was not an epoch of cultural relativism. It is hardly a wonder, then, that Ariadne Warren at the AMA school in Meridian, Mississippi, urged Bardwell, her supervisor, to get a "good revolver" after the Grenada incident: "My private opinion is that the powers of darkness are let loose upon this God-forsaken, distracted, demoralized half-civilized country."[7] Such thoughts were hardly a matter of private opinion: they had been disseminated for well over thirty years, in antislavery publications, the halls of Congress, the churches, and public lecture rooms throughout the North.

As this credo was applied to the freedmen, it took a form expressed by Samuel F. Porter, a teacher in Vicksburg, Mississippi. In 1864, he argued in typical fashion that educational and religious instruction required that slaves, like heathens anywhere, had to be "taken by the hand." Porter was typical of most missionaries, who had not come from well-appointed homes; they knew near poverty themselves. They, like white southerners, were often an agrarian people with a basic earthiness and hard-eyed view of life, which Victorian formality and rigid self-discipline held somewhat from open expression. As a result, they considered their message of uplift an outgrowth of personal experience, not an imposition of social control to replace the chains of bondage. They had discovered self-mastery over "sin" by sheer dint of will. Others—slaves and possibly even southern rebels—should be able to do likewise.[8]

148

Several internal problems also dogged the operations of the missionary agencies and may have affected classroom instruction in ways hard to determine. A common situation was the attitude of male supervisors toward the female teachers who constituted two-thirds of the American Missionary Association's contingent. Single women—"giddy girls," scoffed the Reverend Selah Wright, an AMA functionary—were crowding into the field. The evangelical supervisors fretted about how to handle them. Lively and bright, Oberlin-trained women were especially troublesome. Though often Oberlin alumni themselves, the men were unaccustomed to independent thinking from females. Bardwell in Mississippi, for instance, complained that Adriadne ("Addie") Warren, at Meridian, "has never been satisfied that she was not made a *Man*. She wants to be very independent."[9] She got her wish for freedom when transferred from the safety of Meridian to the federally unoccupied Grenada station.

Another major issue was the relationship of white and black agents sent to the South. Admittedly, the problem was complicated. On the one hand, there was a recognition that the presence of well-dressed, accomplished, young black northern women would set fine examples before the children. On the other hand, success partly depended upon provoking native whites as little as possible. But there was also a genuine dislike of black coadjutors within missionary ranks. The Mississippi case of Blanche B. Harris, age twenty-three, her twelve-year-old sister Elizabeth, and Clara P. Freeman, twenty-two, represented in microcosm the volatility and inherent bigotries that scarred the early mission enterprise. On the way from Oberlin to Natchez, Mississippi, the three women had enraged white passengers by mingling freely in the general company aboard the steamboat. Selah Wright, a former missionary to the Minnesota Obijways, was in charge of the expedition. Wright informed AMA headquarters that "I think it folly to send" such teachers South. Their presence made the trip "unpleasant for all of us."[10]

But the initial difficulties were minor compared with the tendency of black teachers to ally with local blacks who wished to run schools to suit themselves, regardless of white interests. Having been forced to find lodgings in the black quarters of Natchez, the Harris sisters and Clara Freeman naturally had access to pupils who eluded the white instructors. So dangerous was the countryside that teachers tended to congregate wherever town life and military protection were available. As a result, there was a maldistribution of the schoolkeepers, who then had to compete among themselves for the children in the vicinity.

The black teachers had a clear advantage, and in places like Natchez the administrators sought to move the inconvenient supernumeraries elsewhere. "Colored teachers should not be sent to places where there are white teachers," the Reverend Palmer Litts, Natchez supervisor, complained to AMA officials in New York in 1866. He had observed that freedmen selected "as their instructors and leading minds those who . . . are surrounded by the same cloud of ignorance" as themselves. The local black preachers, he reported, were "bombastic and vociferous" and all too ready to conspire with the young black teachers to "prejudice the people against those who would teach them the more perfect way." The classes that the Harris girls and Clara Freeman ran were half again as large as those of the white teachers. Blanche Harris's drew more than one hundred. Yet Litts could not prove his charge of deliberate proselytizing from the white teachers' rolls. In fact, Bardwell conceded in a report to New York City that even little "Lizzie" Harris, the teenager, met the criteria for good teaching and all three maintained "good order in school." Perhaps, he mused, "there has been a little too much yielding to the spirit of caste" in the Natchez contingent.[11]

In addition to Yankee biases carried into the field, the risks of the enterprise set the missionaries on edge at times. Sporadic battles over personalities, wages, sectarian prejudices, missionary jurisdictions, and other matters erupted from time to time, and such distractions were bound to affect the quality of instruction. Also, school supplies were always limited, and disputes arose about favoritism and deliberate neglect. Moreover, teachers feuded over living quarters, which were usually cramped and uncomfortable. The climate bothered those unaccustomed to the heat, and many were unused to the swarms of bugs for which the South was renowned. Discomfort led to discord and hindered teacher cooperation even in the choicest posts. Worse yet, the lower pay women teachers received for the same work as the men aroused resentments and led to poor morale. Anna Snowden of Connecticut had to be fired from the Atlanta station in 1869 because of her "mercenary" attitude. She had protested low female wages and thereby violated a taboo in a cause that insisted upon self-sacrifice. The hothouse atmosphere of teachers' lives, separated as they were from white southern society, created its special strains. On the whole, the schoolchildren were not drawn into these troubles. Yet the disputes no doubt prevented teachers from doing their best work.[12]

Another factor, the subtle signs of discrimination that the children might have quickly perceived, is somewhat harder to document in the classroom itself. One suspects, however, that one reason why black parents so often preferred schoolteachers of their own color was a consequence of conscious as well as unconscious white condescension. Part of the problem was the institutional character of missionary work. It had always been official policy that evangelical agents, wherever their location, should hold themselves aloof from the subjects of their labors. The reason was not solely an arrogant sense of moral superiority but also a deep worry about "going native," that is, taking up drink and other bad habits. It happened every once in awhile, to the horror of pious observers. Dread of losing self-command impelled missionaries to insist upon every social observance that promoted respectability. Besides, obedience to proprieties was thought to encourage virtues of a higher order. The southern enterprise was no different from other missions in this respect. The Reverend A. D. Olds, for example, was a veteran from the pre–Civil War AMA station in Jamaica. "The similarity of the fields is most striking," he reported. Even though he found American blacks readier subjects for uplift than those left behind in the West Indies, neither he nor others thought that intermingling would be wise.[13]

Even though teachers and the black community were supposed to keep a respectful distance between them, the missionaries' leaders up North enjoined them to have no doubts about the educability of the black schoolchildren. Much has already been written about this matter. The record is clear: some missionaries were almost as bigoted as native southern whites, but most, after some seasoning in the classroom, grew cautiously optimistic just as their supervisors expected. Otherwise, their own morale would have atrophied. As one teacher said, "Our trials bring us into sympathy with them." On the whole, teachers concluded that both adults and children who were full-blooded blacks were as qualified to learn as those with some white mixture, a conclusion reached through experience as well as long-standing abolitionist dogma. Mission bodies soon dropped questions about the differences between mulattoes and full-bloods.

Nevertheless, white teachers labored under impressions closely allied with their ambivalent views of black religion. For instance, an almost unanimous verdict was that black pupils fared better in Sabbath schools than in daily classwork because the religious "part of their nature," Lydia Thompson, a white instructor, asserted, "has been the most cultivated."[14] These currents of attitudes outside the classroom doubtless were transmitted inside the school. Missionaries strove for professional ideals, motives that mitigated the effects of their cultural preconceptions. Yet try as they might, white teachers were scarcely immune from the prejudices of their generation.

Sometimes the teachers misinterpreted the signs of progress that they were making because their charges were eager to please, as children generally are, even when they may have missed the major point of the instruction. An example of black attentiveness to white feelings was given in a report of Anna Somers, a Mississippi AMA teacher. She observed that "when their slates or copy books were passed on to me for examination, my face was eagerly watched, to find therein approval or disapproval (they were quick to read the human countenance) and if a word of praise fell from my lips, a look of triumph would so light up their sable faces as to make even them look beautiful."[15] (The last phrase betrayed her. Like so many teachers, she gave the children similarly inadverdent evaluations, whether about racial appearance or mental attribute.)

Indeed, the vitality of black oral tradition did offer advantages in the early steps of learning. For instance, children were remarkably quick-witted about such assignments as memorizing the alphabet, numbers, simple spellings, and short passages of verse and scripture suitable for singing and recital. Recognizing and building upon the observed reaction of northern white children to perform similar tasks, American educators had successfully learned how to make these achievements relatively satisfying and even fun for the pupils. At certain ages, children are particularly eager to absorb facts that lend themselves to group participation. Naming objects, concrete and visible, could be done even in overcrowded classrooms so long as the routine was not mechanical and impersonal. From teachers' reports, it appeared that the first months of education passed relatively smoothly, though the young children were unaccustomed to the prolonged sitting and concentrating.[16]

The group character of early learning was evident when children repeated daily lessons at home. For instance, spelling "the simplest words," observed Anna Harwood, "is a new and apparently inexhaustible source of pleasure and interest to occupy their leisure hours. Parents and children about equally skilled in literature are lost in absorbed attention as they together spell our the wonderful story of A-n-n h-a-d a fast dog." Likewise, Martha L. Jarvis, a black Oberlinite at Meridian, Mississippi, boasted that one pupil had recited twelve biblical verses "without the least hesitation."[17] Phonetic spelling was the method used, so that the children could repeat in unison the proper sound for the syllables. One suspects that even at this level problems arose because of the characteristics of black speech in which the hard "t," "d," and "th" at the end of words was and still is dropped, a vestige of African linguistic habit. The subject has been carefully examined by William Labov, William A. Stewart, David Dalby, and others, but historians have not discussed the stigmatizing effects of these differences nor shown how they affected perceptions of blacks in the past.[18]

But despite these and other cultural problems, the northern school-keepers were optimistic that they could be quickly rooted out. From Port Royal, on the South Carolina Sea Islands, where Gullah dialect made communications more difficult than elsewhere, Mrs. Mansfield French reported to the public in 1863, "You would like to see the men and women 'fighting with the letters,' as they say, so that they may not be 'made ashamed' by their children, who are learning fast." At Craney Island, Virginia, "E.C." remarked, "Our instruction is necessarily mostly oral, as much time would be lost if we trained pupils singly. The little things give us almost undivided attention, and are much stimulated by recitations in concert."[19] Buoyed by these signs of initial mastery, blacks among themselves chided the laggards, a reinforcement for competitive performance that probably stimulated learning. One black girl was overheard to tell a beginner at reading, " 'If I could read as well as you can, I would not say *gwine* for going, *specially* when the white folks take so much pains with you.' "[20]

In imparting how to read, however, teachers soon discovered an unexpected problem, ironically arising from the blacks' ability at quick recall, by which these early triumphs were achieved. S. M. Pearson at New Bern, North Carolina, found that his students "knew by heart the lessons in the 'Picture Primer' which they had and would tell me how much of a book they knew, while in fact they knew not one word."[21] On the other hand, Henrietta Baldwin reported exuberantly from Arkansas that after only seventeen days of instruction her class, with just twenty minutes devoted to any topic, had completed the *National First Reader,* a popular item in pedagogy, and "could write legibly without copy; could numerate; and one of them could write any number less than a thousand."[22]

Whether pleased or confounded, teachers met quick disappointment with the next stage of intellectual development. One disillusioned teacher in Union-occupied New Bern, North Carolina, explained in 1864: "The principal obstacle I encounter is the want of the power of application" in nearly all students. "They will listen greedily to any instruction given them and would gladly spend the whole session writing on their slates, or copying from the blackboard but appear to have but a very slight idea of acquiring knowledge by studying" and working out problems themselves.[23]

Some of the problems were clearly mechanical. Primary among them was the size of the classes—as high as eighty-eight in some cases. Large enrollments had not mattered so much in group exercises on the lower levels. But for the more advanced work in cognition, arithmetic, and composition, the disadvantages and inevitable disciplining distractions of overcrowded classes would be obvious. In addition, the materials were poorly suited to the narrow agrarian world in which the pupils lived. Even at the primary level, the books were often much too advanced. The American Baptist Publication Society, for instance, put out a special *First Reader for Freedmen,* advising teachers to have pupils read "by the eye, without spelling." The abecedarians, the author noted, would name the words "in successive paragraphs." Spelling would come later. It was sound pedagogical practice, but the rural black children must have been mystified by pictures of Xerxes for the letter "X" and "newsboy" for "N". The first assignment alone had eighty-two separate words to be learned.[24] For the more advanced classes, the work was still more out of touch with the experiences available to the youngsters fresh from fields and cabins.[25]

American pedagogy at midcentury was totally unsuited to the rural and penurious character of black life. Assignments to be done at home presented no problems for children living in homes with ample privacy, good lighting, and parental guidance. With chores to perform as well, the farm youngster, though, was at serious disadvantage. Indeed, school attendance itself was necessarily much more irregular in the country and always had been in southern life. Teachers constantly complained that, though class size might remain constant, the membership varied decisively, making it hard even to know the enrollees' names.

In addition, abstract concepts required a special concentration for which the rural setting and black styles of thought were uncongenial. A further problem was that the pedagogy for handling abstractions had not been thoroughly mastered by the mid-nineteenth century. Precision, regularity, and grammatical accuracy as rule, not usage or simple logic, were the demands of the day, but the most efficient means for making them habitual had escaped the American instructors. In prior centuries, even the most sophisticated thinkers had spelled words, for instance, as they saw fit. Contemporaneous white southerners, including judges and generals, were often accustomed to follow the irregular orthographies of the past. How much less prepared were the newly freed slaves with Afro-American dialect to add further complications? Correct spelling and grammar were only the beginnings of pedagogical abstraction.[26]

The capability of applying one set of conditions or rules to make sense of another complex of factors is a cultural function. As a group of educational anthropologists recently concluded, there must be a congruence between the problems that customarily arise in a society and the cognitive skills necessary to meet them. In the world of the rural black schoolchild, very little of what was taught and of its presentation had much relationship to daily existence.[27] The drudgery of manual labor, the lively conversations in the black people's cabins, and the generally nonliterate nature of southern living for both races had almost nothing to do with what instructors talked about, once the concrete naming of things had passed. No wonder black pupils preferred group learning, not individual reflection; concrete experience, not cogitation; copying, not composition; parable, anecdote, and story, not categories, formulas, and abstract rules. Unwittingly then (as now), the child from an affective, noninstrumental environment found in the classroom "a symbolic system" appropriate, perhaps, for middle-class village and city life, but not one that bridged, as two modern linguists surmise, the instructional and linguistic distance "between the house and the school."[28]

Naturally, teachers noted the change in academic morale. Lydia Thompson at Vicksburg remarked, "I find many learn very rapidly for awhile, then seem to fall into a stupid, indifferent state." Particularly troublesome was the introduction of arithmetic. The subject was divided between "mental" and "written" forms. The latter was the older, eighteenth-century style whereby "pupils had to apply their skills to elaborate, supposedly commercial problems," says Daniel Calhoun. Victorian mental arithmetic, however, required reason-giving. Teachers, especially those with little training and innate ability, were often "completely nonplussed in any attempt to explain what they have done," said one critic in 1851, "or analyze the principles upon which it is performed." Mental arithmetic was the first that ought to be mastered, according to convention, though it was in some ways the harder because the rules had to be taken on faith. An earlier generation of masters had taught children to think by "reckoning in their heads," a style that conformed with aptitudes arising from rural life. By the 1860s, though, the topic had become very abstract. Some vainly urged a return to the older ways of "sensible arithmetic," that is, said one, "the addition, subtraction, multiplication, &c, of fingers, corn, beans, apples, blocks, and other sensible or tangible objects."[29] Southern black children were not taught now to cipher with such familiar objects as cotton bales and watermelons.

In fact, the entire discipline of arithmetic, written or mental, was fairly consistently avoided. The teachers' reports tell the story. The well-educated black instructors seemed to do best. Clara Freeman, one of the black teachers of Natchez, for instance, taught forty-four pupils in reading and spelling, fifteen in mental arithmetic, and none in written arithmetic. In one of her classrooms, Blanche Harris, the most accomplished teacher in Natchez, taught thirty-three students in mental arithmetic, seven in written arithmetic, and thirty-six in reading and spelling. Elsie

Spees, a white teacher in Natchez, however, taught no children in either branch of the elementary subject. Instead, she set forty students to reading and spelling. Mary Baker's reports revealed the same disproportions as Elsie Spees's. A check of other statistics from Mississippi shows the same pattern. One must suspect that it was a general phenomenon, though no scholar so far has quantified curricular problems. Charles Stearns, in Augusta, Georgia, generalized: "It seems well nigh an impossibility to teach arithmetic" even to scholars excellent in other respects because they were "deficient in memory." All matters regarding "size, weight, number, order, color, eventuality and individuality" were beyond their comprehension, in contrast to their highly proficient "*reflective*" and oratorical faculties.[30]

In public pronouncements, Freedmen's Bureau supervisors and others did not dwell on these alleged deficiencies. Funds were increasingly hard to obtain from Congress or the public as war enthusiasms diminished. Nonetheless, John W. Alvord, head of the bureau's educational division, admitted that the southern blacks did not "excel in the inventive power, or abstract science, perhaps not in mathematics, though we have seen very commendable ciphering" now and then. Instead, like Stearns, he praised them for having "emotional, imitative, and affectionate" natures with aptitude for "graphic and figurative language" and strong "conceptions of beauty and song." Teachers and administrators, then as now, were not given to self-criticism. It did not occur to them that the deficiency lay at least partly in white method, not in black attribute alone.[31]

Like adults, children everywhere perform those tasks best that mesh with their social and economic experiences. They imitate and aspire for proficiency in adult routines. Other activities, especially classwork that represents a different set of criteria and orientations, are seldom easy to grasp. When white teachers discovered the limitations of black advance in abstract conceptualization, particularly in mathematical subjects, most instructors assumed that the deficiency was racially determined. After all, blacks were supposed to be as docile, imitative, and unreflective as females. "It is sometimes said," declared abolitionist Theodore Tilton, editor of the evangelical *New York Independent,* "the the negro race is the feminine race of the world. This is not only because of his social and affectionate nature, but because he possesses that strange moral, instinctive insight that belongs more to women than to men." This misperception was common in antislavery circles. Science, though, was allegedly "masculine," bold, and thoroughly Anglo-Saxon. This interpretation was often combined with the presumed deleterious effects of slavery, which discouraged deductive reasoning. In addition, there was the natural tendency of simple folk and children to take the easy course, according to current sentiments about the hierarchies of civilizations. As a result, all agreed, blacks simply did not have the mental stamina and "application" to master tough subjects like mathematics.[32]

A recent experiment in Liberia, however, offers a more satisfactory explanation. It illuminates exactly what took place so many years ago in the freedmen's classrooms. An anthropological team asked a group of Peace Corps volunteers to estimate how many cups of uncooked rice would be necessary to fill a particular bowl. All answers were overestimations by at least 35 percent. Giving much speedier replies, members of the Kpelle tribe, in contrast, made guesses only 8 percent from the mark or better. But in the sorting of geometric patterns on a set of different colored cards, the Peace Corps volunteers quickly provided three separate and correct arrangements, as requested, whereas nearly all the Kpelle tribesmen were unable to complete the task without errors about color, shape, and spatial relations, the very specialties in which Stearns had found black deficiency in 1866. The experiment demonstrated that Africans or any other nonliterate group were not hopelessly ignorant children, but rather that abstract conceptualization must conform with cultural exigencies. Using insights from Jean Piaget and others, the anthropologists put aside Western methodologies and devised a form of instruction that built upon the mathematical experiences indigenous to life in central Liberia, a rice-growing region.

Needless to say, Yankees in the Reconstruction South were hardly equipped to undertake such a mission. The same philosophy of cultural imperialism that had sent these folk southward to punish rebels and elevate blacks to New England standards made it unthinkable to bend pedagogy to meet the needs of a basically peasant society with a strong heritage of nonliterate ways of thinking. As the anthropologists conclude about their Liberian investigation, "It is not the case that the noneducated African is incapable of concept-based thinking nor that he never combines sub-instances to obtain a general solution to a problem. Instead, we have to conclude that the situation in which he applies general, concept-based modes of solution are different and perhaps more restricted than the situations in which his educated age mate will apply such solutions." Educational psychology, however, is still in its infancy. Meantime, white cultural assumptions, no less today than yesterday, dominate the manner of instruction, often to the detriment of the black child's self-confidence and intellectual development.[33]

Carter G. Woodson, famed pioneer in Afro-American history, was one of the few American scholars, black or white, to assail the educational curriculum used in the black people's South. In 1933, Woodson argued that Anglo-American pedagogy had long been "an antiquated process which does not hit the mark even in the case of the needs of the white man himself." In addition, he criticized the examples used in black schoolrooms, which denigrated African and slave contributions to history and economic life and celebrated white heroes and tendencies. But above all, he took special aim at the training of blacks in the rudiments of mathematical sciences:

> Even in the certitude of science or mathematics it has been unfortunate that the approach to the Negro has been borrowed from a "foreign" method. For example, the teaching of arithmetic in the fifth grade in a backward county of Mississippi should mean one thing in the Negro school and a decidedly different thing in the white school. The Negro children, as a rule, come from the homes of tenants and peons who have to migrate annually from plantation to plantation, looking for light which they have never seen. The children from the homes of white planters and merchants live permanently in the midst of calculations, family budgets, and the like, which enable them sometimes to learn more by contact than the Negro can acquire in school. Instead of teaching such Negro children less arithmetic, they should be taught much more of it than white children.[34]

The teachers' neglect of mathematics, the single most unmet need of black education, resulted in mass innumeracy, as tragic as illiteracy, a deficiency that has received more attention.[35] It was not planned or calculated as a hidden means of holding back the race. Had blacks done well at arithmetic and poorly at reading, the instructors would have quickly touted the successes, flattering themselves and the students. Nor was it a natural reluctance on the educators' part to pursue difficult topics when demonstrable results could be quickly obtained from easy work with letters. These were indeed factors but, even so, it foundered because the North was not yet prepared for the industrial age, and educational methods had not made the transition successfully. Pedagogy was still shackled to the primary goal of developing moral character, especially for the black race, which was regarded as very backward in that respect. Frugality, precision, initiative, punctuality, honesty, and steadiness of purpose were culturally associated with reading and writing, much less so with the exact sciences in that still unspecialized and religiously minded age. These and other virtues, currently called "bourgeois," were deemed essential to black advance no less than to white accomplishment.[36] Reformist though the missionary teachers were, they could no more break out of their cultural habits and caste expectations than white southerners could from theirs. Moreover, how would it have been possible for Yankee schoolkeepers, most of them females trained in literary and hortatory modes and prevented by customs of gender from developing mathematical skills, to compensate in the classroom for the scientific deficiencies (by white standards) of black children in the rural South? It was a gloomy situation. Only a few instructors, such as Emma Stickney, Clara Anna Harwood, and "Addie" Warren, who promoted mental arithmetic, made much of an effort—at risk to their own reputation as "submissive" females. Others did less. How much more fruitful it seemed to the leaders at Hampton Institute, for instance, to introduce the Negro to "logic and the subjection of feeling to reason" and to "exercise his curiosity, his love of the marvelous, and his imagination as means of sustaining his enthusiasm."[37] Yet as preparation for opportunities, even the minimal ones available to sharecroppers and laborers, learning to keep accounts and do small calculations was just as important as reading and writing, if not more so.

From the black children's perspective, the hidden agenda was how to cope, a task involving much role-playing and craftiness. Exasperated with constant classroom interruptions, implausible alibis for lateness, mind-wandering, or disruption, one missionary in North Carolina complained that "you never know at what point you may expect to find them clear or stark blind," because there was "the most free-and-easy defiance of all rules of discipline or self-regulation." Another exclaimed that the children were "too easily amused," laughed "at trifles," and found almost any excuse for not paying mind to business at hand. These antics were not merely normal reactions of children anywhere.[38] Rather, the obstacles to attentive learning were themselves learning experiences in the children's oral, physical world, which white folks ruled. Knowing when and how to act out or hide feelings, how to provoke authority without going too far—these and other extracurricular doings were the subjects pupils learned at school, though not printed in the *National Reader* or *Sanders' Speller*. Far from understanding the causes of class mischief, teachers thought in terms of a possibly forgivable "manly" reaction to former bondage.[39]

The most unfortunate but least discussed factor in black education has been the natural desire of the blacks to retain a culture and personal autonomy distinctly separate from the white world. Such hopes of the poor have long bedeviled the intrusive evangels of the dominant culture, be they mountain whites, native Americans, or immigrants from abroad. For the blacks, to become well educated was to leave the familiar surroundings of home and community and to risk rebuff and bigotry, all the more galling because of the increased sensitivity that education brings. Even during Reconstruction, when possibilities for advance and recognition were at best slim, black children learned a hidden message: meet your community rules for survival and do not get bleached in the Yankee teacher's educational washroom. You will cut yourself off from your own circle but never be admitted to theirs. Evidence for this drain upon self-confidence cannot be easily found because blacks' conversations among themselves were seldom recorded.

The warnings were given through behavior more often than in words anyway. But occasionally adult blacks voiced the fear of being outdone by the young ones who would learn to despise their parents' country ways. Elizabeth Botume, the great black educator, observed that parents on the sea islands urged their youngsters to school, but the best scholars refused to go back to fieldwork. "This was a serious offense to the old people. 'Do they think I am to hoe with them folks that don't know anything!' exclaimed one of the older boys. 'I know too much for that. . . .' 'Them children discountenance we,' groaned the parents. 'They is too smart; they knows too much.'" Also, inequalities in knowledge among the pupils acted to discourage advance. When some town blacks competed at Elizabeth Botume's school, they boasted of mastering " 'algeeber,' " a subject she did not think her charges ready to tackle. The class was most unhappy to have been so humiliated. Botume complained that the parents were at fault because "home discipline and home instruction" were beyond the simple folks' capacity. She knew that they could not help it, but it was nonetheless their fault.[40]

Yet despite the difficulties, advances were made. Whether evangelicals, black and white, set standards of black educational performance too low or too high, they persisted with all their customary tenacity. Illiteracy in Georgia, for instance, was reduced from 95 to 97 percent in 1860 to 77.3 percent by 1880. Class attendance rates rose from 5 percent in 1870 to 40 percent a decade later in the same state. Similar improvements were made throughout the rest of the South as well. In the District of Columbia, by 1880 only about a quarter of all blacks between ages fifteen and twenty were illiterate. Percentages elsewhere were less dramatically reduced, but in Maryland, for instance, over half the population in the same age group could read and write. Even in South Carolina 26.4 percent had mastered the skills.[41]

Given the high barriers that isolated each participant in the northern teaching enterprise—male and female, Negro and Caucasian, southern and northern—a later age can only marvel that so much was achieved, not how little. The vexations were enormous. The neglect of mathematics was disastrous but probably inescapable. Certainly the complicated task of bringing a race out of slavery was beyond the capacity, knowledge, and intention of that generation of American whites. But the nineteenth-century code of personal heroics, will, and responsibility had ordained that the advocates of emancipation before the war should attempt to fulfill the obligation afterward. Courageous and timid, narrow and visionary, radical and hopelessly conventional, the Yankee missionaries of both races did the best they could. They helped to widen southern black horizons in a world beset with misapprehensions, violent inhumanity, arrogance, and fear. The children knew that domain and its fierce dangers better than their instructors and acted accordingly with valor and persistence that have yet to be appreciated. It may be that those who attended schools against the jeers and violence of white detractors gained more than books alone could give them. Some future historian, one may hope, will find similar marks of achievement in the struggles of teachers and students during the current era. But with more sophisticated means of judging than those available a hundred years ago, what will that historical verdict be?

Notes

1. See John W. Ogbu, *Minority Education and Caste: The American System in Cross-Cultural Perspective* (New York: Academic Press, 1978); Alvin Poussaint and Carolyn Atkinson, "Black Youth and Motivation," in Edgar G. Epps, ed., *Race Relations: Current Perspectives* (Cambridge, Mass.: Winthrop, 1973), pp. 167–77. No current scholars have treated the black child in the Reconstruction classroom, but Ronald E. Butchart, *Northern Schools, Southern Blacks, and Reconstruction: Freedmen's Education* (Westport, Conn.: Greenwood Press, 1980), p. xiii, promises to do so in a forthcoming study.

2. Robert Church and Michael W. Sedlak, *Education in the United States: An Interpretive History* (New York: Free Press, 1976), pp. 117–53; Butchart, *Northern Schools, Southern Blacks, and Reconstruction;* Robert L. Morris, *Reading, 'Riting, and Reconstruction: The Education of the Freedmen in the South, 1861–1870* (Chicago: University of Chicago Press, 1981).

3. Norfolk, Va., editorial, July 2, 1866, quoted in *American Missionary* 10 (August 1866): 174; *Tuscaloosa Observer,* quoted in John B. Myers, "The Education of the Alabama Freedmen during Presidential Reconstruction, 1865–1867," *Journal of Negro Education* 40 (Spring 1971): 169; Wilbur J. Cash, *The Mind of the South* (New York: Knopf, 1941), p. 140.

4. James M. McPherson, *Ordeal by Fire: The Civil War and Reconstruction* (New York: Knopf, 1982), p. 574; William Preston Vaughan, *Schools for All:*

The Blacks and Public Education in the South, 1865–1877 (Lexington: University Press of Kentucky, 1974), p. 13.

5. James D. Anderson, "Ex-Slaves and the Rise of Universal Education in the New South, 1860–1880," in Ronald K. Goodenow and Arthur O. White, eds., *Education and the Rise of the New South* (Boston: G. K. Hall, 1981), p. 9.

6. John P. Bardwell to George Whipple, April 28, May 4, 21, 26 (quotation), 1866, Mississippi, American Missionary Association MSS (microfilm), Dillard University, New Orleans (hereafter Miss., AMA MSS).

7. Ariadne Warren to Bardwell, May 6, 1866, Miss., AMA MSS. See also Bardwell, letter to editor, *American Missionary* 10 (June 1866): 138, and Anna Clara Harwood to Whipple, April 30, 1866, Miss., AMA MSS.

8. Samuel F. Porter to Whipple, April 5, 1864, Miss., AMA MSS; James M. McPherson, *The Abolitionist Legacy: From Reconstruction to the NAACP* (Princeton: Princeton University Press, 1975); and on missionary backgrounds, see Oberlin College Alumni Files, Oberlin College Archives.

9. Bardwell to Whipple, March 10, 1866, Wright to Whipple, March 19, 1866, "Addie" Warren to Whipple, March 26, May 6, 1866, Joseph Warren to Whipple, May 15, 1866, and Major Jonathan J. Knox to Samuel Hunt, May 25, 1866, Miss., AMA MSS; Sandra E. Small, "The Yankee Schoolmarm in Freedmen's School: An Analysis of Attitudes," *Journal of Southern History* 45 (August 1979): 381; Morris, *Reading, 'Riting, and Reconstruction*, pp. 54–84.

10. Wright to Whipple, April 7, 1866, Miss., AMA MSS. But see Rupert S. Holland, ed., *Letters of Laura M. Towne . . .* (Cambridge, Mass.: Riverside, 1912), p. 146; Small, "Yankee Schoolmarm," 391–92.

11. Palmer Litts to Whipple, 1865, March 7, April 27, 1866, Litts to Samuel Hunt, April 2, 1866, Wright to Whipple, November 11, 1865, April 27, 1866, Bardwell to Whipple, March 2, 1866, Blanche V. Harris to Michael E. Strieby, June 24, 1864, Harris to Whipple, January 23, March 10, 1866, Miss., AMA MSS; Teachers' Monthly Reports, October 1865–March 1866, ibid. For biographies of these individuals, see Oberlin College Alumni Files.

12. Jacqueline Jones, *Soldiers of Light and Love: Northern Teachers and Georgia Blacks* (Chapel Hill: University of North Carolina Press, 1980), pp. 173–83; Willie Lee Rose, *Rehearsal for Reconstruction: The Port Royal Experiment* (Indianapolis: Bobbs Merrill, 1964), pp. 229–35, 372–74; Small, "Yankee Schoolmarm," pp. 381–402.

13. A. D. Olds to Whipple, April 16 (quotation), June 1, July 22, 1863, A. B. Harwell to Whipple, January 19, July 6, 1864, Anna M. Keen to J. R. Shipherd, February 4, 1868, Miss., AMA MSS.

14. Litts to Whipple, July 11, 1865, Wright to Strieby, November 20, 1865 (quotation), Mary O. Baker to Whipple, September 6, 1864, Bardwell to Whipple, March 26, 1866, Anna M. Keen to Shipherd, February 4, 1868, ibid.; Wright, letter, December 10, 1865, in *American Missionary* 10 (January 1866): 37–38; Joel R. Williamson, "Black Self-Assertion before and after Emancipation," in Nathan I. Huggins, Martin Kilson, and Daniel M. Fox, eds., *Key Issues in the Afro-American Experience* (New York: Harcourt Brace Jovanovich,

1971), pp. 213–19; Lydia Thompson, May 1864 (quotation), Teachers' Monthly Report, Miss., AMA MSS.

15. Anna Somers to Hunt, June 1, 1866, Miss., AMA MSS; see also Daniel Calhoun, *The Intelligence of a People* (Princeton: Princeton University Press, 1973), p. 75; Jack Goody and Ian Watts, "The Consequences of Literacy," in Jack Goody, ed., *Literacy in Traditional Societies* (Cambridge: Cambridge University Press, 1968), pp. 56–68; David Riesman, *The Oral Tradition, the Written Word and the Screen Image* (Yellow Springs, Ohio: Antioch College Press, 1956); Daniel F. McCall, "Literacy and Social Structures," *History of Education Quarterly* 11 (Spring 1971): 85–92.

16. See Litts to Whipple, July 11, 1866; "The Condol School Exhibition," enclosure in Nathan T. Condol to Whipple, April 21, 1866, Bardwell to Whipple, June 30, 1866, Wright to Bardwell, November 11, 1865, Helen M. Jones to Wright, January 13, 1866, Miss., AMA MSS; Rose, *Rehearsal for Reconstruction*, p. 230.

17. Anna C. Harwood to Whipple, February 1, 1866, Martha L. Jarvis to Whipple, June 30, 1866, Miss., AMA MSS.

18. See William Labov, "The Logic of Nonstructured English," in Frederick Williams, ed., *Language and Poverty: Perspectives on a Theme* (Chicago: Markham, 1970), pp. 153–89, and William A. Stewart, "Toward a History of American Negro Dialect," ibid., pp. 351–79; David Dalby, "Black through White: Patterns of Communication in Africa and the New World," in Walt Wolfram and Mona E. Clark, eds., *Black-White Speech Relationships* (Washington, D.C.: Center for Applied Linguistics, 1971), pp. 99–137; Thomas Kochman, "Toward an Ethnography of Black American Speech Behavior," in Norman E. Whitten, Jr., and John F. Szwed, eds., *Afro-American Anthropology: Contemporary Perspectives* (New York: Free Press, 1970), pp. 149–55.

19. Letters, "E.H.F.," May 15, 1863, "E.C.," March 16, 1863, in *Third Series of Extracts from Letters Received by the Educational Commission for Freedmen, from Teachers and Superintendents at Port Royal and Its Vicinity* (Boston: John Wilson & Son, 1863), pp. 2–3 (hereafter *Extracts*, with date).

20. C. E. Croome to James Horace James, November 23, 1863, in *Extracts* (1864), p. 10.

21. Pearson to James, December 22, 1863, ibid., pp. 10, 11.

22. *Second Annual Report of the Western Freedmen's Aid Commission* (Cincinnati: A. P. Thompson, 1865), p. 38.

23. Letter, "A.C.G.C.," March 1864, in *Extracts* (1864), p. 12.

24. *The First Reader for Freedmen* (Philadelphia: American Baptist Publication Society, 1866), pp. 11, 12.

25. See, for instance, Charles W. Sanders, *Sanders' New Speller, Definer and Analyzer . . .* (Chicago: S. C. Griggs, 1861), a text with 429 exercises. Other books employed were Charles W. Sanders, *The School Reader; McGuffey's Reader; The National Reader; Webster's Reader;* and Arnold H. Guyot, *Physical Geography* (New York: Armstrong, 1866).

26. Calhoun, *Intelligence of a People*, pp. 87–88, 123.

27. Michael Cole et al., *The Cultural Context of Learning and Thinking: An Exploration in Experimental Anthropology* (New York: Basic Books, 1971), pp. 230–33.

28. See Eleanor R. Leacock, "Abstract versus Concrete Speech: A False Dichotomy," in Courtney B. Cazden et al., eds., *Functions of Language in the Classroom* (New York: Teachers College Press, 1972), pp. 111–34; Basil B. Bernstein, "A Critique of the Concept of Compensatory Education," in ibid., pp. 135–51; and Basil B. Bernstein and Dorothy Henderson, "Social Class Differences in the Relevance of Language to Socialization," *Sociology* 3 (January 1969): 17 (quotation). See also Calhoun, *Intelligence of a People*, pp. 116–17, and for overview of recent investigations, Michael Cole and Barbara Means, *Comparative Studies of How People Think: An Introduction* (Cambridge, Mass.: Harvard University Press, 1981), esp. pp. 49–51.

29. These quotations and arguments are all from Calhoun, *Intelligence of a People*, pp. 103–6.

30. Charles Stearns, *The Black Man of the South and the Rebels* . . . (New York: American News Co., 1872), p. 394. See Teachers' Monthly Reports for 1865–66, Miss., AMA MSS; Elsie Spees's report, February 20, 1863 (1864?), and Mary Baker, May 1, 1864, ibid. The subject of geography was also greatly neglected.

31. John W. Alvord, *First Semi-Annual Report on Schools and Finances of Freedmen, January 1, 1866* (Washington, D.C.: U.S. Government Printing Office, 1868), p. 11.

32. Tilton, quoted in George M. Fredrickson, *The Black Image in the White Mind: The Debate on Afro-American Character and Destiny, 1817–1914* (New York: Harper & Row, 1971), p. 115; Stearns, *Black Man*, pp. 190–91; Calhoun, *Intelligence of a People*, pp. 23, 124, 199–200, 201, 334.

33. Michael Cole and John Gay, *The New Mathematics and an Old Culture: A Study of Learning among the Kpelle of Liberia* (New York: Holt, Rinehart, and Winston, 1967), p. 1; Cole et al., *Cultural Context of Learning*, p. 225 (quotation); see also Gordon W. Allport and Thomas F. Pettigrew, "The Trapezoidal Illusion among Zulus," in Ihsan Al-Isa and Wayne Dennis, eds., *Cross-Cultural Studies of Behavior* (New York: Holt, Rinehart, and Winston, 1970), pp. 30–48.

34. Carter G. Woodson, *The Mis-Education of the American Negro* (Washington, D.C.: Associated Publishers, 1933), pp. xii, 4. Of course, there were always notable black geniuses in all fields, including mathematics.

35. But see Patricia Cline Cohen, *A Calculating People: The Spread of Numeracy in Early America* (Chicago: University of Chicago Press, 1983).

36. See Barbara L. Finkelstein, "Pedagogy as Intrusion: Teaching Values in Popular Primary Schools in Nineteenth-Century America," *History of Childhood Quarterly* 1 (Winter 1974): 349–78; "The Moral Dimensions of Pedagogy: Teaching Behavior in Popular Primary Schools in Nineteenth-Century America," *American Studies* 15 (Fall 1974): 79–89.

37. *Hampton Institute: Catalogue of the Hampton Normal and Agricultural Institute for the Academical Year 1870–71* (Boston: T. R. Marvin, 1871), p. 22, Anna Clara Harwood, September 1865, Teachers' Report, Natchez: 24 mental arithmetic, 0 written arithmetic; 78 reading and writing; Ariadne Warren, 5 mental arithmetic, 0 written arithmetic; Emma Stickney, 5 written arithmetic, 38 mental arithmetic, December 1865. Totals for Natchez were 170 reading and spelling; 10 mental arithmetic; 15 written arithmetic; 44 geography. See Miss., AMA MSS.

38. "W.F.A." (probably William F. Allen), April 1, 1864, in *Extracts* (1864), p. 15. See Rose, *Rehearsal for Reconstruction,* pp. 115, 265–67, 313–14; Stickney to Whipple, March 14, 1866, Litts to Whipple, July 11, 25, 1865, Harwood to Whipple, September 1, 1866, Warren to Whipple, January 29, 1866, Martha L. Jarvis to Whipple, January 31, 1866, John Eaton to Whipple, September 11, 1863, Miss., AMA MSS; Eugene D. Genovese, *Roll, Jordan, Roll: The World the Slaves Made* (New York: Pantheon, 1974), p. 167; Elizabeth Botume, *First Days amongst the Contraband* (Boston: Lee & Shephard, 1893), p. 104.

39. Bardwell to Strieby, December 24, 1864, Miss., AMA MSS; letters, "M.G.K.," June (?), 1864, and "W.F.A.," April 1, 1864, in *Extracts* (1864), p. 15.

40. Botume, *First Days,* pp. 274–76.

41. Jones, *Soldiers of Light and Love,* p. 229. Unfortunately, the 1870 census did not give percentage figures for illiteracy. See *Ninth Census of the United States* (1870), pp. 452–57, but see *Tenth Census* (1880), *Compendium,* pt. 2, pp. 1650–53.

Women and the Progressive Impulse in Southern Education

Joseph F. Kett

During the last fifteen years the work of Anne F. Scott, J. Morgan Kousser, Dewey W. Grantham, and other scholars has established that Progressivism had a southern wing. Not only were some southerners interested in regulating the railroads and trusts, but there were also vigorous southern advocates of such humanitarian causes as settlement houses, the abolition of child labor, better schools, and public health. This configuration of humanitarian causes can best be termed "social Progressivism." Although suffused with the same moral earnestness that marked Progressivism in general, social Progressivism was distinctive in its focus on issues that usually pertained to the welfare of children, the family, and the neighborhood—issues long identified with the sphere of women. Unlike the Populists of the 1890s, social Progressives did not see themselves as personally oppressed, nor did they consider an intensification of class conflict a necessary step toward social justice. Rather, they sought to ameliorate social conditions without fundamentally altering the distribution of political and economic power among classes. In contrast to other forms of Progressivism and to the Populist revolt of the 1890s, social Progressivism provided middle- and upper-class women with a spacious theater for their reformist activities. Just as women played a vital role in the humanitarian, social-welfare wing of northern Progressivism, they often provided the impetus behind the social wing of southern Progressivism. Alongside Jane Addams, Florence Kelley, and Sophonisba Breckenridge are such southern women as Madeline McDowell Breckenridge (Sophonisba's sister-in-law), Julia Tutwiler, Louise B. Poppenheim, Celeste Parrish, and Mary Cooke Branch Munford.[1]

These correspondences between northern and southern Progressivism are not surprising, for any number of institutions served to link reform-minded southern women with their northern counterparts. The Chautauqua movement of the late nineteenth century was one source of contacts between women of different sections. Named for the lake in southwestern New York where the movement started, Chautauqua became the center of a drive for popular adult education during the 1870s and 1880s and by 1900 had spawned more than sixty independent offshoots. During the 1890s many upper-class southern women made annual hegiras to these Chautauquas, where they not only savored lectures on history or literature but stayed long enough in the North to study that section's superior public schools.[2]

Philanthropic foundations also linked northern and southern women. During the 1890s Robert Curtis Ogden of New York City used his private railroad car to bring wealthy ladies and gentlemen from the North to the South to promote improved education for blacks. The outgrowth of this effort was the first Conference on Education in the South, held at Capon Springs, West Virginia, in 1898. The executive committee of this conference became the Southern Education Board in 1901; in 1903 it was absorbed by the General Education Board. The latter was primed, in turn, by a bequest of more than a million dollars from John D. Rockefeller. Both boards downplayed the importance of educational betterment for blacks but sought to rally southerners to improve their schools. They struck responsive chords, as shown, for example, by the establishment in 1904 of the Cooperative Education Association of Virginia to advance the work of the boards in promoting school improvement.[3]

In addition to the Chautauquas and philanthropic foundations, other agencies linked northern and southern Progressives. Some southern Progressives were educated at northern colleges and universities. Madeline McDowell Breckenridge went to Vassar; Celeste Parrish attended Cornell and the universities of Chicago and Michigan. Northern Progressives often lectured in the South, for example, Madeline McDowell Breckenridge used her connections to bring Jane Addams, Owen Lovejoy, Ben Lindsay, and other stalwarts of northern social Progressivism to speak in Lexington, Kentucky. Through these various agencies, southern Progressives became familiar with the reform agenda of social Progressivism: better schools and playgrounds, the abolition of child labor, establishment of juvenile courts, improved care for dependent and defective children, prison reform, and public health.[4]

In addition to their similar agendas, Progressives in each section embraced essentially the same ideology. They sought not merely to eradicate specific evils but to create a society marked by consensus and cooperation. Progressives routinely spoke of the lack of civic consciousness in the electorate, which they traced to ignorance or to excessive attachment to class, party, or sect. Numerous Progressive agencies aimed to promote identification with the larger community: settlement houses, Progressive schools, playgrounds, even the Boy Scouts and Campfire Girls. At a glance, these institutions appear to have encouraged nothing more than allegiance to themselves, but Progressives did not see it that way. They believed, rather, that feelings of "loyalty" or community developed toward play groups, school groups, or neighborhood groups could be extended to the entire community by proper direction. Progressive social psychologists such as Charles Horton Cooley argued that the self was social, that personality was not fixed at birth but developed through interaction with others, and that the social dimensions of selfhood could be progressively enlarged by educating the public in the interrelationship of social problems—by getting working mothers, for example, to recognize that their absence from the home contributed to the delinquency of their children.[5] In this respect, social Progressivism was fundamentally an educational movement, although I do not mean to suggest that Progressives had no other goals than the improvement of public schools or that they were indifferent to legislation. Rather, social Progressives usually preferred solutions to social problems that maximized popular participation. When they approached the subject of public health, for example, they emphasized health education. In New York City, S. Josephine Baker introduced "baby health stations," which dispensed both milk and advice. When Progressives thought about the theater, they tended to favor "community drama," which often took the form of staging huge masques and pageants in public stadiums and enlisting thousands of people as actors. Similarly, they envisioned the public school not only as a place where children learned to interact with other children and to explore miniaturized versions of their adult roles, but also as "community centers" or evening settlement houses, where parents would meet to discuss neighborhood problems and to hear teachers and other school officials celebrate the value of education.[6]

This educational motif reflected several realities. First, social Progressives not unreasonably thought that the apathy and ignorance of a largely immigrant population were obstacles to social reform and had to be eroded by the techniques of mass education. Second, the maximization of popular participation through educational campaigns provided social Progressives with a role to play in the solution of problems. Even in the northern cities where they were strongest, social Progressives were often marginal people—ministers, former ministers, and women—without political constituencies. Education and philanthropy were among the few roles traditionally open to such people, but social Progressives were reluctant to accept either of these roles in its traditional form. Progressive social workers were in flight from both the image of the schoolmarm and that of the lady bountiful. Part of their genius lay in forging new institutions through which they could play a significant social role and, in a sense, new intellectual occupations such as psychiatric social worker, civic league secretary, or recreation association president.

All of these new occupations demanded clients, who could be led—educated—to desire and accept the social services offered. Individuals had to be taught to recognize their need for services. They had to be made to feel dependent. Social Progressives were uncomfortable with the term "individualism." Rather, their favorite words were "community," "socialization," "cooperation," and "interdependence." A society marked by interdependence was one in which most people felt dependent. Social Progressives tended to define social solutions in ways that both maximized popular participation and emphasized dependency. For example, they contributed to a major redefinition of juvenile delinquency during the early 1900s. Whereas delinquents had traditionally been viewed as wild, vicious, and usually male, Progressives insisted that they were maladjusted, vulnerable, physically and emotionally weak, often mentally retarded, and even diseased. They also emphasized that girls as well as boys were inclined to delinquency, a linkage that appeared to reinforce their case, for girls had long been thought of as more vulnerable than boys.[7]

These ideas and methods were not unique to northern Progressives. Southern Progressives shared many of the same beliefs. The speeches of president Edward Kidder Graham, who as head of the University of North Carolina pushed that institution toward extension work and allied it with Progressivism, were filled with calls for "cooperative socialism," by which Graham meant neither Marxian nor utopian socialism but the Progressivism just described.[8] The Southern Sociological Congress, organized at Nashville in 1912, not only embraced many of the causes of northern social Progressivism but also its techniques. When it called for improved public health, for example, it emphasized "health parades," the dissemination of "health messages," traveling exhibits, the enlistment of local citizens in community surveys, and other techniques of mass mobilization.[9] The idea of attaching playgrounds to public schools became one of Madeline McDowell Breckenridge's first causes in Lexington.[10] Playgrounds were not merely places where children could let off steam but agencies for teaching cooperation through play. Southern Progressives were also ardent supporters of improved public education; this was their first and perhaps greatest cause. Like northern Progressives, they wanted to abolish or at least restrict child labor so that children could go to school, to increase expenditures for schools, and to force children to attend them.

At the root of these similarities between northern and southern Progressivism lay not merely shared intellectual experiences but leaderships recruited from the same social strata. The centers of southern Progressivism were the towns and cities of the South. Southern Progressives had close ties to business, manufacturing, and the professions, embraced major components of the New South creed, and stood at a much greater psychic than temporal distance from the Populist revolt of the 1890s.

Were there, then, any significant differences between the two branches? The same scholars who have helped us to understand the contours of southern Progressivism have identified at least two. First, southern women had to confront a tradition that pronounced them to be ladies, unfit for the rigors of public life. Before they could enter politics, they had to leave the pedestal.[11] Second, southern women who expected to achieve any success as reformers had to tread cautiously around racial issues. Keeping quiet about race in the South in 1900 or 1910 meant not challenging the disfranchisement of most blacks (along with many whites) that had occurred during the late nineteenth century. With few exceptions, southern Progressives allowed themselves little more than a cautious accommodationism on racial issues.[12]

These were important differences, but only up to a point. Anyone familiar with the agonies Jane Addams experienced in trying to identify a suitable career for herself and with the hate mail she received from ward heelers in Chicago will recognize that earnest northern women no less than dainty southern ladies faced obstacles at the end of the nineteenth century when they sought to forge public roles for themselves. The problem, in other words, existed in the North as well as in the South. Further, although northern Progressives were neither willing nor able to disfranchise blacks, they generally did not make combating racial discrimination one of their priorities. Indeed, like southern Progressives they were willing to restrict the size of the electorate by immigration restriction rather than outright disfranchisement.

In sum, neither the pedestal nor race established a profound disjunction between northern and southern Progressivism. There was, however, one notable difference. Southern Progressives had to swim in a different ocean, to confront a radically different society than the one northern Progressives lived in. Starting with notions virtually identical to those of northern

Progressives and viewing themselves, at least initially, as merely engaged in a less developed form of the social work that was emerging in northern cities, southern social Progressives were repeatedly forced to adapt to the peculiar exigencies of their society. Poverty, of course, was part of the difference, but probably not the key one. The South was poorer than the North, but northern Progressives actually believed that the North was poorer or at least that most really poor people were in the North. Mesmerized by the industrial city, they could not believe that conditions elsewhere could be worse.[13] Both northern and southern Progressives viewed their clients as extremely needy. The real difference was that the southern population was much more rural and dispersed. In 1900 only 16 percent of the South's population lived in places of twenty-five hundred or more people, compared to 40 percent for the remainder of the country, and only three cities in the South (New Orleans, Louisville, and Memphis) had one hundred thousand or more inhabitants.[14]

The dispersed nature of the southern population created several problems for Progressives. It was obviously difficult to deliver services to a rural population, but, more fundamentally, it seemed almost impossible to get potential clients to recognize the value of services. Although northern social Progressives believed that modern cities were fragmented places, lacking an adequate conception of community, they were confident that they could build on the "natural" sentiments in favor of a stronger communal bond that were already present. Northern social Progressives viewed cities as favorable testing grounds for their ideas. Urban dwellers were already dependent on public services; they needed the trolley to get to work, for example. In addition, social Progressives such as Jane Addams believed that immigrants came from tightly knit villages in the Old World and thought that their tightly knit neighborhoods in the New World were a sign of their natural receptivity to community life. The prominent Progressive sociologist Edward A. Ross described southern Europeans as "less individualistic" than northern Europeans and as "more gregarious and dependent."[15] In contrast, southern Progressives faced the apparently dauntless individualism of the southern farmer.

The work of J. Mills Thornton and Harry Watson has effectively traced the antebellum roots of this individualism. More recently David Carlton has demonstrated its tenacity among poor whites who left southern farms for mills during the Progressive Era. Individualism is a term which Americans have traditionally applied to the entire nation, but it is becoming clear that southern individualism was a breed apart. Throughout the North and in the towns and cities of the South the individualist was a go-getter who outstripped his friends in business skill and outgained them in wealth. But in the rural South individualism has long described a different configuration of attitudes in which poverty among whites was an acceptable if not desirable condition as long as it was not attended by dependency. What made the South different, of course, was that every white southerner knew that under him was a caste of black people who, even if they might not feel dependent, could be forced to act in a dependent manner. The individualism of the white southerner, in other words, was defined by negative reference; it was the opposite of the groveling dependency which the caste system imposed upon blacks.[16]

Although historians have recently sharpened our understanding of individualism in the South, Progressives were no strangers to it. Those who did not experience it firsthand could read about it in the spate of books on southern mountain people which appeared during the early 1900s, most notably John C. Campbell's *The Southern Highlander and His Homeland*. As Campbell wrote, the dominant trait of the southern highlander was "independence raised to the fourth power."[17] Northern Progressives could impute a love of community to immigrants, but southern Progressives could make no such assumptions. They confronted a population that was not only rural and dispersed but could and did explode in fury at the condescension implicit in the uplift campaigns of social Progressives. As Carlton shows, in South Carolina the mill workers who backed Cole Blease wanted no part of the efforts of Progressives to restrict child labor, not merely because they expected their children to contribute to the support of the family but because they correctly identified the hidden agenda behind child labor restriction—to sever the tie between mill children and their supposedly shiftless parents.[18]

Southern social Progressives thus confronted a situation that differed in important ways from that facing most northern Progressives. The South was not just conservative or backward but often consciously antithetical to the changes social Progressivism sought to impose. Northern Progressives were not unfamiliar with opposition, so we should view this difference as one of degree rather than of kind, but, sufficiently augmented, differences in degree can become differences in kind, and, as the case of southern education suggests, such a situation occurred in the South.

Unlike their northern counterparts, social Progressives in the South did not inherit from the nineteenth century a centralized system of compulsory education. The distinctive feature of southern education in 1900 was its localism. The basic unit of administration in the South was neither the state nor the county but the local district. As late as 1906, for example, Kentucky had more than eight thousand school districts, each generally responsible for its own standards or lack of them.[19] The goal of southern Progressives was not so much to create schools, of which there were already an abundance, but to reduce local influence and strengthen state and especially county supervision. The apple of their desire was the consolidated school firmly under county control. Such a school, drawing students from a relatively wide area, would be large enough to allow grading and the introduction of textbooks and to attract good teachers. It would not only bear the marks of strong leadership and purposeful education, but it would build a firmer feeling of community identification. Children from the villages and hollows would meet children from the towns, play with them on athletic teams, and build lasting friendships. There would be no losers, but the country children would be the clear winners, for they would gain the viewpoint of the town people.[20]

The consolidated school thus became an agent of socialization, a term which Progressives used not only in its narrow sense of getting children to play and to cooperate with other children but also in the broader sense of inducing rural people to identify with modernizing forces emanating from towns and cities. Rural southerners could reasonably contend, of course, that they already had a community, that they cooperated to maintain rural schools just as they cooperated to maintain the Baptist church. But these were not the forms of community that Progressives could identify with. Progressives preferred to talk of the "larger" community, by which they meant feelings of solidarity not merely among rural people but between rural people and townspeople, the true modernizing and progressive agents in the South. Most southern Progressives came from towns and cities rather than farms, and they viewed merchants, manufacturers, and professionals as modernizing forces. Consolidated schools, as a corollary, were not merely agencies of basic education but engines for the extension of Progressive values to the rural population.

None of these changes would occur, however, unless enthusiasm for consolidated schools could be engendered in the South. In contrast to northern Progressives, who never defined their task as fundamentally one of reaching a dispersed and rural population, southern Progressives had to engage in extension activity or be doomed to insignificance. Although the task was immense, it provided reform-minded women with an extensive sphere of activity. Northern Progressives usually treated their southern counterparts as poor relations, and southern Progressives such as Mary Cooke Branch Munford saw themselves as engaged in "less advanced and less highly developed forms" of social and educational work than were northern women.[21] Yet because advocacy of education in the South was less specialized, less tied to the narrow disciplines being spawned by schools of pedagogy in the North, it was accessible to women. The professionalization of education and social work came much more slowly to the South than to the North, and, as a result, southern educational reform gave extensive scope to the activities of women who, though inheriting strong traditions of evangelical advocacy (kept burning by the contemporary temperance crusades), lacked either specialized pedagogical training or easy access to state educational administrative agencies.

During the early 1900s the school improvement leagues that proliferated in southern states became key agencies for mobilizing popular opinion on behalf of educational reform along Progressive lines. School improvement leagues sought to beautify schools by painting them and planting grass in their yards, but their long-term goals were much more ambitious. Once beautified, the rural schools would become, Progressives hoped, a central institution for the entire rural community, a magnet that would pull rural people out of their individualistic isolation and make them recognize their ties to others. It was not enough for individuals to assist schools; the entire community had to identify with them.[22] And, as Edgar Gardner Murphy wrote, "The agents of the community are the women of the South."[23] Progressives believed that the school improvement leagues were creating a collective conscience among southern women by making possible (to a greater extent than the urban-based women's clubs) "the intermingling of women from all sections of the State."[24]

Denied a significant role in the actual administration of schools on the state or municipal level, indeed forced to accept an even smaller role than their northern counterparts, southern women proved themselves inventive at finding ways to induce interest in education among a rural population. Their efforts in the field of "propaganda" (a term that lacked pejorative connotations before the world war) drew on a specific method, which, though it appealed ultimately to Progressives everywhere, began in the South. The beautified schoolhouse was, in a sense, a demonstration of the advantages of progress that was designed to appeal as much to the imagination as to the reason. As such it resembled and indeed borrowed from the demonstration method of agricultural improvement devised by Seaman A. Knapp and embodied in Knapp's Farmers' Cooperative Demonstration Work (FCDW). Launched in Texas in 1903, FCDW spread quickly throughout the lower South, then to the upper South, and finally to the North. It was the first movement for mass education in American history to originate in the South and to prove more effective there than in the North. By inducing poor southern farmers to allow him to try improved methods of agriculture on their land and at his expense, Knapp was able to surmount one of the long-standing obstacles to the extension of scientific agriculture into the South: the indifference of poor southern farmers to advice in newspapers, circulars, books, or other species of print culture. Unlike other agencies of agricultural extension, it did not depend either on literacy or on an anterior interest on the part of farmers in agricultural improvement. All it did was to show a farmer on his own land that one method might be better than another.[25]

Although Knapp's demonstration projects did not directly engage women, they became the basis for so-called "home demonstration work" even before home economics became a federally subsidized division of the Agricultural Extension Service created by the Smith-Lever Act in 1914. This act provided women with abundant opportunities to be paid for organizing canning clubs, sewing clubs, and what was to become 4-H work for boys and girls. The women who became involved in the cause of home economics were the foot soldiers of social Progressivism in the rural South. Although the term "home economics" today conjures up images of young would-be ladies being taught to place the fork on the left and the spoon on the right, this was hardly its aim in 1914. Nor is its aim encompassed entirely by saying that home demonstration work sought to render farmers' wives more efficient homemakers, for it also aimed to organize farm women and youth to overcome their presumed indifference to cooperation. In other words, its goal was not only to make the entire farm family think more scientifically and efficiently about production within the home but to link farm people together, to make them develop a sense of belonging to a community. As a speaker before the Southern Sociological Congress meeting in Houston in 1915 proclaimed, the real purpose of corn and tomato clubs was not instruction in growing better corn or tomatoes; that was "little more than a byproduct." Rather, the value of these clubs was that they "have furnished wholesome, happy cooperation,—in other words recreation. The clubs have broken down the isolation that is the curse of rural America."[26] Similarly, a contemporary described the values of home demonstration agents as to " 'organize and cooperate.' Isolated existence is doomed and it is time that we take our places among members of social groups."[27]

Even during the 1920s educational reform and social work in the South remained less professionalized than their northern counterparts and continued to provide scope for the energies of reform-minded women. Inasmuch as most historians have viewed the professionalization of education and social work as a challenge to the broad impulse of Progressivism, it may well be true that Progressivism in its pure form hung

175

on longer in the South than in the North. Certainly the task of assuaging rural individualism continued to animate the efforts of southern Progressives during the 1920s.[28] Indeed, it is possible to see among southern Progressives during the 1920s signs of growing optimism that the battle might be won, that the individualistic whites in the rural areas, once viewed as resolutely set against reform, were coming around. A glimpse of the change may be found in a cause embraced by many social Progressives in the South—community drama.

Community drama often took the form of masques and pageants that engaged local citizens as actors. These and other varieties of community drama constituted a mythic form of the demonstration method. The extension divisions of state universities, which were not only important arms of southern Progressivism but also far more accessible to women than the regular faculties of universities, were especially active in advancing community drama. As the case of a play called *Signal Fires* suggests, Progressives viewed drama as more than an art form. Written during the early 1920s and promoted by the extension division of the University of Virginia, *Signal Fires* was described as a "Masque of Service with a pageant of the lives of Florence Nightingale and Sadie Heath Cabaniss."[29] Its specific goal was to arouse popular support for establishment of a chair of nursing at the University of Virginia at a time when public health nurses were becoming actively engaged in the administration throughout the South of the Sheppard-Towner Maternity and Infancy Care Act of 1921, the first incursion of the federal government into the field of social welfare. Unfortunately, the goal of dramatizing so humdrum a cause as the establishment of a professorship and standardized examinations proved too much for its author, Louise Burleigh. But the awkward, stilted prose and situations of *Signal Fires* should not conceal its Progressive goal. As Burleigh wrote in her book *The Community Theatre in Theory and Practice* (1917): "The Community Theatre is a house of play in which events offer to every member of the body politic active participation in a common interest." It was an agent of "the movement of social reorganization led by the social scientist."[30]

Burleigh was a northerner, a graduate of Radcliffe, and an ardent follower of the dramatist Percy MacKaye; far from springing spontaneously from Virginia's soil, *Signal Fires* was a commissioned play. Community drama got its start in northern cities, particularly in settlement houses, during the first decade and a half of the twentieth century; many of the most lavish masques and pageants, such as MacKaye's "Caliban of the Yellow Sands," were staged in crowded metropolises with casts of thousands. Yet the future of community drama lay less in northern cities, where it was unable to compete effectively with commerical theater, than in the South, where commercial theater was rare. It was not merely that the South offered less competition for community drama; for in the Progressive imagination the "folk" of the South, the southern poor, seemed to offer more suitable material for drama than any subjects in northern cities. It is not surprising that the most enduring legacy of the movement for community drama came from the South, specifically from the Carolina Players and Bureau of Community Drama established at the University of North Carolina by Frederick Koch in 1918.

Koch came to Chapel Hill from the University of North Dakota, where he had begun to formulate his ideas about "folk drama," dramas about simple, elemental people who passed long, bitter winters in little sod shanties.[31] As Koch defined it, the essence of a folk drama lay "in man's desperate struggle for existence and in his enjoyment of the world of nature. The term 'folk' with us applies to that form of drama which is earth-rooted in the life of our common humanity."[32] Koch's legendary success at North Carolina resulted not only from his organizational efforts but from his ability to attract and inspire native North Carolinians with the ideal of the folk. His most famous students were Paul Green (whose *In Abraham's Bosom* won the Pulitzer Prize in 1926), Lulu Vollmer, and Hatcher Hughes, but many other Carolinians were attracted by Koch's ideals, for example Bernice Kelly Harris, who wrote *Folk Plays of Eastern North Carolina.* Many of her plays were performed in her hometown of Seabord and brought later to the annual festivals of the Carolina Dramatic Association at Chapel Hill.[33]

Koch did more than provide creative southerners with opportunities to develop their talents. Plays such as Lulu Vollmer's *Sun-Up* (first performed in 1923) effectively dramatized the humanity as well as the ignorance and misery of southern poor whites. At the end of *Sun-Up* the widow Cagle, exhausted by her misfortunes, voluntarily submits to the law. As dramatists projected a more tender image of poor whites during the 1920s, reformers shifted to new tactics. Home demonstration agents of the Agricultural Extension Service continued to encourage more efficient housewifery but began to add programs in rural music, arts and crafts, and drama, with the justification that these were merely reviving the traditional culture of the southern folk.[34] The agencies that inspired and promoted these programs—the Agricultural Extension Service, the extension divisions of state universities, women's clubs, and parent-teacher associations—all had impeccable Progressive credentials, but their programs now revealed less of the heavy-handed assimilationism that marked earlier Progressive attitudes toward rural southerners.

This substitution of cultural pluralism for assimilationism was not without irony, for it came at a time when the radio and highway were eroding many of the barriers that had long made the rural South difficult for reformers to penetrate. Southern Progressives had favored modernization, but when it came it was not always because of their efforts nor did it necessarily take forms with which they could identify. Throughout rural America, Eduard C. Lindeman wrote in 1927, "gasoline stations seem to grow up on every corner as naturally as the toadstool emerges from warm humus." The symbols of beauty that now blazoned forth from the sides of barns read "Hot-dogs, Balloon Tires, Lucky Strikes . . . and That School-girl Complexion."[35] Perhaps the very fact that rural southerners were now embracing their own version of assimilation stimulated the efforts of reformers to revive the old ways. The irony was that by the time reformers were trying to revive folk dancing, the farmer and his wife wanted to go to the movies.

Notes

1. Anne F. Scott, *The Southern Lady: From Pedestal to Politics* (Chicago: University of Chicago Press, 1970), pp. 119–20, 143, 148, 158–59; J. Morgan Kousser, "Progressivism—For Middle Class Whites Only: North Carolina Education, 1880–1910," *Journal of Southern History* 46 (May 1980): 189–94; Dewey W. Grantham, *Southern Progressivism: The Reconciliation of Progress and Tradition* (Knoxville: University of Tennessee Press, 1983); see also William A. Link, "Public Schooling and Social Change in Rural Virginia, 1870–1920" (Ph.D. dissertation, University of Virginia, 1981).

2. Amory D. Mayo, *Southern Women in the Recent Educational Movement in the South,* reprint ed. Dan T. Carter and Amy Friedlander (1892; rpt. Baton Rouge: Louisiana State University Press, 1978), p. 57.

3. Charles W. Dabney, *Universal Education in the South,* 2 vols. (Chapel Hill: University of North Carolina Press, 1936), 2:7–128, 324–25; Link, "Public Schooling," chap. 4.

4. Sophonisba Breckenridge, *Madeline McDowell Breckenridge: A Leader in the New South* (Chicago: University of Chicago Press, 1921), pp. 47–48.

5. Charles H. Cooley, *Human Nature and the Social Order* (New York: Charles Scribner's Sons, 1902); Cooley, *Social Organization: A Study of the Larger Mind* (New York: Charles Scribner's Sons, 1910); R. Jackson Wilson, *In Quest of Community: Social Philosophy in the United States, 1860–1920* (New York: Wiley, 1968); Jean B. Quandt, *From the Small Town to the Great Community: The Social Thought of Progressive Intellectuals* (New Brunswick: Rutgers University Press, 1970).

6. See, for example, Charles L. Robbins, *The School as a Social Institution: An Introduction to the Study of Social Education* (Boston: Allyn and Bacon, 1918).

7. Joseph F. Kett, *Rites of Passage: Adolescence in America, 1790–Present* (New York: Basic Books, 1977), chap. 8.

8. Edward K. Graham, *Education and Citizenship and Other Papers* (New York: G. P. Putnam's Sons, 1919), pp. 94–95 and passim.

9. James E. McCulloch, ed., *The New Chivalry—Health: Southern Sociological Congress, Houston, Texas, May 8–11, 1915* (Nashville: N.p., 1915), p. 536.

10. Breckenridge, *Madeline McDowell Breckenridge,* p. 48.

11. Scott, *Southern Lady,* p. 181.

12. Kousser, "Progressivism," pp. 181–82. Kousser presents a more negative impression of Progressive attitudes on race than is given here, as does Louis Harlan, *Separate and Unequal: Public School Campaigns and Racism in the Southern Seaboard States, 1901–1915* (Chapel Hill: University of North Carolina Press, 1958), p. 264. Their conclusions apply to many Progressives, but it is risky to encompass them all in a generalization.

13. James T. Patterson, *America's Struggle against Poverty, 1900–1980* (Cambridge, Mass.: Harvard University Press, 1981), pp. 10–11.

14. Grantham, *Southern Progressivism,* p. 276.

15. Edward A. Ross, *Social Control: A Survey of the Foundations of Order* (New York, 1901), p. 440.

16. J. Mills Thornton, *Politics and Power in a Slave Society: Alabama, 1800–1860* (Baton Rouge: Louisiana State University Press, 1978); Harry L. Watson, *Jacksonian Politics and Community Conflict: The Emergence of the Second Party System in Cumberland County, North Carolina* (Baton Rouge: Louisiana State University Press, 1981); David L. Carlton, *Mill and Town in South Carolina, 1880–1920* (Baton Rouge: Louisiana State University Press, 1982).

17. John L. Campbell, *The Southern Highlander and His Homeland* (New York: Russell Sage Foundation, 1921), p. 91.

18. Carlton, *Mill and Town in South Carolina,* chap. 5.

19. "Reports from the States: Kentucky," in Southern Education Association, *Journal of Proceedings and Addresses of the Seventeenth Annual Meeting . . . Montgomery, 1906* (Asheville, N.C.: Southern Education Association, 1906), p. 86.

20. For a full statement of these objectives, see J. D. Eggleston, Jr., "Consolidation and Transportation in Virginia," *Rural Life Conference Held at the University of Virginia Summer School, July 13–15, 1910, Alumni Bulletin, University of Virginia,* 3d ser., 3 (July 1910): 254–56. See also C. J. Galpin, *Rural Life* (New York: Century, 1918), p. 166; Mary Mims with Georgia Williams Moritz, *The Awakening Community* (New York: Macmillan, 1932), p. 119.

21. Mary Cooke Branch Munford, "Women's Work in the Educational Prog-

179

ress of the South," in *The South in the Building of the Nation,* 12 vols. (Richmond: Southern Publication Society, 1909), 10:640.

22. "Women's Meetings," *Proceedings of the Eleventh Conference for Education in the South, Memphis, Tenn., April 22–24, 1908* (N.p.: Executive Committee of the Conference for Education in the South, 1908), pp. 113–29.

23. Edgar Gardner Murphy, "The Southern Education Board," *Proceedings of the Tenth Conference for Education in the South, Pinehurst, N.C., April 9, 1907* (N.p.: Executive Committee of the Conference for Education in the South, 1907), p. 40.

24. "Women's Meetings," p. 117.

25. Roy V. Scott, *The Reluctant Farmer: The Rise of Agricultural Extension to 1914* (Urbana: University of Illinois Press, 1970), chaps. 8–9.

26. Warren Foster, "A Working Program for Rural Recreation," in McCulloch, ed., *The New Chivalry—Health,* p. 325.

27. J. S. Peters and W. F. Stinespring, "An Economic and Social Survey of Rockingham County," *University of Virginia Record: Extension Series* 9 (September 1924): 127–28.

28. The administration of the Sheppard-Towner Maternity and Infancy Care Act of 1921 illustrates the effects of rural individualism; see J. H. Mason Knox, "Itinerant Conferences—Standards of Examination," *Proceedings of the Third Annual Conference of State Directors in Charge of the Local Administration of the Maternity and Infancy Act,* U.S. Department of Labor, Children's Bureau Publication 157 (Washington, D.C.: U.S. Government Printing Office, 1926), pp. 80–82.

29. Louise Burleigh, "Signal Fires: A Masque of Service with a Pageant of the Lives of Florence Nightingale and Sadie Heath Cabaniss," *University of Virginia Record: Extension Series* 8 (Fall 1924): 6–28.

30. Louise Burleigh, *The Community Theatre in Theory and Practice* (Boston: Little, Brown, 1917), p. xxvii.

31. Samuel Selden, assisted by Mary Tom Sphangos, *Frederick Henry Koch, Pioneer Playmaker: A Brief Biography* (Chapel Hill: University of North Carolina Press, 1954), pp. 8–9.

32. Ibid., p. 61.

33. Ibid., pp. 64–65.

34. Marjorie Patten, *The Arts Workshop in Rural America: A Study of the Rural Arts Program of the Agricultural Extension Service* (New York, 1937), pp. 9, 12, 18–19.

35. Eduard C. Lindeman, "The Future of Agriculture and Rural Life," *Rural America* 5 (October 1927): 22.

"Colored Ladies Also Contributed": Black Women's Activities from Benevolence to Social Welfare, 1866–1896

Kathleen C. Berkeley

The members of the Daughters of Zion of Avery Chapel made a momentous decision at their June 1867 quarterly meeting. The church-based mutual aid society voted to hire Dr. S. H. Toles as the organization's personal physician. Beginning July 1, 1867, Dr. Toles, a black man free before 1860 and a native of Ohio, would receive a yearly salary of two hundred dollars. In exchange, he was expected to provide free medical care to all ailing members of Avery Chapel, one of the several African Methodist Episcopal churches of recent origin in Memphis, Tennessee.[1] Dr. Toles's first annual report to the society underscores the importance of the women's efforts to safeguard the health and well-being of a community denied equal access to public-supported professional health care.[2] Between July 1, 1867, and June 30, 1868, Dr. Toles treated 260 patients and reported only two fatalities. In addition to supplying the services of a physician, the organization disbursed $248.50 within a three-month period to indigent members of the congregation.[3] To sustain their benevolent activities (which included education and mission work) the women pooled their meager resources, solicited voluntary contributions from the congregation, and sponsored a series of fund-raising events such as fairs, picnics, and balls. Despite the outlay of almost $450, the Daughters of Zion remained solvent at the close of the 1868 fiscal year. A credit of $140.20 was posted to the society's account in the local branch of the Freedman's Savings and Trust Company.[4]

The collective efforts of a group of black women recently freed from slavery to provide aid for the sick and impoverished was by no means exceptional in Memphis. The Avery Chapel chapter of the Daughters of Zion, with its 304 dues-paying members in 1868, had dozens of counterparts sprinkled across the city. Almost every black church in town depended upon the services of a ladies aid society to look after cases of distress within its congregation.[5] Nor was the situation in Memphis unique. Scholars studying the transition from slavery to freedom in other southern communities are struck by the presence of a black institutional infrastructure consisting of churches, schools, orphanages, presses, political organizations, and benevolent societies.[6]

In fact, the abundant literature on the emancipation experience has provided the context for a lively debate in historical circles. For although scholars have corroborated the existence of a distinct black infrastructure in enclaves settled by former slaves, no one is certain how it was built. The central question remains, who supplied the leadership? From that basic query several others follow. Was guidance supplied by the federal government under the auspices of the Freedmen's Bureau? Or did participation in community-building projects reflect the class divisions that were beginning to emerge in postwar black society? Did the more prosperous blacks in the community, the majority of whom were free before the Civil War, manage the organizations for the benefit of the more impoverished members, who tended to come from the ranks of the former slaves? Or were these institutions genuine working-class cooperatives?[7] Finally, how solid were these structures? After all, if they depended upon the support of a class of people who faced chronic economic deprivation, one might suspect them to be short-lived.

In a recent essay, Armstead Robinson suggested a new approach for conceptualizing the emancipation experience.[8] His framework not only allows for a synthesis of existing literature but it also creates a model for future scholarship. As Robinson analyzed the institution-building process among blacks in Reconstruction-era Memphis, he discovered a split between the religious-benevolent functions of the community and its political activities. This division reflected the class distinctions that were beginning to characterize postwar black society. Working-class blacks, because of their precarious economic existence, recognized the necessity for sharing their limited assets. These people concentrated their efforts on creating a network of churches, each with a laity strongly committed to mission, education, and benevolence work. Blacks from the more privileged ranks remained aloof from these churches and their auxiliaries. These nascent middle and upper classes were attracted to the pressing political and legal questions of the day and demonstrated their class-specific interests by participating heavily in local political organizations sponsored by the Republican party. Thus a schism existed between the private needs of some blacks and the public concerns of others—a schism rooted in rapidly diverging class-based interests.[9]

How does this dichotomy relate to the Daughters of Zion of Avery Chapel or any of the other female benevolent societies operating in Memphis? Robinson alludes to the answer. Because he is more interested in class-specific concerns than gender-specific issues, his analysis of institution-building excludes the daily activities of working-class women. Readily admitting the limits of his methodology, Robinson asks how our understanding of the complexities of the transition from slavery to freedom might be enhanced by highlighting rather than obscuring gender.[10] One example will suffice as a response to Robinson's query. In discussing the decision of former slave preachers to abandon white-owned churches in favor of black-controlled structures, Robinson marveled at how quickly "bush arbors" were transformed into permanent edifices. How were recently freed slave preachers able to purchase lots and erect their own churches? Exploring this question through the lens of women's history not only widens but sharpens our vision of the past. For example, in the case of the most famous black church in Memphis, Beale Street Baptist Church, partial credit belongs to the black women who met after services one warm Sunday afternoon in June 1865 to organize the Baptist Sewing Society. Dedicating their collective efforts to securing funds for a permanent church, the women raised more than five hundred dollars during the first nine months of the society's existence. By April 1867, the five-thousand-dollar mortgage on the lot was paid in full, a thousand-dollar nest egg lay gathering interest in the Freedman's Savings and Trust Company, and a temporary building housed both a meeting hall for worship and a classroom for religious and secular instruction. Finally, two female members of the congregation presided over the "week school."[11]

Concern for the neglect of gender as an appropriate window to the past highlights a historical truism. Women of color remain the most invisible group in American history. Why? Because most scholars tend to focus on race and class-specific issues rather than gender-specific issues. Among historians interested in the Afro-American past, the continued use of the generic—slave, freedman, black—obscures gender differences by reinforcing the assumption that the experiences of black women under slavery and in freedom did not differ significantly from those of their male counterparts.[12] The notion that racism could have a differential impact upon the lives of black men and women received scant attention in Afro-American historiography, with the single exception of the literature on the sexual abuse black women suffered at the hands of white men. Thus when efforts to alleviate racism required collective action, the assumption was that black men and women invariably stood together.[13]

The recent marriage of Afro-American and women's history has produced a spate of works over the last decade challenging this interpretation.[14] While women's historians argued forcefully for the existence of both an autonomous female culture and politics, practitioners of black women's history began to discover that race-specific issues did not always outweigh gender-specific concerns when the need for organizing arose in the black community. The works of Gerda Lerner, Beverly Jones, Rosalyn Terborg-Penn, Sharon Harley, and Cynthia Neverdon-Morton (to name but a few) went beyond the bounds of "contribution history."[15] These authors found that black women had done more than merely contribute to the development of an institutional infrastructure within their local communities (an admirable accomplishment in and of itself). More important, black women were often in the vanguard in founding and sustaining autonomous organizations designed specifically to improve social conditions within their respective communities.[16] Black women, it appears, were busy carving out their own separate spheres of activity in freedom. In creating autonomous institutions to solve the problems caused by inadequate health care services, substandard housing, economic deprivation, and segregated schools, black women served notice that they felt a special responsibility to provide social welfare programs for their communities. Apparently they believed they alone could fulfill this need.[17]

Where did the impetus for creating autonomous black female institutions originate? The answer is rooted within the heritage of slavery as well as the duality black women experienced as members of two subordinate groups in American society. Jacqueline Jones's research on black women, work, and family values under slavery has shown that the slave community maintained the traditional division of labor between the sexes whenever possible. "Like women in almost all cultures," Jones informs us, "slave women had both a biological and social 'destiny.'"[18] In the quarters, black women shouldered the responsibility for nurturing and caring for the health and well-being of both the family and community.

As blacks traveled the road to freedom, the values and customs of the slave community persisted. Some thirty-plus years after emancipation, when Mary Church Terrell (the first president of the National Association of Colored Women [NACW]) described the forces that motivated black women to engage in collective action, she spoke of the symbiotic relationship between the biological and social responsibilities of womanhood.[19] Addressing the Nashville convention of the NACW in 1897, Terrell remarked that black women were called to serve their people because they were "the mothers, wives, daughters, and sisters of our race." Further on in her speech she elaborated upon this theme: "This [the NACW] is an association of colored women because our peculiar status in this country at the present time seems to demand that we stand by ourselves in this special work for which we have organized."[20] The interplay between racism and sexism defined the problems confronting black women. In seeking a solution to this twin dilemma they advanced a strategy of "social housekeeping," which did not appear to challenge prescriptive behavior.[21]

The formation of the NACW in 1896 culminated a thirty-year struggle by black women to achieve common objectives.[22] Day nurseries for working mothers, orphanages, homes for the aged and the infirm, hospitals, cemeteries, night schools, and scholarship funds were high priorities for female activists. Although the agenda of black women essentially remained unchanged during the transitional years, the stage they chose for collective action seemed to shift away from grass-roots, church-based organizations to a more formalized, centralized, and secular-based network at the state and national levels. By the early part of the twentieth century, the NACW had emerged as the leading organization for social change among black women. In 1914, the organization claimed fifty thousand dues-paying members and more than a thousand affiliated clubs.

Until a decade ago, little was known about the activities of the NACW except for the laudatory and uncritical reports of the black women who pioneered in the movement. Partly in response to Gerda Lerner's challenge to take seriously the benevolent work of black women, we have witnessed the growth of a body of literature on the black women's club movement during the Progressive Era. In addition to uncovering the myriad programs and institutions sponsored by the NACW, a portrait of its leadership is at last coming into focus.[23]

The typical leader was among the first generation of black women born in freedom. Originally from the South, she seldom remained there but sought opportunity either in the West or North. If she lived below the Mason-Dixon line, she tended to reside in one of the large urban centers on the periphery of the region. A member of the black middle class, she earned a college education and more than likely taught school before retiring upon marriage. Her husband held a prestigious position within the black community either as an educator, lawyer, doctor, politician, businessman, or minister. Although she rejected the biological role of motherhood, she accepted and indeed exploited to her advantage the social obligations and responsibilities of that role as justification for her activism. The interpretive literature suggests that the black female activist of the 1890s represented a "new woman," one who "eschewed the more traditional female societies such as sewing circles, church clubs, and sisterly orders." Supposedly, the creation of the NACW elevated black women's benevolent activities to a higher plane of social welfare.[24]

How, then, does one assess the historical relationship between the refined, educated, middle-class activists of the NACW and the anonymous women who founded the Daughters of Zion of Avery Chapel in Memphis, Tennessee? In asking that question we have come full circle and returned to the queries posed at the beginning of this essay. Did working-class or middle-class women form the backbone of those early sewing circles, church clubs, and sisterly societies? Did the split that mirrored class divisions within black America also characterize black women's benevolent activities by the close of the nineteenth century? Or does a straight line connect the emergence of local benevolent societies during the Civil War–Reconstruction era with the formation of a national network of social welfare programs during the Progressive Era? After all, how dissimilar were the problems confronting black women in both eras? Had the formalization of Jim Crow laws after 1890 really altered the day-to-day realities of life for most blacks? Had not a policy of partial exclusion coupled with segregation (especially with regard to social services) always existed in the New South?[25]

Although black women appear to have had a continuous record of self-help since emancipation, no one has documented the strength of this movement or followed its course of development from the grass-roots to the federation stage. As far as we know, no official historian recorded the meetings and activities of these early societies; if she did, the records have not survived. At the other end of the spectrum, the existence of a permanent headquarters in Washington, D.C., a national newsletter, and an official history have made the task of rescuing the NACW and its leadership from obscurity easier.[26] Thus source limitations have been the primary justification for ignoring the early community work of black women,[27] yet this rationale cannot hold up under the close scrutiny of historians trained in the methods of community studies. Both local and federal records for the Civil War–Reconstruction era contain an embarrassment of riches on the public work of black women. Newspapers, city directories, municipal and county records, the Freedmen's Bureau papers, and the signature books and deposit ledgers of the Freedman's Savings and Trust Company are but a few of the sources one might consult.

The remainder of this essay will follow the emergence and development of self-help societies in one locality—Memphis, Tennessee—in an effort to bridge the gap in the historical literature. Although the officers of the Daughters of Zion of Avery Chapel were not present at the historic meeting in July 1896 at which the NACW was formed, Memphis women were represented. Two other ladies' societies, Coterie Migratory Assembly and Hooks School Association, sent a small delegation of women to Washington, D.C.[28] Thus a link, however tenuous, does exist between the local activities of black women in Memphis and the work of the national federation.

Memphis was chosen for study because the city offers a favorable laboratory for analyzing the collective activities of black women who directly experienced the sometimes bumpy transition from slavery to freedom. First, Memphis was a major port city on the Mississippi River during the late antebellum era servicing the needs of the mid-South's plantation-based cotton economy.[29] On the eve of the Civil War, the city's black population was overwhelmingly slave: there were fewer than 200 free blacks out of a total black population of 3,882 (blacks made up 17 percent of the total urban population).[30] Second, the war wrought dramatic changes in the demographic composition of the city. The disruption of trade and transportation networks and the destruction of crops and livestock severed vast numbers of slaves from the soil of nearby counties. Memphis became the likely destination of these runaways and contrabands, especially after the city's capture by northern troops in June 1862. The records of the Union army occupation forces document the rural, slave background of the city's newest residents. Thus we can be reasonably sure that it was an unskilled, peasant population relatively unfamiliar with urban folkways. According to a Union army census taken in the summer of 1865, there were approximately 15,828 "freed people living in or about Memphis," with an additional 681 freedmen located on nearby President's Island.[31] By 1870 blacks totaled 38 percent of the city's population.[32] Finally, postwar Memphis was headquarters for the federal government's Reconstruction efforts in West Tennessee. Thus the city was home to occupation forces until 1869 and in addition housed a Freedmen's Bureau office, a branch of the Freedman's Bank, and a Republican party–sponsored newspaper whose editor faithfully reported the social as well as political activities of the black community.

A major question addressed in this essay is whether the social conditions that called forth black female activism changed over the thirty-year period under examination. To try to answer that question, I will trace the development of black women's benevolent societies within a context that explores the evolution of a New South social welfare policy that adversely affected blacks, a program that combined aspects of exclusion and segregation.[33] In the following pages, I will suggest that such a policy either provided no services to the black community or provided services of questionable quality. Thus former slaves were compelled to turn inward; working-class blacks shouldered the burden of providing themselves with desperately needed social services. Black women, because of their socioculturally defined duties as the mothers and wives of the race, assumed a primary responsibility for this awesome task.

The influx of thousands of former plantation blacks created numerous problems for the succession of Union army generals placed in charge of occupied Memphis. It is by now a familiar story that the solution for caring for these people evolved along with their status, first as fugitive slaves, then as contrabands of war, and finally as freedmen.[34] In July 1862, Congress authorized President Lincoln to allow local field commanders to employ fugitive slaves, who in return received food, clothing, and shelter. Any revenue earned beyond the cost of the slave's subsistence remained with the army. Masters who sued and won the return of their property were entitled to the wages that had accrued. Military commanders moved quickly to institute this program to ease the release of food to the runaways. In Memphis, General William Sherman, who took command of the city in the fall of 1862, issued an order implementing this program less than a month after its approval in Congress.[35]

To prevent the growing numbers of blacks from hampering military activities, eventually they were herded into a string of centrally located contraband/freedmen's camps. Colonel John Eaton, the chaplain assigned to General Ulysses S. Grant's army in Tennessee, assumed the title of superintendent of freedmen and took charge of directing relief operations for the former slaves. By March 1865, Eaton's agency had become a subdepartment of the newly created Freedmen's Bureau. Memphis, Tennessee, was selected as one of the camp sites intended to serve the mid-South. On February 4, 1863, the new commander of the city, General James Veatch, placed an army chaplain named Fiske in charge of the seven thousand former slaves residing in or near the city.[36]

In keeping with mid-nineteenth-century laissez-faire attitudes toward social welfare, the federal government sought to encourage a self-help philosophy among the former slaves.[37] The desire to foster self-sufficiency while discouraging dependence upon public charity led those in charge of black relief to view any aid as a temporary, emergency measure. Orders from the War Department, like the one Chaplain Fiske of Memphis received in February 1864, repeatedly stressed that "rations must be for short periods of time."[38] To drive home the point that the freed people must be responsible for their own welfare, white soldiers visited the freedmen's camps in Memphis in August 1865 with a strict warning: only those with "permanent employment so as to be able to take care of themselves during the coming winter would be allowed to remain in the city."[39] The following month the assistant commissioner of the Freedmen's Bureau for Kentucky and Tennessee made plans to suspend the disbursement of rations to freedmen. "No more rations will be issued to the freed people of this sub-division after the twentieth [of September]," stated the letter sent to Lieutenant Potter, the local bureau agent for Memphis and its surrounding environs.[40]

General O. O. Howard, the head of the Freedmen's Bureau, was proud that his was not a "pauperizing agency." Only a small percentage of blacks ever received assistance from the government. By Howard's own estimate, only one out of every two hundred freedmen relied upon public relief.[41] In Memphis, according to the reports of the Freedmen's Home for 1865, former slaves fared only slightly better than the regional average indicates. Approximately 774 persons received assistance from the Freedmen's Bureau each month; 66 percent (521) of the recipients were black, and the remainder were white war refugees. The 521 freedmen who received aid represented only 3.1 percent of the black population residing in Memphis by the close of 1865. Over the next two years public assistance for blacks dropped off precipitously. Even as funding dried up, poor blacks found themselves competing with and losing their earlier advantage to needy whites. Shortly after Dr. Toles assumed his duties for the Daughters of Zion he issued a preliminary report in which he castigated the bureau for its favoritism toward poor whites. Producing figures to support his claim, Toles charged that "poor whites had received twice the aid the colored people had."[42]

The black community always bore part of the responsibility for the care of its aged, infirm, and dependent young. Even as the federal government appealed for private assistance from northern churches, missionary, and freedmen's aid societies, public officials took the necessary steps to transfer some of the burden to the freedmen. After 1862, to help defray the costs of providing for dependent blacks, the federal government relied upon enforced contributions from the freed people. In the "Department of Mississippi, Tennessee, and Arkansas, medical care depended upon the direct contributions of the freedmen. The director of the freedmen's work in that area levied a tax on the wages of the able-bodied to support the sick."[43] When the Memphis Freedmen's Bureau made plans to dismantle its hospital system during the fall of 1865, agents attempted to turn the care of sick blacks over to local civilian authorities. When they refused, bureau officials organized the Freedmen's Sanitary Commission and Hospital Fund. Staffed originally by the handful of prosperous blacks who made up the city's pre-1860 free black community, the commission received authorization from the military to levy and collect a dollar tax on all blacks between the ages of eighteen and sixty living either in Memphis or within a mile radius of the city. To ensure compliance, sanitary agents were empowered to impose heavy fines on all those who sought to evade the tax.[44]

Elite blacks soon divested themselves of the onerous and sometimes irksome responsibility of overseeing the distribution of the freedmen's hospital fund. Social class tensions, which divided other urban black communities, were at work in Memphis as well.[45] In the bluff city, upper-class blacks took great pains to avoid any activity or institution that would bring them into proximity with working-class blacks. Thus sometime during 1866, Joseph Clouston, one of the most visible and prosperous among the city's free blacks, signed over the hospital fund to the Reverend Page Tyler. The two men were very different. Clouston, a mulatto, owned a successful string of barber shop concessions in the more prestigious hotels in Memphis. In 1860 Clouston was worth $20,000 in real estate and $12,000 in personal property. The dark-complexioned Tyler was born in bondage in Kentucky in 1818 and moved to Memphis shortly after the war ended. By 1866 the former slave preacher presided over the African Methodist Episcopal (AME) congregation of Avery Chapel. Recognizing the important work black women performed as the coordinators of relief, Reverend Tyler quickly relinquished control of the freedman's hospital fund to the Daughters of Zion's president, Martha Ware, and the secretary-treasurer, Jeannie Beckford.[46]

For dependent blacks whose care could not be discharged to the newly freed community, the federal government had a contingency plan: the care of indigents would be turned over to southern state or local authorities. Initially hostile to the concept, southern whites eventually agreed to accept responsibility for black relief but on a segregated basis.[47] Recent studies have linked the decline in black life expectancy in the twenty years after the Civil War to the inadequate health care blacks received in segregated public facilities.[48] In addition to the acknowledged substandard care blacks received in postwar southern institutions, another dimension to this subject merits further exploration. Once southern whites assumed the reigns of government, were blacks substantially un-derrepresented among those persons receiving public assistance? Did a policy of partial exclusion coexist alongside the practice of segregation?

The answer, if we may generalize from the Memphis experience, is affirmative. Blacks were underrepresented as recipients of the city's nascent social welfare program. Established by city ordinance on December 10, 1860, the Memphis City Charity Hospital was consistent in the post-war era in its discrimination against blacks.[49] For example, during a three-and-a-half-year period from March 1868 to December 1871, the Memphis City Charity Hospital admitted 2,695 persons. Of that number 248 or 9 percent were black. In the same period, foreign-born whites accounted for 1,299 or 48 percent of those admitted. The remaining 1,148 (43 percent) were native-born whites. Between August 8, 1869, and October 15, 1870, the largest single group receiving municipal aid was the Irish (30.5 percent). When one realizes that blacks accounted for 38.4 percent of the city's population in 1870 and Irish for 7.1 percent, the inequities seem more pronounced.[50]

Thus the interplay between white institutional racism and class antag-onisms within the black community left former slaves with no alternative but to rely upon their own meager resources for survival. To cushion themselves against privation caused by chronic unemployment, sickness, or the death of the main breadwinner, the freed people discovered the necessity for collective action. Pooling their often limited material re-sources, former slaves developed and sustained a panoply of support in-stitutions in post–Civil War Memphis. An analysis of the deposit ledgers of the Freedman's Savings and Trust Company indicates that black churches lent encouragement to the creation of this infrastructure.[51]

From 1866 until 1874, when the bank went bankrupt, 220 black orga-nizations deposited funds in the Memphis branch. Ninety-seven (44 per-cent) of the accounts belonged to black churches. The various Baptist and AME churches led the way, followed by the two Congregational churches. Significantly, the Presbyterian congregation, home to the re-ligious devotions of the more prosperous blacks, did not put its funds in the bank. Church accounts were used to make improvements on build-ings and to support private secular schools. An additional 20.9 percent (forty-six) of the accounts were deposited by church-related benevolent societies such as the Daughters of Zion, the Advent Benevolent Society (also female), the Sons of Ham, and the Sons and Daughters of Cannon. Thus almost two-thirds of the organizations with accounts in the bank had a direct religious affiliation. Of the remaining accounts, 12.7 percent were secular-based self-help societies (the Union Forever Society and the Farmer's Relief Number 2); 8.2 percent were self-improvement associations (the Young Ladies of Purity and the Le Moyne Literary Society). Trade societies accounted for 7.7 percent of the accounts (the Laboring Ladies Society and the New Memphis Laborer's Society); fraternal lodges (King Solomon's Lodge) and their female auxiliaries (Queen Esther's Court) constituted the remaining 6.4 percent (see Table 1).[52]

Women shared in the organizational life of the black community as leaders of the various societies and as members of the rank and file. Autonomous female institutions constituted 29.1 percent (sixty-four) of the accounts deposited in the Freedman's Savings and Trust Company; an additional 4.1 percent (nine) of the deposits were listed as joint male/female enterprises. The list of officers drawn from a sample of the "mixed societies"—the Providence Chapel School Fund, the Central Baptist Church Sunday School Collection, and the Avery Chapel School Committee—indicates that women served with distinction as leaders of these joint ventures.[53]

That women assumed leadership positions in roughly one-third of the black associations reflects a continuity in the values and customs acquired under slavery. In bondage, the habits of mutuality were preached and practiced in two institutions: the barely visible slave church and the family. Slave preachers, who were almost always male, nonetheless stressed in their sermons the complementary aspect of the relationship among the individual, the family, and the community. This concept found reinforcement in slave religion by the customary use of the terms "sister" and "brother." Because black women used their special knowledge of

Table 1. Deposits in the Freedman's Savings and Trust
Company, by Affiliation: Memphis, Tennessee, 1866–1874

Depositors	Percent	Number
Church accounts	44.0	97
Church-based mutual relief and educational societies	20.9	46
Secular-based mutual relief associations	12.7	28
Work/trade associations	7.7	17
Fraternal lodges	6.4	14
Self-improvement societies	8.2	18
Total accounts		220

Source: Signature Books, Freedman's Savings and Trust Company, Record Group 101, National Archives, Washington, D.C.

herbs and roots to cure illnesses, they were often accorded a powerful position in black religion as conjurers.[54] Finally, within the realm of the family, the black man and woman had "reciprocal obligations towards one another":[55] he assumed the role of provider and protector, and she functioned as the nurturer and caretaker.

The black churches served as the organizational base for the women's benevolent activities. Of the autonomous female associations in Memphis, 84.4 percent were linked to a local Baptist or African Methodist Episcopal church (see Table 2). Apparently almost every black congregation in town had a female benevolent society. The numerous chapters of the United Daughters of Ham, the Sisters of Zion, the Daughters of Zion, and the Ladies Benevolent Society numbers 1, 2, and 3 ministered to the needs of the sick and impoverished and consoled the bereaved. They also sponsored the churches' mission and educational work. All of these duties fell within the scope of traditional female obligations.

To determine who guided these organizations, a profile of the typical black female activist's social class orientation can be drawn from easily quantifiable data. The signature books of the Freedman's Savings and Trust Company yielded a list of fifty-seven women who served as leaders of the various benevolent societies. Because some of the officers maintained personal accounts at the bank, descriptive information was available on several of them.[56] In addition, city directories and the U.S. census manuscripts were used to corroborate data or supply missing information. Whenever possible I noted the woman's occupational status to place her within a social class. I substituted the husband's occupation in the rare occasions when the wife's was unknown. Occupational data were supplied for 59.6 percent (thirty-four) of the women. To provide more detailed analysis of female leadership patterns, the officers were divided

Table 2. Female Organizational Accounts, Freedman's Savings and Trust Company: Memphis, Tennessee, 1866–1874

Depositors	Percent	Number
Baptist societies	53.1	34
African Methodist Episcopal societies	31.3	20
Secular lodges	4.7	3
Secular mutual relief societies	3.1	2
Secular self-improvement associations	4.7	3
Work/trade associations	3.1	2
Total	100	64

Source: Signature Books, Freedman's Savings and Trust Company, Record Group 101, National Archives, Washington, D.C.

into three categories: community influentials, community activists, and elite. Community influentials were defined simply as all women who served as officers. Community activists were those chosen to lead their respective societies at least twice. The elite category consisted of women elected to office more than three times.[57]

The results reveal a great deal about the inner workings of a black community consisting largely of unskilled former slaves.[58] Women from the professional classes participated in female-directed self-help societies but rarely as members of the elite cadre. Instead, these women tended to serve their community as influentials and activists. Predictably, of the nine women in this social class, seven were teachers, including Mary Burton, who served as vice-president of the Sun Beam Society. The other two women in this category were the wives of professional men: a minister and a politician. Only Mrs. Edward Shaw, the politician's wife, served at least three terms as an officer of the Sisters of Ham. Skilled workers such as seamstresses Martha Ware and Julia Johnson (presidents respectively of the Daughters of Zion of Avery Chapel and the Advent Benevolent Society) were more often than not drafted into the elite circle of women. But the bulk of the women who served as leaders of the benevolent societies, especially at the elite level, came from the ranks of the unskilled. Almost two-thirds (61.5 percent) of the leadership elite worked as laundresses, ironers, and domestics (see Table 3).

Although benevolence in Memphis depended upon a class of black women who undoubtedly endured long hours of work at extremely low pay, the women and their societies persevered. Their endurance is all the

Table 3. Occupational Distribution of Black Female Community Influentials, Activists, and Elites: Memphis, Tennessee, 1866–1874

Occupational Groupings	Influentials		Activists		Elites	
Professional	26.5%	(9)	38.1%	(8)	7.7%	(1)
Managerial	–		–		–	
Entrepreneurial	2.9%	(1)	4.8%	(1)	–	
White collar	–		–		–	
Skilled	20.6%	(7)	14.3%	(3)	30.8%	(4)
Semiskilled/service	8.8%	(3)	14.3%	(3)	–	
Unskilled	41.2%	(14)	28.6%	(6)	61.5%	(8)
Totals		(34)		(21)		(13)

Sources: Signature Books, Freedman's Savings and Trust Company, Record Group 101, National Archives, Washington, D.C.; Memphis City Directories, 1860–80; U.S. Bureau of the Census, Manuscript Schedules, 1870.

more impressive because difficult economic times confronted Memphis throughout the decades of the 1870s and 1880s. The panic of 1873 and the subsequent depression, which dragged on until 1879, contributed to chaotic financial conditions in the city. Ultimately, the city government declared itself bankrupt. In 1879 the municipal charter was revoked, and Memphis became a taxing district of Shelby County.[59] Of more immediate importance to the city's black population and the women's benevolent activities were two other related and cataclysmic events: the failure of the Freedman's Savings and Trust Company and the yellow fever epidemic.

When the Memphis branch of the Freedman's Savings and Trust Company closed its doors to anxious depositors in July 1874, the funds to sustain benevolence in the black community vanished. While the officers of the mutual aid societies struggled to keep their organizations afloat, the demands for benevolence increased. Memphis was visited by a series of yellow fever epidemics throughout the 1870s. Residents who could afford to flee the disease-ravaged city did so while the poor, both black and white, remained trapped. Medical care was at a premium in the black community. In the aftermath of the epidemics, the survivors bore the responsibility for providing for the widowed and orphaned.[60]

The women's benevolent societies demonstrated their resiliency in the face of these tragedies by continuing to meet and dispense aid and comfort to the needy. What enabled such organizations as the Sisters of Zion of North Memphis and the Daughters of Zion of Avery Chapel to weather the storms of depression, bankruptcy, and disease which fell heavily upon the black community? No doubt as the women stood together in the larger fight against racism, they drew strength from their shared social obligations as the mothers of their race.

During the 1890s a movement arose among black middle-class female activists for the formation of a national network to coordinate benevolent activities at the community level. Although unity was the primary objective, the federation made no attempt to standardize social welfare programs, preferring instead to sponsor projects that reflected the needs of black people arising from local conditions. Nevertheless, a continuity of interests could be discerned, for education and the care of the sick, the young, and the elderly were high-priority issues at all levels of organization and across the nation.[61]

Although additional work is needed before we can reach a definitive conclusion about the complex relationship between the NACW and its affiliates, two misperceptions can be rectified. A careful reading of the official history of the NACW indicates that the refined, educated, prosperous women who ran the federation did not look with disdain upon the self-help activities of working-class women. On the contrary, the membership policy of the NACW encouraged all "Negro women's groups" to join the national. From the more traditional church clubs, sewing circles, and sisterly societies to trade unions, self-improvement/literary associations, and college organizations, "all may affiliate with the National Association of Colored Women without losing their identity."[62]

At the same time, the leadership of the NACW carefully nurtured its relationship with the traditional institution associated with benevolence in the black community—the black church. Evidence of this link is that the initial organizing meeting that led to the formation of the NACW on July 19, 1896, took place at the 19th Street Baptist Church in Washington, D.C. The following year the convention was held in Nashville, Tennessee, at the Howard Chapel of the Congregational Church. At that time, the organization decided to meet biennially. The delegates to the 1899 convention found a warm welcome at Quinn Chapel in Chicago, Illinois. Over the next thirty years, eight of the fifteen national meetings were held in black churches.[63]

The choice of meeting sites and the willingness of the national leadership to encourage laboring-class women to affiliate with the NACW suggests the need to revise the view that the NACW was an elitist organization. Rather than arguing for a divergence between local and national benevolent activities of black women based upon the ethos of competing class interests, we ought to see a convergence of class interests based on the more pressing concerns of race and gender. Thus the formation of the NACW in 1896 represented an effort on the part of middle-class black women to build an alliance with working-class women. Viewed from this perspective, the NACW emerges as an organization that sought to bridge class divisions within the female world of black America. What drew these two disparate classes of women together in the 1890s? Perhaps the harsh realities of racism muted class tensions. By the beginning of the twentieth century, laboring-class and middle-class black female activists had joined together in support of each other's social work efforts for the greater good of the community.

Notes

1. *Memphis Post,* June 6, 20, 1864.
2. For two different interpretations of health care for freedmen see Howard Rabinowitz, "From Exclusion to Segregation: Health and Welfare Services for Southern Blacks, 1865–1900," *Social Service Review* 48 (September 1974):

327–54, and Gaines M. Foster, "The Limitations of Federal Health Care for Freedmen, 1862–1868," *Journal of Social History* 48 (August 1982): 349–72.

The Memphis Charity Hospital was established by city ordinance on December 10, 1860. In the postwar era, discrimination in admittance exacerbated the difficulties of the black community in receiving public-supported medical care. See the abstracts of the Memphis City Minute Books, December 10, 1860, Memphis and Shelby County Archives.

3. *Memphis Post,* July 9, 1868. It is not clear whether Dr. Toles treated 260 or 278 patients. The total number listed is 260, but the newspaper's tally is 278.

4. See the deposit ledgers, Freedman's Savings and Trust Company, Memphis Branch, 1866–74, Record Group 101, National Archives, Washington, D.C. For a history of the Freedman's Savings and Trust Company see Carl R. Osthaus, *Freedmen, Philanthropy, and Fraud: A History of the Freedman's Bank* (Chicago: University of Chicago Press, 1976).

5. The United Brothers and Sisters of Zion also hired the services of a physician, Dr. C. Baker, to care for ailing members of the congregation. The *Memphis Post,* a Republican newspaper, faithfully printed the benevolent activities of black women. See issues of October 4, 1867, June 1, 1868; also *Memphis Bulletin,* August 3, 1864.

6. See the following post–Civil War southern community studies: Joel Williamson, *After Slavery: The Negro in South Carolina, 1861–1877* (Chapel Hill: University of North Carolina Press, 1965); Peter Kolchin, *First Freedom: The Response of Alabama's Blacks to Emancipation and Reconstruction* (Westport, Conn.: Greenwood Press, 1972); John Blassingame, *Black New Orleans* (Chicago: University of Chicago Press, 1973), and "Before the Ghetto: The Making of the Black Community in Savannah, Georgia, 1865–1880, *Journal of Southern History* 6 (Summer 1973): 463–88; Edward Magdol, *A Right to the Land: Essays on the Freedmen's Communities* (Westport, Conn.: Greenwood Press, 1977); C. Peter Ripley, *Slaves and Freedmen in Civil War Louisiana* (Baton Rouge: Louisiana State University Press, 1976); and Howard Rabinowitz, *Race Relations in the Urban South, 1865–1900* (New York: Oxford University Press, 1978).

7. In his discussion of "friendly societies," E. P. Thompson argues that these associations grew out of collective values rooted in working-class culture (*The Making of the English Working Class* [New York: Vintage Books, 1966], pp. 418–29).

8. Armstead L. Robinson, "Plans Dat Comed from God: Institution Building and the Emergence of Black Leadership in Reconstruction Memphis, 1865–1880," in Orville Vernon Burton and Robert C. McMath, Jr., eds., *Toward a New South? Studies in Post–Civil War Southern Communities* (Westport, Conn.: Greenwood Press, 1982), 71–102.

9. Private here refers to internal-oriented functions within black society, whereas public concerns and activities are those that necessitated interaction with white society.

10. Robinson, "Plans Dat Comed from God," p. 98.

11. *Memphis Post,* March 6, October 30, 1866, April 1, June 18, 1867; also see the deposit ledgers, Freedman's Savings and Trust Company, Memphis Branch, account number 115, August 29, 1867.

12. Jacqueline Jones makes this point in " 'My Mother Was Much of a Woman': Black Women, Work and Family under Slavery," *Feminist Studies* 8 (Summer 1982): 235–70.

13. Historians, Catherine Clinton argues, have downplayed the extent to which black women were subjected to sexual abuse by white men. At the same time, a "blaming the victim syndrome" occurred whereby black women also suffered violence at the hands of jealous white women. White women displaced their anger at the illicit sexual relationship between black women and white men by assaulting powerless black women. See Catherine Clinton's "Caught in the Web of the Big House: Women and Slavery" in this volume.

14. The editors of *Feminist Studies* devoted most of an issue to the topic of a separate female culture. See Ellen DuBois et al., "Politics and Culture in Women's History: A Symposium," *Feminist Studies* 6 (Spring 1980): 26–64, and Estelle Freedman, "Separatism as Strategy: Female Institution Building and American Feminism," *Feminist Studies* 5 (Fall 1979): 512–29. The practitioners of women's history also were guilty of the sins of omission. Until recently and with few exceptions, women's history has meant the study of native-born white middle- to upper-class women from the New England and Mid-Atlantic states. The possibility that regional distinctions existed among women as well as the more obvious ones of race, class, and ethnicity received scant attention.

15. See Gerda Lerner, *The Majority Finds Its Past: Placing Women in History* (New York: Oxford University Press, 1979), pp. 63–111; Beverly Jones, "Quest for Equality: The Life of Mary Church Terrell, 1863–1954" (Ph.D. dissertation, University of North Carolina, Chapel Hill, 1980), and "Mary Church Terrell and the National Association of Colored Women, 1896 to 1901," *Journal of Negro History* 67 (Spring 1982): 20–33; Rosalyn-Terborg Penn and Sharon Harley, eds., *The Afro-American Woman: Struggle and Images* (Port Washington: Kennikat Press, 1978); Sharon Harley, "Beyond the Classroom: Organizational Lives of Black Women Educators," *Journal of Negro Education* 51 (Summer 1983): 254–65; Cynthia Neverdon-Morton, "Self-Help Programs of Black Women, 1895–1925," *Journal of Negro Education* 51 (Summer 1983): 207–21; and Bettye Collier-Thomas, "The Impact of Black Women in Education: An Historical Overview," *Journal of Negro Education* 51 (Summer 1983): 173–79.

16. Neverdon-Morton, "Self-Help Programs," p. 207.

17. Harley, "Beyond the Classroom," p. 256.

18. Jones, " 'My Mother Was Much of a Woman,' " pp. 235–69, quotation on p. 253.

19. Mary Church Terrell, *A Colored Woman in a White World* (New York: Arno Press, 1980).

20. Quoted in Jones, "Quest For Equality," pp. 41–42.

21. See Mary Ryan's discussion of "social housekeeping" in *Womanhood in America: From Colonial Times to the Present*, 3d ed. (New York: Franklin Watts, 1983), pp. 198–210. In discussing the organizational activities of black female educators, Sharon Harley refers to this strategy as a justification for black female activism in the public arena ("Beyond the Classroom," p. 256).

22. Tullia Kay Brown Hamilton, "The National Association of Colored Women, 1896–1920" (Ph.D. dissertation, Emory University, 1978).

23. Two contemporary accounts of the NACW are Elizabeth Lindsey Davis, *Lifting as They Climb: The National Association of Colored Women* (Washington, D.C.: National Association of Colored Women, 1933), and Fannie Barrier Williams, "Club Movement among Colored Women," in L. W. Gibson and W. H. Crogman, eds., *The Colored American from Slavery to Honorable Citizenship* (Atlanta: J. L. Nichols, 1903), pp. 197–231; Lerner, *The Majority Finds Its Past*, pp. 83–93; see also the sources listed in note 15.

24. Hamilton, "National Association of Colored Women," pp. 38–53. Hamilton's quantitative analysis of the NACW's leadership validates the conclusions drawn by Gerda Lerner and Beverly Jones about the middle-class backgrounds of the organization's leadership. Also see Kathleen Berkeley, " 'Colored Women in a White World': Race and Gender as Organizing Principles in the Black Community, 1880–1980" (paper presented at the Conference on Women's Culture in American Society, Los Angeles, March 1981). The possibility that the rank and file of the movement (in the local affiliates) were working-class women while the leadership of the federation (national level) drew support from the elite classes should be explored. Willie Mae Coleman makes this point in her dissertation, "Keeping the Faith and Disturbing the Peace: Black Women from Anti-Slavery to Women's Suffrage" (Ph.D. dissertation, University of California, Irvine, 1982), pp. 79–80. The quote is from Jones, "Mary Church Terrell," p. 20.

25. Gerda Lerner and Beverly Jones suggest that conditions worsened for blacks by the Progressive Era because of the codification of Jim Crow practices. They of course subscribe to C. Vann Woodward's interpretation of a flexible system of race relations during Reconstruction. For this thesis, see Woodward, *The Strange Career of Jim Crow*, 3d ed. (New York: Oxford University Press, 1974). Recent research has modified this interpretation. At least in southern cities by the early 1870s a formal system of exclusion and/or segregation existed. See Rabinowitz, *Race Relations in the Urban South*.

26. Coleman, "Keeping the Faith," pp. 79–80. The quote is from Lerner, *The Majority Finds Its Past*, p. 84.

27. Hamilton, "National Association of Colored Women," p. 11.

28. Coleman, "Keeping the Faith," p. 138.

29. See Kathleen Berkeley, " 'Like a Plague of Locusts': Immigration and Social Change in Memphis, Tennessee, 1850–1880" (Ph.D. dissertation, University of California, Los Angeles, 1980), and Charles Williams, Jr., "Two Black Communities in Memphis, Tennessee: A Study in Urban-Socio-Political Structures" (Ph.D. dissertation, University of Illinois, 1982), pp. 20–41.

30. U.S. Bureau of the Census, Manuscript schedules for the free and slave populations, Shelby County, Tennessee, 1860.

31. Brigadier General Davis Tillson to Captain W. T. Clark, August 15, 1865, Memphis, Tennessee, Records of the Bureau of Regugees, Freedmen and Abandoned Lands, Record Group 105, National Archives, Washington, D.C. Three-fourths of the migrants during the war years were women and children, many of them unfit to labor in military camps and on abandoned plantations. See Berkeley, " 'Like a Plague of Locusts,' " pp. 145–47.

32. U.S. Bureau of the Census, Manuscript schedule, Shelby County, Tennessee, 1870.

33. Rabinowitz, *Race Relations in the Urban South*.

34. The classic source on the changing legal status of blacks during the Civil War is Louis Gerties, *From Contraband to Freedmen: Federal Policy towards Southern Blacks, 1861–1865* (Westport, Conn.: Greenwood Press, 1973).

35. Berkeley, " 'Like a Plague of Locusts,' " p. 145.

36. Ibid., p. 146.

37. Robert Bremner, *The Public Good: Philanthropy and Welfare in the Civil War Era* (New York: Alfred A. Knopf, 1980).

38. Order 4, February 7, 1864, from General Lorenzo Thomas by order of the secretary of war, Mississippi Valley Collection, Memphis State University.

39. General Davis Tillson to Brevet Brigadier General Morgen, Headquarters, District of West Tennessee, August 2, 1865; General Tillson to Captain Clark, September 11, 1865, Record Group 105, National Archives.

40. Superintendent of Refugees, Freedmen and Abandoned Lands to Lieutenant Potter, September 18, 1865, ibid.

41. Bremner, *Public Good*, p. 125; Lois E. Horton and James Oliver Horton, "Race, Occupation, and Literacy in Reconstruction Washington, D.C.," in Burton and McMath, eds., *Toward a New South?*, pp. 135–51.

42. Monthly Reports of the Refugees and Freedmen's Homes, Memphis, Tennessee, May–December 1865, Record Group 105, National Archives.

43. Foster, "Limitations of Federal Health Care for Freedmen," p. 355.

44. Berkeley, " 'Like a Plague of Locusts,' " pp. 171–72, *Memphis Post*, April 20, 1866; see the Proceedings of a Meeting by the Trustees of the Freedmen's Sanitary Commission, Memphis, December 4, 1867, Record Group 105, National Archives.

45. Thomas Holt, *Black over White: Negro Political Leadership in South Carolina during Reconstruction* (Urbana: University of Illinois Press, 1977); Robinson, "Plans Dat Comed from God," pp. 71–102; Berkeley, " 'Like a Plague of Locusts,' " pp. 170–77.

46. The information on Joseph Clouston and Reverend Page Tyler is drawn from the deposit ledgers of the Freedmen's Savings and Trust Company, Memphis Branch; The U.S. Bureau of the Census, Manuscript schedules, free population, 1860, and the U.S. Bureau of the Census, Manuscript schedules, Shelby County, Tennessee, 1870.

47. Rabinowitz, "From Exclusion to Segregation."

48. Edward Meeker, "Mortality Trends of Southern Blacks, 1850–1910: Some Preliminary Findings," *Explorations in Economic History* 12 (January 1976): 13–42; Anne S. Lee and Everett S. Lee, "The Health of Slaves and the Health of Freedmen: A Savannah Study," *Phylon* 38 (June 1977): 170–80; Foster, "Limitations of Federal Health Care for Freedmen," pp. 370–72.

49. Memphis Charity Hospital Records, Memphis City Minute Book Abstracts, Memphis and Shelby County Archives, Memphis, Tennessee.

50. Memphis City Charity Hospital Admittance Records, March 1868–December 1871, ibid.
Why the indigent, sick Irish received a disproportionate share of public assistance owes more to the peculiarities of urban politics in postwar Memphis than to native-born white tolerance for the foreign-born. The Civil War had created a vacuum in the ranks of the city's political leaders. After 1861 control over municipal affairs shifted away from the domination of native-born white southern elites to a coalition of foreign- and northern-born middle-class shopkeepers whose roots also lay in prewar Memphis. Between 1861 and 1869 the small group of antebellum prosperous Irish residents made up almost one-quarter of the city's political leadership. Obviously, it was well within their authority and power to make public facilities available to their larger working-class constituency. Undoubtedly, long-standing ethnic and racial tensions added to the disinclination of the municipal leadership to care for indigent blacks. See Berkeley, " 'Like a Plague of Locusts,' " pp. 298–373.

51. Carl Osthaus's study of several of the Freedman's Bank branches led him to conclude that the "bulk of the depositers were unskilled laborers, servants of one kind or another or farm workers" (*Freedmen, Philanthropy, and Fraud*, pp. 81, 92). Robinson's study confirms that working-class former slaves used the Freedman's Bank but that the more prosperous blacks who were free before 1860 shunned its services ("Plans Dat Comed from God," pp. 71–102).

52. My calculations differ slightly from Robinson's.

53. Files of the Freedman's Savings and Trust Company, Memphis Branch; see esp. accounts 517, 2879, and 3258.

54. For an analysis of slave religion see Carter G. Woodson, *History of the Negro Church* (Washington, D.C.: Associated Publishers, 1921); Thomas O. Fuller, *History of the Negro Baptists of Tennessee* (Memphis: Haskins Print, 1935); Albert J. Raboteau, *Slave Religion: The "Invisible Institution" in the Antebellum South* (New York: Oxford University Press, 1979); and Eugene Genovese, *Roll, Jordan, Roll: The World the Slaves Made* (New York: Pantheon, 1974), pp. 232–34, 255–79. For the black family see Jones, " 'My Mother Was Much of a Woman,' " and Herbert Gutman, *The Black Family in Slavery and Freedom, 1750–1925* (New York: Pantheon, 1976).

55. Jacqueline Jones argues that in freedom the traditional sexual division of labor reinforced black patriarchy and denied black women a position of power within their community. She focuses on the role of the black church in reinforc-

ing the subservience of black women. I think that this interpretation needs to be reexamined, especially in light of the evidence presented in this essay. Benevolent societies associated with the churches enabled black women to form an independent power base within their communities. Willie Coleman makes this point in "Keeping the Faith," p. 78. For an analysis of the relationship between the patriarchial church and the emergence of "domestic feminism," see Carrol Smith-Rosenberg, "Beauty, the Beast, and the Militant Woman: A Case Study in Sex Roles and Social Stress in Jacksonian American," *American Quarterly* 23 (1971): 562–84, and Barbara T. Berg, *The Remembered Gate: Origins of American Feminism, the Woman and the City, 1800–1860* (New York: Oxford University Press, 1978).

56. The signature books of the Freedman's Savings and Trust Company contained information on the account holders, often including age, color, occupation, birthplace, master's name, current residence, marital status, number, names, and ages of children, parents' names, and siblings' names.

57. See Walter S. Glazer, "Participation and Power: Voluntary Associations and Functional Organizations of Cincinnati in 1840," *Historical Methods Newsletter* 5 (September 1972): 151–68, as a model for analyzing leadership patterns.

58. For an in-depth analysis of the working-class origins of the black population in Memphis see Berkeley, " 'Like a Plague of Locusts,' " pp. 192–94, and Robinson, "Plans Dat Comed from God."

59. For an analysis of the economic woes of Memphis during the 1870s, see Berkeley, " 'Like a Plague of Locusts,' " pp. 300–302, 331–34, 336–38.

60. Historians of epidemiology argue that blacks tended to be immune to the ravages of yellow fever because they developed a genetic resistance to the disease (yellow fever is a viral disease native to Africa). Whites, however, had no advantage and were at the mercy of the disease. Mortality statistics support this hypothesis, but statistics on the percent of the population that came down with the disease present a different picture. According to the Board of Health records for the state of Tennessee, 80 percent of the black population and 98 percent of the white population contracted yellow fever in Memphis during the 1878 epidemic. During the 1879 epidemic, of the cases reported to the local Board of Health, 43.4 percent occurred in the black population and 56.6 percent in the white population. Because the city was abandoned during the epidemic to the poor, the majority of whom were black, it is possible to argue that the black community suffered more from the effects of the disease than did the white community. At the onset of the 1879 yellow fever season, for example, the city's population was reduced from 38,400 to 13,600. Two-thirds of those who remained were black (according to the 1878 city census, blacks accounted for 32.6 percent of the total urban population). For more information see *The First Report of the State Board of Health of the State of Tennessee, April 1877– October 1880* (Nashville: Tavel and Howell, 1880), pp. 106, 399–402; G. B. Thornton, "Yellow Fever Epidemic in Memphis, 1879," *Public Health Reports*

and Papers in the American Public Health Association 5 (1879): 111–20; and
G. B. Thornton, "Death Rate in Memphis," *Mississippi Valley Medical Monthly,*
July 1881, pp. 1–7. In the latter source, Thornton reported that the annual
death rate for blacks was 44.8 percent per 1,000 of the total population and
that the comparable figure for whites was 24.4 percent.

61. In 1930 the NACW narrowed the scope of its activities and called for
"uniformity of thought and action." Thereafter each state had to sponsor two
departments (1) Mother, Home, and Child and (2) Negro Women in Industry.
See Davis, *Lifting as They Climb,* pp. 88–90.

62. A survey of the first delegates to the 1896 convention found a surprising
number of church groups present. See Davis, *Lifting as They Climb,* pp. 11–13,
91–92.

63. Ibid, pp. 21, 41–42, and Coleman, "Keeping the Faith," pp. 78–79.

The Effects of the Civil War and Reconstruction on the Coming of Age of Southern Males, Edgefield County, South Carolina

Orville Vernon Burton

This essay suggests that the Civil War and Reconstruction had a differential impact upon black and white youth and their emergence as leaders in the postwar period.[1]

Edgefield County, South Carolina, was noted for its leadership role in both the antebellum and postbellum periods and thus provides a good area for a case study.[2] As South Carolina led the South, first in nullification, then in proslavery and prosouthern arguments, and finally in secession, so Edgefield led South Carolina. Edgefield was the home of two Civil War governors, Francis W. Pickens and Milledge Luke Bonham.[3] Former Confederate generals Matthew Calbraith Butler and Martin Witherspoon Gary directed the Edgefield Plan to redeem the state by reasserting the conservative white elite in 1876.[4] Edgefield was also the home of Benjamin Ryan Tillman, who spearheaded the farmer protest of the 1890s.[5] Edgefield District has claimed one of South Carolina's two U.S. senators from the election of George McDuffie in 1842 until James Henry Hammond's withdrawal as the Civil War approached, and during Redemption and withdrawal of federal troops from the state, with Matthew Calbraith Butler, and later with Ben Tillman, who served into the twentieth century, and today with J. Strom Thurmond.[6]

But this sequence of leadership omits the role of black youths and their interaction with their white counterparts, their adjustment to freedom, and the way the absence of slavery's constraints affected their actions and in turn the behavior of young whites. These questions will be considered within the context of postbellum South Carolina, and, in particular, Edgefield County. Examining how these two groups responded to unique conditions and investigating the interactions between them reveal something of the lives of youth in the postbellum South and how the rivalry between young whites and blacks contributed to the fierce competition for political and economic power in Reconstruction Edgefield.[7]

Overwhelming historical evidence shows that the black community adjusted remarkably well to the shock of emancipation in the immediate post–Civil War era. In every southern state, former slaves assumed a variety of social and political roles.

There are many examples of very young Edgefield former slaves asserting themselves in the postwar era. During the time when youth are expected to be undergoing a long period of indecision and self-examination, approximately ages fifteen to twenty-five, these Afro-Americans were teaching, making money, and gaining political power. The stability of the black community after the Civil War helps explain this precociousness. During slavery, values of mutuality and self-help in the Afro-American community served to soften some of the most oppressive aspects of the peculiar institution. The Civil War and emancipation disrupted this community, but it emerged eager to affirm its new rights. Common problems, relative homogeneity, strong kinship ties, developing economic and occupational possibilities, and an open political leadership during Reconstruction fostered a sense of belonging among blacks, promoting that all-important stability. During and after slavery, young blacks internalized a powerful work ethic, as well as a dedication to family members, which contributed to the solidarity of the black community in Edgefield. This stability is reflected in the high persistence rate among blacks. Between 1870 and 1880, slightly more black household heads persisted in Edgefield than did white household heads (45 to 43 percent). Younger married male and female Afro-Americans who died in 1879 had generally lived in Edgefield longer than their counterpart white cohorts.[8]

Other demographic comparisons of blacks and whites in Edgefield point to the earlier independence of young blacks. White children were more likely than black children to continue living with parents after they reached the age of eighteen, and the racial difference increased as the age of the household head increased. Young black males set up households while working as farm laborers and tenants, and young black women found employment as domestics. Young white males, however, remained in their parents' homes, working on the family farms until they inherited or bought land, and young white women lived with their parents until marriage. Black men who married for the first time in the census year of 1870 were an average of two years younger than whites (blacks, aged twenty-three; whites, aged twenty-five). Black brides at age nineteen averaged a year younger than whites (twenty) at first marriage.

Another important source of strength for young black leaders was their commitment to the church. This institution's emphasis on such traditional kinship structures as patriarchy and the continuing importance of the father figure in church services particularly inspired young black males to apply religious ethics to political problems. The churches helped many young black leaders see that their authority was not dependent upon whites but derived directly from the black religious community and the autonomy of their own families. Thus church and family were regarded both as sources of and spurs to black freedom and dignity.

In 1867 the founders of the Macedonia Black Church, which withdrew from the white-dominated Edgefield Village Baptist Church, included older leaders Peter Johnson and George Simkins, but also conspicuous were young schoolteachers Robert A. Green and Lawrence Cain, Cain's younger brother Henry, Paris Simkins, and his younger half-brother Andrew Simkins. These religious leaders, who were under twenty-five, became important elected officeholders and political leaders in Edgefield.[9]

Black religious organizations also enhanced black leadership by encouraging education. Churches often initiated efforts to establish schools. Black Baptists in Edgefield believed that "illiterate men are injurious in the pulpit." Just two decades after emancipation the local Baptists insisted that ministers pass examinations on "Orthography, Writing, English Grammar, Arithemetic, Geography, and the Scriptures" before being licensed to preach.[10]

As exemplified in the twentieth century by Edgefieldian Benjamin E. Mays, a close relationship existed between the ministry and teaching. Young black men often taught school in rural areas such as Edgefield to earn money to attend college and seminary. Some young black Edgefield teachers were the sons of preachers. The linkage of churches and schools becomes clear in the Freedmen's Bureau papers. Even after the establishment of a public school system, many black schools were still connected with churches; sometimes the church building was the school, and sometimes the church owned the school building. The manuscript teachers' reports for Edgefield for 1869 and 1870 reveal that many black churches and congregations supported the public school system.[11]

White churches and schools did not have close ties. According to the teachers' reports for Edgefield, no public white school was church-related. In the Graniteville and Langley mills, school buildings were provided by the company. White schools enjoyed the support of individual benefactors, whereas black schools represented a community effort, often organized through the churches.

Ample evidence exists, particularly in the educational and political arenas, to demonstrate that rapid gains in these areas were more the result of the self-sustained activity of former slaves than of assistance from the Freedmen's Bureau or northern aid societies. Throughout northwestern South Carolina, blacks, individually and collectively, contributed their money and labor to build new schools, hire black teachers, and organize responsible supervisory committees. Historian of education James D. Anderson persuasively argues that "the ex-slaves were the central force in the South's postwar movement for universal education."[12] As social historian Herbert Gutman suggests, this activity was not a bizarre manifestation of the elation associated with emancipation; it was deeply rooted in communal values established decades earlier by ancestors of freedmen.[13]

One of the reasons for the remarkable initiative of the black community in creating a free school system for its people was the enthusiasm of its youth for education. Author Harriet Beecher Stowe said of these youth: "They rushed not to the grog-shop, but to the schoolroom—they cried for the spelling book as bread, and pleaded for teachers as a necessity of life."[14] John Alvord, who became the superintendent of schools for the Freedmen's Bureau, marveled, "Throughout the entire South an effort is being made by the colored people to educate themselves. In the absence of other teaching, they are determined to be self-taught; and everywhere some elementary text-book, or the fragment of one, may be found in the hands of negroes."[15]

In Reconstruction Edgefield, blacks established public and church schools to educate their young. By 1871 freedmen had established ten Baptist churches within the Edgefield Baptist Association's boundaries and seventeen Sunday schools, all but one managed by blacks.[16] As Ronald Butchart has shown and as I have noted elsewhere, these Sunday or Sabbath schools were precursors of free schools, providing basic instruction in reading and writing.[17] Thus if we count these Sunday schools, former slaves in Edgefield, like freedmen in other regions of the South, initiated their own school system. Although the literacy rate among blacks was considerably lower than among whites in Edgefield even after Reconstruction, the rate of increase among blacks during the ten years after the Civil War, especially those younger than thirty, was remarkable.[18]

The assertiveness of young freedmen in seeking an education was only in part slavery's legacy. It was also an attempt to declare their freedom, to distance themselves from bondage. In endeavoring to shake off the shackles of oppression, the former slaves viewed a liberal education as an affirmation of their freedom. They embraced it with a passion and reverence comparable only to the love they held for their families and religion. Black youth, particularly, recognized the practical importance of education and literacy in enabling them to read labor contracts and ballots. And not surprisingly, in both economic and political affairs, young blacks in Edgefield were consistently effective during Reconstruction in achieving their desired ends.

Young Lawrence Cain provides a good example. Cain, considered the "pet" of an Edgefield white, served in the Union army. At the age of twenty-two, just a year after the war's end, Cain invited the white community to observe the progress of the young black scholars he had taught in the local school he had established. This activity did not endear him to his former master. Later, the editors of the *Edgefield Advertiser* could find no words adequate to defame him when he began to organize local blacks politically and ran successfully in several elections. In 1868, Cain and several other young blacks were elected to the state legislature. By 1870, in addition to being one of the black community's leading political figures, Cain had become a landowner and had declared personal assets in the local tax records. While serving as state senator from Edgefield he received his law degree. As a colonel, he also commanded the black militia in Edgefield.[19]

Paris Simkins, eleven years old at the start of the Civil War, was the son of a slave and his mother's owner, the white editor of the *Edgefield Advertiser,* Arthur Simkins. After Paris's birth, his mother, Charlotte, married another slave, George Simkins, who was a leader among the slave members of the Edgefield Baptist Church. While a child under slavery, Paris had learned the rudiments of education from a slave carriage driver who taught him in secret after midnight. He was taken to the battlefront as a barber with Edgefield's Confederate troops and after the war opened a barber shop in Edgefield. The white Baptist minister Luther Rice Gwaltney aided young Simkins in furthering his education. After the war, Paris and his younger half-brother Andrew, who was later the first black superintendent of education in Edgefield, became political activists. Paris joined Lawrence Cain as one of the two major Republican political leaders in Edgefield. While serving in the South Carolina House of Representatives, Paris Simkins graduated with a law degree from the University of South Carolina on December 12, 1876. Simkins was second in command, a lieutenant colonel, in the black militia. With an infant in his arms, he single-handedly faced down a band of white Ku Klux Klansmen by preaching a sermon to the intimidators and shaming them into withdrawing without harming him.[20]

Cain and Simkins were not the only blacks to enjoy youthful success in Edgefield. From the town of Hamburg, in the southwestern part of the district, Samuel J. Lee and John Gardener were elected to the state legislature in 1868. Respectively twenty-three and twenty-five years old when elected, Lee and Gardener were known for their keen minds and their courage. Samuel J. Lee had been born a slave in 1844 on Samuel McGowan's plantation, just across the county line in Abbeville District. In 1870 Lee listed his occupation as "commissioner of county" and had accumulated a real and personal estate valued at almost a thousand dollars. Before long he would own a lot in town and a farm of more than a hundred acres. Lee also had a reputation for being a skillful debater and public speaker and for courage in standing up to whites. These qualities must have contributed to his success, for in 1872 he was chosen as Speaker of the South Carolina House of Representatives and after Reconstruction built a sizable law practice in Charleston.[21] Like Lawrence Cain, John Gardener was a schoolteacher. He, too, was literate and proud of his accomplishments as a teacher of Edgefield's black children. Service in the Union army during the war provided him with enough money to purchase land. By the time he was twenty-five he had a personal fortune valued at about fifteen hundred dollars. Like Lee, he was known as a black man who would not tolerate abuse from whites. When a white man rebuked some of Gardener's students for frightening his team of horses, Gardener defended them. The ensuing argument became heated, and the white man attacked the unarmed Gardener, severing his jugular vein. Gardener survived but was unable to run for reelection. He was the only black representative elected in 1868 who did not return to office in the 1870 election, but he remained active in local politics and became the intendant of Hamburg.[22] The section of Edgefield District where Hamburg was located became part of the new county of Aiken in 1871, thus opening more offices for young Edgefield former slaves. Vigorous political campaigns led by youthful freedmen characterized Reconstruction in the county from 1872 through 1876.[23]

With strong family and community support, a few young blacks emerged from slavery with a rudimentary education and confidence in their ability to usher in a new era for former slaves.[24] Most of these men,

Edgefield's black political leaders, were under twenty-five when they began their political careers.

To put into perspective some of the gains made by blacks in Edgefield during Reconstruction, more comparisons between the black and white communities are needed. After the Civil War, blacks outnumbered whites 25,417 to 17,040, and a large number of blacks attended schools during Reconstruction, though a lower percentage than whites. Of the adult males, 80 percent of the whites and 95 percent of the blacks engaged in agriculture. In 1870, only 3 percent of Edgefield's blacks owned land, compared to 65 percent of white household heads. If we focus only on persons younger than thirty, these percentages shift dramatically. Both absolutely and relatively, there were more young black household heads than young white household heads. Also, young blacks were surprisingly wealthy relative to their white counterparts (see Table 1).

In general, the economic life cycles of young blacks and whites show that economically, socially, and politically young blacks dominated their race whereas for whites power was spread among age groups or concentrated among older men. This situation had not always been true among whites. In the antebellum period, young men, often in their early twenties, were the political leaders of the South. In South Carolina in particular, many nullifiers were in their twenties. Among the firebrands most fiercely promoting the Confederate cause from Edgefield were Martin Witherspoon Gary and Matthew Calbraith Butler. Yet during Reconstruction, until the leading prewar patricians and an emerging generation of planters joined together to reassert their economic and political dominance, the voices of very few youthful white leaders were heard.

David Donald made a similar point in his essay "A Generation of Defeat." He suggested that white men between the ages of seventeen and thirty during the Civil War were traumatized by the defeat of the Confederacy and the emancipation of slaves.[25] This group apparently suffered a crisis of confidence that contributed to the South's slowness to recover economically from the war. But in Edgefield it seems that an even more circumscribed group than the seventeen-to-thirty-year-olds experienced great difficulty in adjusting to the radically different postwar conditions. Those prewar Edgefield leaders, many in their late twenties and early thirties during Reconstruction, did not abdicate their responsibilities. Martin Witherspoon Gary, Matthew Calbraith Butler, George Tillman, and others remained active in Edgefield's economic and political affairs and were among those who spearheaded the drive for Redemption in the late 1870s and led the Red Shirt Campaign in 1876.

Another group, those in their teens to very early twenties, who before

Table 1. Wealth of Black and White Males under Thirty Years of Age (percentages)

Year	1850	1860	1870	1880
Whites				
Household heads	21.2	21.6	23.1	25.4
Real estate owned	10.1	9.1	12.8	NA*
Total white wealth (real and personal estate)	NA	9.9	14.1	NA
Household heads who own real estate	43.3	39.8	34.8	NA
Household heads thirty years of age and older who own real estate	63.9	68.8	60.3	NA
Blacks				
Household heads	NA	NA	30.5	34.7
Real estate owned	NA	NA	21.8	NA
Total black wealth (real and personal estate)	NA	NA	18.5	NA
Household heads who own real estate	NA	NA	1.0	NA
Household heads thirty years of age and older who own real estate	NA	NA	1.9	NA

*NA: not available from census returns that year.
Source: Edgefield County data base.

the war were too young to assume political duties, were stunted by the Civil War and Reconstruction. This group had experienced the unsettling life on the home front during the Civil War. As the war dragged on, these youth witnessed avarice, land speculation, loss of individual autonomy, desertion from the army, and a secularization of religion.[26] To the twin traumas described by Donald can be added military occupation, black assertiveness and political dominance, and economic setbacks, including the great depression of 1873. This list of demoralizing developments could be lengthened, and it substantiates an argument, in an Elkins-like analogy to "dumping the bucket of culture," that at the very least those youngsters who did not go to battle suffered a devastating experience during the Civil War and Reconstruction.[27]

If anyone underwent a crisis of confidence it was the adolescents, who as a result of the Civil War fell just short of enjoying the fruits of leadership. Their future was before them, with thoughts of marvelous heroics dancing in their heads, but the abrupt and painful reversals they experienced either delayed their entries into professional and political life or doomed them forever to forbear from these activities.

Although candidates for political office in antebellum South Carolina were required to own a considerable amount of property,[28] many men under thirty could easily meet these qualifications. Most of Edgefield's antebellum leaders were young scions of wealthy families who had established themselves in the professions while their northern counterparts were still pondering the question of their future. In 1850, 305 people under the age of thirty owned nearly a tenth of the real estate owned by whites, and that age group constituted more than a fifth of all household heads in Edgefield. Nearly half of these household heads owned real estate compared to about two-thirds of older household heads (see Table 11.1). The statistics for 1860 show similar trends. In addition, in the latter decade young whites accounted for 17.4 percent of all slaveowners; these 273 persons owned 2,114 slaves. Thus as masters at least, these young whites were accustomed to command and control.

The data from the years immediately after the Civil War tell a remarkably similar story. Although black youth owned a much larger percentage of total black wealth than did white youth of the total white wealth, the proportion held by white youth increased slightly in the postbellum period. It is surprising that, although they had become proportionately more wealthy, younger whites were unlikely to run for public office during Reconstruction and even for some years after Redemption. In contrast, during Reconstruction and until the great mass exodus of blacks from Edgefield in 1881–82, many of the Afro-American leaders were young.[29]

One would expect that the removal of the wealth qualification would encourage more young white men to run for office. Instead, during Reconstruction and the years following, rarely did several white candidates vie for the same office. Certainly the age requirements, twenty-five years for a state senator and twenty-one for a state representative, of the 1868 constitutional convention did not deter them.[30] Before the Civil War, the constitution of 1790 had required that legislators be white and twenty-one for the House and thirty for the Senate.[31] Hence the age requirement for senators had been lowered.

In 1860, when he was elected to the state legislature, Matthew Calbraith Butler was only twenty-four years old. Martin Witherspoon Gary lost his first bid for the legislature in 1858, when he was twenty-six, but he was elected in 1860. Francis W. Pickens was elected in 1832 at age twenty-five.[32] Preston Brooks was twenty-five when elected to the legislature in 1844.[33] All four were successful lawyers and had held high rank in the state militia; Pickens, Brooks, and Butler were successful planters as well before they ran for office. The fathers and close relatives of all four also had held elected public offices such as state legislator, governor, and congressman. From 1865 until Pitchfork Ben Tillman's revolution in the 1890s, except for Butler, who was elected again in 1865, no white candidate ran for the state legislature again who was under thirty years of age. Invariably whites were in their forties or older when they ran for the state legislature (George Tillman, who had been a state legislator before the war, was reelected when thirty-eight in 1865 along with M. C. Butler, another Civil War veteran, in his thirties when reelected in 1876).

Not only does this pattern contrast sharply with that of the antebellum period, but during Reconstruction former slaves—twenty-three-year-old Samuel Lee, twenty-five-year-old John Gardener, twenty-three-year-old Paris Simkins, and twenty-nine-year-old John Green—won election to the state legislature from Edgefield. Black carpetbagger Robert Brown Elliott was twenty-nine when he represented Edgefield in the U.S. Congress. Scores of younger blacks filled various county and municipal leadership roles. The militia and the state guards, previously training grounds for young whites with leadership ambitions, were now composed mostly of young blacks. And preliminary investigation of illegal and clandestine paramilitary organizations suggests that whites too young to fight in the Civil War did not participate in them but that these groups, like the one commanded by Matthew Calbraith Butler, which massacred six blacks at Hamburg in early July 1876, were composed of Civil War veterans.[34]

Not only were there no younger candidates for the legislature until Tillman's revolution and generally no more candidates than there were positions, but the voter turnout for the elections was much lower than in the antebellum years. Apparently, not just the younger elite but most whites withdrew from the political process in the postbellum period.[35]

The declining number of young professionals, lawyers, doctors, and preachers in Edgefield from 1850 to 1880 follows the same trend as that for candidates for public office. As Table 2 illustrates, the age distributions rose sharply in the 1870s and only began to move toward the younger ages in 1880. In 1870 no preachers or lawyers were under thirty years of age, whereas in 1850 nine of twenty-six attorneys were under thirty years of age. (Census ages tended to be heaped on fives and tens; if thirty and under is considered the cutoff point, more than half, fifteen, were in that category.) Four of thirty-one preachers and twenty-six of sixty-seven doctors were under thirty in 1850 (thirty-one of sixty-seven of those thirty and under); in 1870 only three out of forty-three were.

The practice of law during this period is especially interesting. U.S. senator and South Carolina statesman William C. Preston (with whom

Table 2. White Youth in the Professions, 1850–1880

Occupation	Year	Number	Age Range	Percent under 30	Median Age
Lawyer	1850	26	20–50	34.6	30.2
	1860	27	22–46	51.9	28.3
	1870	11	31–59	0	42.0
	1880	20	23–63	40	35.5
Doctor	1850	67	19–60	38.8	31.7
	1860	70	22–60	32.9	34.2
	1870	43	26–63	7.0	42.8
	1880	33	25–67	12.1	46.7
Preacher	1850	31	26–82	12.9	48.7
	1860	26	21–66	23.0	38.5
	1870	12	30–73	0	48.5
	1880	22	25–90	22.7	34.5

Source: Edgefield County data base.

James Henry Hammond read law) explained that "the object of a Southern man's life is politics and subsidiary to this end we all practice law."[36] Nineteen-year-old Francis W. Pickens told his fellow college students: "The great talents of the nation are drawn into politics. There is nothing that has so great a charm for ambition as power in government." Antebellum Edgefield was noted for its able attorneys. In his 1859 history of the South Carolina bar, John Belton O'Neall wrote that "from 1820 to 1832 no interior Bar of South Carolina presented abler counsellors than there appeared often in the Edgefield Courts." Leadership was almost synonymous with lawyers in antebellum South Carolina. In the same volume, O'Neall celebrated antebellum leaders of Edgefield as a "brilliant galaxy."[37] In 1860, no attorney in Edgefield was older than forty-six; more than half were under thirty.

Another useful index of the development of youth might be found by determining the number of new practitioners in a given field from one census year to the next. A consistent maturation process across years would be indicated by roughly equal rates of turnover. As a result of Civil War casualties, one would expect the turnover rate to increase from 1860 to 1870. Exactly the opposite occurred, providing evidence of the disruption in the development process of postbellum white youth. In 1860, 29 percent of the Edgefield lawyers had also practiced in 1850. In 1870, 55 percent of the attorneys had practiced law in 1860. Figures for 1870 to 1880 show a movement back to the prewar pattern; a fifth of the attorneys in 1880 had practiced in 1870, and 38 percent of the new lawyers in 1880 were under thirty years of age. Thus Redemption appears to represent both a reassertion of white power and a reemergence of white youth.

Since the absolute numbers became smaller in 1870, especially for lawyers, one has to consider that perhaps the men who would have become lawyers were killed in the Civil War. Such was not the case. The proportion of the population from 1850 to 1880 in the age cohorts fifteen to nineteen and twenty to twenty-nine, the proportions for black and white, male and female for Edgefield and for South Carolina are basically the same (within a percentage difference varying from 27 to 29 percent). In addition, except for 1850 to 1860, the real population of whites grew in every census enumeration, even though a large part of the population was taken away in the southern part of the district with the formation of Aiken County in 1871.[38]

Since both absolutely and proportionately postbellum whites under thirty headed a greater number of Edgefield households than in the antebellum decades, we must consider other possibilities. Ten years is a long time in the lives of people, even telescoping their lives into the ten-year periods marked by the census. The revolution that occurred during Reconstruction in Edgefield did not begin until 1870. It was in 1872 that Edgefield's Afro-Americans became the dominant political force within the Republican party and demanded their political plums. In 1876 the Reconstruction revolution was violently turned around. By the time of the next census enumeration many of the advances made by Afro-Americans in the nonagricultural occupations were no longer visible. During Reconstruction, however, at least four blacks in Edgefield obtained law degrees, and at least three of the four had been slaves until the end of the war.[39] Could it be that the young black leadership not only displaced white youths in the political arena but were beginning to displace them in the professions that traditionally in South Carolina were the means to political power and office?

Traditional institutions of elite training—the state militia and the University of South Carolina—were also disrupted. Classical education, designed to prepare students to command in any situation, had dominated antebellum South Carolina College. After the Civil War, when the white elite lost control, the school turned to more modern, specialized education, with much more emphasis on agriculture and technical subjects.[40]

A survey of postbellum undergraduate enrollment at the University of South Carolina shows that the war had taken its toll of the state's white youth. When the university reopened in 1866, most students were eighteen or nineteen, with one or two years of military service behind them. Yet of those who attended in 1861–62, the last year before the university closed, only six returned in 1866. Few veterans of three or four years continued their education after the war. Even those who attended the university seemed to have little direction or enthusiasm. Although poverty and poor preparation may have been part of the explanation, the university's historian, Daniel Hollis, has suggested that apathy was more likely the problem. From 1866 to 1870, although the number of registrants was fairly large, only thirteen A.B. degrees were awarded. Undergraduates often took courses aimlessly without attempting to meet degree requirements. One student "graduated" from five different colleges and had more than enough courses to earn a degree, but, because he lacked many of the required courses, could not receive an A.B. Many students sought practical training in mathematics and engineering but were disappointed in South Carolina's scant offerings in these fields.[41]

The schools of law and medicine fared no better. When the law school opened in 1866 it enrolled four students. The medical school, which also opened in 1866, graduated four doctors of medicine in 1868 and three more in 1869. The training given to these future lawyers and doctors was inadequate at best. Lack of funds made it difficult to attract good instructors, and sparse student enrollment indicated a general lack of interest in professional education.[42]

As whites in the state tried to withdraw from politics by boycotting the election of delegates to the 1868 Constitutional Convention, young white South Carolinians withdrew from South Carolina College when blacks entered in 1873. With the removal of federal troops after the inauguration of Rutherford B. Hayes in 1877, the Republican institution that had enabled former Edgefield slaves to obtain law degrees closed. It did not open until three years later, and then as a college primarily for farmers and mechanics.[43] Thus the antebellum institution that had served to bring up-country and low-country youths together and had enabled both privileged youth such as Louis Wigfall and Maximilian Laborde and those less fortunate such as George McDuffie and James Henry Hammond to prove their intellectual skills and make important connections with others was unavailable for postbellum whites until after 1880.[44]

A few examples contrasting Edgefield youth before and after the war help illustrate some of the theses of this essay. Comparison of the active political life of James Henry Hammond during the years of South Carolina's greatest political strength before the Civil War and the lackluster lives of his sons after the war is further evidence of the effects of the Confederate defeat on South Carolina's youth. James Henry Hammond at eighteen earned an A.B. degree from South Carolina College and at twenty-one was successfully practicing law in Columbia. He edited a major nullification newspaper and was a militia officer at an early age. At twenty-seven, just two years over the age of eligibility, he was elected to the United States Congress. Like many of his fellow southerners in the antebellum period, Hammond came of age when he was already a leading politician in his state.

For his sons it was different. Paul, the youngest, failed as a planter and died a confessed morphine addict at the age of forty-nine. Spann, the second oldest surviving son, was fairly successful financially and lived quietly as a lawyer and town magistrate. Despite political ambitions before the war, Spann never again was active in public life. Harry, the eldest, tried to make some public contributions but was frustrated at every turn. He expected to be confirmed as superintendent of the 1880 U.S. Census, but President Rutherford B. Hayes withdrew his name at the last moment. In 1883, the South Carolina Department of Agriculture published a 726-page handbook, which included the names of the governor and the commissioner of agriculture but not its editor and major author—Harry Hammond. Although it eventually became known as the "Hammond Handbook," these failures and frustrations were symbolic of the difficulties borne by the younger Hammonds. Furthermore, even if Harry had been successful in his few political endeavors, his contributions still would have paled in comparison to those of his father.[45]

Father-son comparisons may not be the best. Examples are Edgefield's antebellum fire-eater, Louis T. Wigfall, and its favorite "New South" son, Daniel Augustus Tompkins. Having manipulated the editors of the *Edgefield Advertiser* so that he controlled editorial policy during the 1840 gubernatorial campaign, the youthful Wigfall gloated late one night as he wrote, "You have *my full consent* to divulge my name at *any time* it *may suit your purposes!* I am twenty one years of age & have a right to support who I please & I hope I shall always have the *heart* to serve my *friends* when ever it is in my power—or rather, to attempt it, for the *actual service* is more dependant upon the *head* than the *heart*." Tompkins, born in 1851, was too young for service in the Civil War. He entered South Carolina College in 1867 and left in 1869. During Reconstruction he attended the Rensselaer Polytechnical Institute, where he fretted that he did not display the dignity that northerners did in the company of the other students and at social occasions. He discovered that among northern people of "refinement," the "emotional parts of one's nature is not expected to be shown." Tompkins blamed his shortcomings in society on his Edgefield upbringing, where the country people did not restrain themselves. Instead of participating in the Red Shirt Campaign of 1876, Tompkins wrote about it as a correspondent for a northern newspaper.

He moved around frequently after leaving Rensselaer, trying to get established in the steel business in the North and then in the South, showing a certain amount of indecision.[46]

Another interesting contrast is between George Tillman and his younger brother Ben. George Tillman was born in 1826 and by the time he was twenty-two had established a profitable law firm in Edgefield village. At twenty-eight he entered the state legislature and was elected senator in 1865 over the Civil War general R. G. M. Dunovant. He was a leader of the Redemption movement and challenged the most formidable black vote-getter, Civil War hero Robert Smalls, in the campaign of 1876 for Congress. George won in 1878 through a campaign of intimidation and fraud; he served seven terms in the U.S. Congress.[47]

In contrast to George, Ben Tillman was slow in establishing his public career. He was forty-three years old before he ran for public office, but when elected governor in 1890, Ben made up for lost time. Born in 1847, he was thirteen when the Civil War began and eighteen in 1865. Ben had not enlisted in Confederate service but stayed in school and helped his mother until he was seventeen. A few days before he was to enlist he contracted an eye disease, which ultimately cost him one eye. His biographer reports that Ben basically tended to his own affairs in Edgefield. He became a successful farmer during those trying times. He participated in Redemption but as an underling, not a leader. He was thirty-five before election to the captaincy of the Edgefield Hussars, a local militia group. He participated in the local Democratic party organization, but it was through his agricultural organization that he rose to political prominence. And it is important that the route he took differed from that of the antebellum politician.[48]

John Gary Evans was born during the Civil War. He was reared in his Uncle Martin Witherspoon Gary's home in Edgefield. He was too young to comprehend the defeat of the Confederacy. The victory of Redemption and his coming of age reflect a return to the antebellum pattern. Representing the generation of whites once removed from the disillusionment of the Civil War and the postbellum years, he established himself at an early age. He had a successful law practice by the time he was twenty-three years old. Before he was twenty-seven, Evans had served as director of three railroads, founded the Aiken Mining and Porcelain Company, and directed the Bank of Aiken. In 1894, this young Tillmanite was elected governor of South Carolina when only thirty.[49]

The Civil War and Reconstruction wrought much change in the coming of age of black and white youth in Edgefield. These events had a measurable social impact in the way they disrupted the continuity of the

emergence of South Carolina leaders. Accompanying the extensive physical and economic damage of the Civil War was the emotional dislocation
that affected black and white youths.

Notes

The author would like to express his appreciation to Steven Preskill, Joseph
Fratesi, Frederic C. Jaher, Barbara Kerwin, and Georgeanne Burton for their
help with this article.

1. For "coming of age" see Joseph F. Kett, *Rites of Passage: Adolescence in
America, 1790 to Present* (New York: Basic Books, 1977), esp. p. 35.

2. On Edgefield's production of state and national leaders see especially Richard Maxwell Brown, *Strain of Violence: Historical Studies of American Violence and Vigilantism* (New York: Oxford University Press, 1977), pp. 67–90.
See also the first chapter of my book, *In My Father's House Are Many Mansions: Family and Community in Edgefield, South Carolina* (Chapel Hill: University of North Carolina Press, forthcoming).

3. John Boyd Edmunds, "Francis W. Pickens: A Political Biography" (Ph.D.
dissertation, University of South Carolina, 1967). Edmunds has revised his dissertation into a manuscript chronicling antebellum South Carolina politics entitled "The Politics of Destruction: Francis Pickens and the Carolinians." For
Bonham see Milledge Louis Bonham, "The Life and Times of Milledge Luke
Bonham," undated typescript, Papers of Milledge Luke Bonham, South Caroliniana Library, Columbia, S.C.

4. See Vernon Burton, "Race and Reconstruction: Edgefield County, South
Carolina," *Journal of Social History* 12 (Fall 1978): 42–45.

5. Francis Butler Simkins, *Pitchfork Ben Tillman: South Carolinian* (Baton
Rouge: Louisiana State University Press, 1944); Diane Neale, "Benjamin Ryan
Tillman: The South Carolina Years, 1847–1894" (Ph.D. dissertation, Kent State
University, 1976).

6. Edwin Luther Green, *George McDuffie* (Columbia: State Company,
1936); James G. Banks, "Strom Thurmond and the Revolt against Modernity"
(Ph.D. dissertation, Kent State University, 1970). Hammond has had several
biographers: Elizabeth Merritt, *James Henry Hammond, 1807–1864* (Baltimore: Johns Hopkins Press, 1923); Robert Cinnamond Tucker, "James Henry
Hammond: South Carolinian" (Ph.D. dissertation, University of North Carolina, 1958); Carol Bleser, *The Hammonds of Redcliffe* (New York: Oxford
University Press, 1981); and Drew Gilpin Faust, *James Henry Hammond and
the Old South: A Design for Mastery* (Baton Rouge: Louisiana State University
Press, 1982).

7. I have explored the competition between blacks and whites in "Race and
Reconstruction" and in my dissertation, "Ungrateful Servants? Edgefield's Black

Reconstruction, Part 1 of the Total History of Edgefield County, South Carolina" (Ph.D. dissertation, Princeton University, 1976).

8. All statistics are from my Edgefield County data base and are derived from using SPSS and SAS statistical packages. A brief description of the data base is appended to *In My Father's House*. I can provide more detailed descriptions for the costs of copying and mailing.

9. Edgefield Village Baptist Church Records, November 1867 and July 13, 1869, Baptist Historical Collection, Furman University, Greenville, S.C.; Hortense Woodson and church historians, *History of Edgefield Baptist Association, 1807–1957* (Edgefield: Edgefield Advertiser Press, 1957), p. 221.

10. Quotations from Afro-American Baptist associations to which Edgefield churches belonged: Little River Baptist Association Minutes, August 23–25, 1877, p. 4, also September 1886, p. 7, American Baptist Historical Society, Colgate Rochester Theological Seminary, Rochester, N.Y.; George Rawick, *The American Slave: A Composite Autobiography*, sup. ser. 1, vol. 3, *Georgia* (Westport, Conn.: Greenwood Press, 1977), p. 305.

11. Benjamin Elijah Mays, *Born to Rebel: An Autobiography* (New York: Scribner's, 1971). See Burton, "Ungrateful Servants," chap. 5, S. Walker to Brvt. Brig. Gen. Ben P. Hunkle, October 1866, and Annual Report of the Bureau District of Anderson, pp. 771, 883–84, in Records of the Bureau of Refugees, Freedmen and Abandoned Lands, Record Group 105, National Archives, Washington, D.C.; Teachers' Reports, Edgefield, 1868–70, five folders, Superintendent of Education Papers, Records of the Department of Education, South Carolina Department of Archives and History, Columbia.

12. James D. Anderson, "Ex-Slaves and the Rise of Universal Education in the New South, 1860–1880," in Roland Goodenow and Arthur O. White, eds., *Education and the Rise of the New South* (Boston: G. K. Hall, 1981), pp. 2–3, 10.

13. Herbert G. Gutman, *The Black Family in Slavery and Freedom, 1750–1925* (New York: Pantheon, 1976), and "Passageways" (Paper presented at a conference on the First and Second Reconstructions and cited in Anderson, "Ex-Slaves and the Rise of Universal Education").

14. Stowe quoted in Anderson, "Ex-Slaves and the Rise of Universal Education," p. 2.

15. Alvord quoted in ibid., p. 3.

16. "The Religious Instruction of the Colored People," a report by Luther Broadus, 1871, Edgefield Baptist Association Records, Baptist Historical Collection, Furman University; Woodson et al., *History of Edgefield Baptist Association*, pp. 57–59.

17. Ronald Butchart, "Educating for Freedom: Northern Whites and the Origins of Black Education in the South, 1862–1875" (Ph.D. dissertation, State University of New York at Binghamton, 1976), pp. 418–23; Burton, "Race and Reconstruction," p. 33.

18. Literacy rates for household heads in 1870 were 4.4 percent for Afro-

Americans and 84.1 percent for whites. In 1870, black household heads younger than thirty years of age had a literacy rate of 4.5 percent and comparable aged white household heads had a rate of 84.3 percent. In 1880, 16.4 percent of all Afro-American household heads were literate compared to 86.6 percent of whites. In 1880, 20.3 percent of black household heads less than thirty years old were literate compared to 86 percent of white household heads of the same age.

19. The information on the black and white leaders in Edgefield County comes from a prosopographical profile that I have constructed. Demographic, economic, political, and social information was gathered from all sources available to construct a collective biography of leaders in the antebellum and postbellum county. For Cain see *Edgefield Advertiser,* July 11, 1866, December 15, 1870, January 12, 19, 1871, January 25, February 29, and March 21, 1872, January 16, and February 3, 1873; John Reynolds, *Reconstruction in South Carolina, 1865–1877* (Columbia: State Printing Co., 1905), p. 365; Thomas Holt, *Black over White: Negro Political Leadership in South Carolina during Reconstruction* (Urbana: University of Illinois Press, 1977), p. 76.

20. Boothe Simkins et al., "The Life of Paris Simkins," unpublished biography, Papers of Paris Simkins, in possession of C. B. Bailey, Sr., Columbia, S.C.

21. George Brown Tindall, *South Carolina Negroes, 1877–1900* (Columbia: University of South Carolina Press, 1952), p. 146; Edgefield County Deed Book, SSS, pp. 344–45, TTT, pp. 447–48, and OOO, pp. 624–25; Julian Landrum Mims, "Radical Reconstruction in Edgefield County, 1868–1877" (M.A. thesis, University of South Carolina, 1969), p. 33; Joan Reynolds Faunt and Emily B. Reynolds, *Biographical Directory of the Senate of the State of South Carolina* (Columbia: University of South Carolina Press, 1964), p. 191.

22. *Edgefield Advertiser,* April 21, and October 6, 1870.

23. For documentation of local political successes for blacks see Burton, "Race and Reconstruction" and "Ungrateful Servants."

24. On slave literacy see Janet Cornelius, " 'We Slipped and Learned to Read': Slave Accounts of the Literacy Process, 1830–1865," *Phylon* 44 (September 1983): 171–86, and Robert William Fogel and Stanley Engerman, *Time on the Cross:* Evidence and Methods—a Supplement, 2 vols. (Boston: Little, Brown, 1974), 2:196.

25. David Herbert Donald, "A Generation of Defeat," in Walter J. Fraser, Jr., and Winfred B. Moore, Jr., eds., *From the Old South to the New South: Essays on the Transitional South* (Westport, Conn.: Greenwood Press, 1981), pp. 3–20.

26. Burton, "The Civil War in the Confederate Interior: From Community to the Nation—The Transformation of Local Values in Edgefield, South Carolina" (Paper presented at the Southern Historical Annual Meeting, November 1984, Charleston, S.C.).

27. Stanley M. Elkins, *Slavery: A Problem in American Institutional and Intellectual History* (Chicago: University of Chicago Press, 1959).

28. Ralph A. Wooster, *The People in Power: Courthouse and Statehouse in the Lower South, 1850–1860* (Knoxville: University of Tennessee Press, 1969), pp. 8–9.

29. For the black exodus from Edgefield see Burton, "Ungrateful Servants," pp. 166–78.

30. South Carolina, State Board of Agriculture, *South Carolina: Resources and Population, Institutions and Industries* (Charleston: Walker, Evans & Cogswell, 1883), pp. 481, 482.

31. "Constitution of South Carolina—1790," Article 1, sections 6 and 8, reprinted in Francis N. Thorpe, comp., *The Federal and State Constitutions, Colonial Charters, and Other Organic Laws of the States, Territories, and Colonies Now or Heretofore Forming the United States,* 7 vols. (Washington, D.C.: U.S. Government Printing Office, 1909), 6:3260.

32. Edmunds, "Politics of Destruction," p. 18.

33. Robert Neil Mathis, "Preston Smith Brooks: The Man and His Image," *South Carolina Historical Magazine* 79 (October 1978): 300–301.

34. Peggy Lamson, *The Glorious Failure: Robert Brown Elliott and the Reconstruction in South Carolina* (New York: Norton, 1974), p. 118. On the Hamburg riot, see Burton, "Race and Reconstruction," pp. 42–43.

35. Voter turnout was estimated by using the male population as reported in the censuses. For an excellent reinterpretation of the voter turnout for the antebellum elections for the legislature see J. William Harris, "A Slaveholding Republic: Augusta's Hinterlands before the Civil War" (Ph.D. dissertation, Johns Hopkins University, 1982), pp. 240–42.

36. William C. Preston to George Ticknor, March 2, 1824, Papers of William C. Preston, South Caroliniana Library, Columbia, S.C.; Francis W. Pickens, *Anniversary Address Delivered to the Clariosophic Society, South Carolina College, February 22, 1827* (Columbia: Printed by Sweeny and Sims at the Telescope Press, 1827). On the prominence of attorneys in antebellum South Carolina's leadership see especially Harold S. Schultz, *Nationalism and Sectionalism in South Carolina, 1852–1860: A Study of the Movement for Southern Independence* (Durham: Duke University Press, 1950), p. 7, and Green, *George McDuffie,* pp. 17, 19.

37. John Belton O'Neall, *Biographical Sketches of the Bench and Bar of South Carolina,* 2 vols. (1859; rpr. Spartanburg: Reprint Company, 1975), 2:223, 279.

38. Figures for age cohorts fifteen to nineteen and twenty to twenty-nine for 1870 and 1880 are based on sample townships within Edgefield and from an estimate of the cohorts from the South Carolina published returns. I have coded everyone in the 1870 and 1880 population censuses but have not been able to obtain funds to have the data entered onto the computer for manipulation to get the precise Edgefield demographics.

A check for practicing attorneys in 1860 among those who died in the Civil War suggests that middle-class farmers, especially church members, were much more likely to be killed in the war. Young lawyers, however, were among the first to enlist. Both Matthew Calbraith Butler and Martin Witherspoon Gary were promoted to general. Butler lost part of his leg.

39. See Burton, "Ungrateful Servants," esp. chaps. 3 and 5. John Mardenborough was a practicing attorney in Edgefield District as late as 1876. Samuel J. Lee moved from Hamburg to the town of Aiken and practiced law in Aiken County after 1871, and Lawrence Cain and Paris Simkins received their law degrees near the end of Reconstruction.

40. J. Howard Marshall, "Gentlemen without a Country: A Social and Intellectual History of South Carolina, 1860–1900" (Ph.D. dissertation, University of North Carolina, 1979), pp. 5, 8, 30, 32, 208.

41. Daniel Walker Hollis, *University of South Carolina*, vol. 2, *College to University* (Columbia: University of South Carolina Press, 1956), pp. 26, 33–34. In the antebellum period some Edgefieldians attended college but never received degrees, usually because of disciplinary problems or matters of honor, rather than indecisiveness. Indeed, the reasons for not receiving the degree were the opposite of passivity—determined and deliberate actions such as those of Preston Brooks and Francis Pickens. See Mathis, "Preston Smith Brooks," pp. 298–99; Edmunds, "Politics of Destruction," pp. 8–9; Hollis, *University of South Carolina*, vol. 1, *South Carolina College* (Columbia: University of South Carolina Press, 1951) pp. 138–39.

42. Hollis, *University of South Carolina*, 2:38–39.

43. Ibid., pp. 78, 81.

44. Alvy L. King, *Louis T. Wigfall: Southern Fire-eater* (Baton Rouge: Louisiana State University Press, 1970), pp. 12–19 (see esp. p. 17 on Wigfall's reflection that a great benefit of college was personal contacts); Maximilian Laborde, *History of the South Carolina College, from Its Incorporation, Dec. 19, 1801, to Dec. 19, 1865* (Charleston: Walker, Evans, and Cogswell, 1874), pp. ix–xi; Joseph Ioor Waring, *A History of Medicine in South Carolina, 1825–1900* (Columbia: R. L. Bryan, 1967), pp. 255–56; Green, *George McDuffie*, pp. 14–17; Edmunds, "Politics of Destruction," pp. 5–8; Faust, *James Henry Hammond*, pp. 13–23; Bleser, *Hammonds of Redcliffe*, p. 4; Tucker, "James Henry Hammond," pp. 1, 5–9.

45. Faust, *James Henry Hammond*, pp. 29–57; Bleser, *Hammonds of Redcliffe*, pp. 4, 6, 137–38, 140.

46. Louis T. Wigfall to John Manning, February 17, 1840, Williams-Chesnut-Manning Family Papers, South Caroliniana Library; Howard Bunyan Clay, "Daniel Augustus Tompkins: An American Bourbon" (Ph.D. dissertation, University of North Carolina, 1951), esp. pp. 2, 5–13, 18–19; D. A. Tompkins to Harriet Brigham, 7 June 1874, Papers of Daniel Augustus Tompkins, Perkins Library, Duke University, Durham, N.C.; George Tayloe Winston, *A Builder of the New South: Being the Story of the Life Work of Daniel Augustus Tompkins* (Garden City, N.Y.: Doubleday, 1920), esp. chap. 1.

47. Julian L. Mims, "The Life and Politics of George Dionysius Tillman,

1826–1902" (manuscript submitted May 9, 1972, as a graduate seminar paper, in possession of the author); see also relevant sections in Simkins, *Pitchfork Ben Tillman.*

48. Simkins, *Pitchfork Ben Tillman,* esp. p. 56, and Neale, "Benjamin Ryan Tillman."

49. Carlanna Hendricks, "John Gary Evans: A Political Biography" (Ph.D. dissertation, University of South Carolina, 1966); Marshall, "Gentlemen without a Country," p. 68; Simkins, *Pitchfork Ben Tillman,* pp. 216, 274–81.

Folks like Us: The Southern Poor White Family, 1865–1935

J. Wayne Flynt

John William DeForest was an unlikely person to understand poor white family life. A native of Connecticut, while serving in 1866 as Freedmen's Bureau agent in Greenville, South Carolina, he recorded his observations of poor whites who desperately sought rations and assistance from him. They were "low-downers" who had little respect for human life and shunned work. The women were "ungainly," "stooping and clumsy in build," the mothers "yellow-faced," "gaunt and ragged." Two such women visited his office with a young girl in tow. One of the women in "that dull, sour, dogged tone of complaint which seems to be the natural utterance of the low-down people" charged that her "man has run me off." She had lived with him without benefit of matrimony because he was already married; the best he would offer her was a ninety-nine-year contract in writing. She had pressed him to marry her and borne him a child, but he expressed his gratitude by taking up with a married woman.[1]

Such family decadence neither caught the attention nor dampened the enthusiasm of Saffold Berney, an Alabama exponent of the New South, who described poor whites twenty-six years later. Thousands upon thousands of children and young women waited in poverty and idleness for philanthropic mill owners to hire them. "It is astonishing," he gushed, "how rapidly these little folks learn to 'keep up an end' . . . to piece a yarn . . . to spin, to reel, to warp, to weave . . . to perform the multifarious duties which go to make up the daily routine of a well ordered mill."

DeForest's lazy, shiftless ne'er-do-wells were transformed by the mills into "comfortably dressed, well fed, cheerful young people of both sexes . . . bright . . . good tempered, orderly, obedient young folks" passing "rapidly among their exquisite machines, sometimes singing in concert, and content— the very people who have had all their lives long nothing to do!" And such folk were naturally grateful. Strikes were "unknown among these really worthy people, who fill their appropriate squares in the great chess board of life, dutifully and gladsomely, as good citizens, as much worthy of respect and consideration as the merchant princes of the land."[2]

Both images are exaggerated and simplistic, but neither is entirely wrong. Poor white families contained millions of persons, and the patterns of their lives were complex. Some evidence is quantifiable and specific, but much is impressionistic and general.

The fact of being poor was the one constant in an otherwise diverse story. To pick one state as an example, Alabama poor whites worked primarily in four occupations: as tenant farmers, textile workers, lumbermen, and coal miners. Tenancy was primarily an occupation of young white families. Of Alabama's 166,420 tenant farm families in 1930, 53 percent were white. In 1940, 87 percent of Alabama farmers under the age of twenty-five were tenants. Tenant families were larger than those of landowners, and their housing was poorer. Less than 2 percent of tenant houses had running water in 1940; less than 1 percent had a flush toilet (only 71 percent had an outside privy, leaving 29 percent with neither toilet nor privy). Above all, tenants were mobile, and landless whites were twice as likely to move as blacks. In 1940 some 46,000 tenant families had occupied the farms on which they lived for less than fifteen months.[3]

The origins of the poor white class are diverse. Severe deprivation followed the Civil War, driving poor whites from the hills, piney woods, and wiregrass regions in search of food and work. This migration appears to have been as extensive as the temporary dislocation of emancipated blacks. One careful historian of the upheaval in Alabama estimates that between 10 and 15 percent of the white population migrated out of the South.

In the wiregrass region of southeastern Alabama, for instance, Simeon Ward and his brother Moses left their younger children in Pea Ridge with relatives and moved their wives and older sons near Andalusia, where they found jobs as timber workers.[4]

The dislocation of families which afflicted the Wards was widespread. Poor whites moved almost as often as they bore children. With no more than several pieces of homemade furniture and a few farm animals to detain them, moving for a sharecropper was as simple as "calling the dog and spitting in the fire."[5]

Mrs. E. J. Alexander of Perry County, Alabama, had been born in Texas, the daughter of a carpenter. Her family had moved frequently in search of a better life. Children were uprooted from school and friends, loaded aboard wagons, and shifted from town to town. She had lived nowhere longer than a year before her marriage. Then, like her father before her, she lived a gypsy life, moving with her tenant farmer husband from farm to farm, "hoping by each move to better their conditions." They established the chronology of their lives by the names of the landlords whose land they rented: the Francis place, the Johnson place, the Bell place. Such mobility took its toll. Mrs. Alexander admitted in 1938: "I ain't old, just forty-two, but I feel pretty old. If I could have looked ahead I guess maybe I would have picked a different road."[6]

Nor did their frequent moves reduce their isolation. Jack Kytle lived on the banks of the Coosa River in northeastern Alabama in the 1930s. He had never been to a movie or heard a radio, which was no surprise because only 20 percent of Alabama's tenant families had radios in 1940.[7] He lived with his father, mother, and two sisters in a shack that could be reached only by horse, boat, or buggy. One sister had pellagra, and the family existed mainly on a small patch of corn, which they made into whiskey. No one in the family could read or write. Their isolation was so complete that the first time Kytle heard an airplane "I honest-t'-God thought it was Ol' Man Stamps sawmill biler a-blowing up."[8] One appeal of the mine or mill village was the new opportunities which a more stable and sociable life afforded families.

The cycle of life in such families differed more in degree and chronology than in broad design. Birth, childhood, adolescence, courtship, marriage, and old age proceeded like the cycle of their crops.

Their troubles began at birth. Childbirth could be terrifying to any woman during these years, but to the poor woman, whose only attendant was usually a midwife, it posed a special danger. Oral histories recorded in the 1930s demonstrate clearly that southern poor whites understood next to nothing about birth control. One white sharecropper described her marriage and the brief good times that followed: "Then the first baby came on. . . . After that, things didn't go so good. Another baby come on and we had our hands full." A young white man on relief remembered that his first child was born the year he married and babies had come at two-year intervals ever since.[9] Julia Rhodes, a textile mill worker in Alexander City, Alabama, had married at age fifteen and borne her first baby a year later. When interviewed in 1938, she had eight children ranging in age from an infant to a nineteen-year-old boy.[10]

Some poor whites justified their large families in the same way they did so many of life's burdens: large families were a blessing from the Lord. A northern Alabama coal miner and member of the Church of God justified his five sons and one daughter by condemning birth control as an attempt to thwart God's will.[11]

Lack of information about birth control was more often the problem than religious objection to it; and ignorance about how to prevent large families, which snuffed out hope of a better life, caused strife in poor white families. Two examples were reported in a volume of Federal Writers' Project interviews published in 1938.

Sarah Easton was a plump, strong North Carolina woman who worked with her husband as a farm laborer. A year after her marriage Lucy was born, followed by Macy a year and a half later. Sarah became ill, her husband was disappointed because both children were girls, and he complained that babies were arriving too fast to feed, especially when his wife's pregnancy kept her from the fields. He began to drink harder: "He always drunk some but now he was like a hog in a bucket of slops." While drunk, he tried to run her off. When she became pregnant again, she feared to tell him. Instead, she visited a neighborhood "granny woman," who prepared a brew of cotton root tea. The medicine aborted the baby and nearly killed her in the process. When she finally told her husband what she had done, he wept and said that it was his sin instead of hers. She saw the irony of it all: "He is funny like that. He didn't think it was wrong to cuss, drink, and work me to death, but he thought it was awful to git rid of a baby or to impose on a dumb animal." He need not have worried. Months later she was pregnant again. He kissed her and consoled: "God knows, Sarah, I love the brats but I'm worried about how to look after them." When she presented him with a boy, he rejoiced until the next poor tobacco crop, then spent every cent on a drunken spree: "He come home about midnight as drunk as a dog and as broke as a beggar. . . . I suddenly took a notion that I could beat the stuffin' out of him, and I did. I got a barrel stave and I turned him across the table bench and I blistered his rump. I made him pretty sore but it ain't done no good." Following the birth of her son, she presented her husband with twin girls. But "them was my last because before they was a year old I had appendicitis and when the doctor operated he tied my tubes so I couldn't have no more."[12]

The son of an Alabama tenant farmer who became a labor organizer and jack-of-all-trades reacted to the crisis of having babies in a different way. He quit cotton mill work when he was seventeen and wound up working at Coney Island, where he met and married the Roman Catholic daughter of a Pennsylvania coal miner. Trouble began when he moved to California to take a job, leaving his bride behind. When she finally joined him she insisted on separate beds. His interpretation of these events became a justification for his violence:

I didn't like that; I believe a man and his wife should sleep in the same bed. But she wouldn't have it, and she wouldn't have any sex either. The truth was she was afraid she'd get pregnant and it'd hurt her business [beautician]. She didn't want to spoil her figure either. She didn't know anything about birth control and I didn't either at the time. Well things got worse and worse and we was scrappin' all the time and finally we had a break-up.

She moved downstairs in the same building'— . . . and I stayed upstairs. It was bad. Because of my religious trainin' [Episcopalian] I felt that I shouldn't step out on her. . . . Even if she wouldn't be a wife to me I felt I couldn't go back on my vows I'd made in church. Well I couldn't satisfy myself and I'd nearly go crazy. Some nights I'd just go out of my head and I'd go downstairs and beat on her door beggin' her to let me in. One night I just had to break her door right in and we had a big fight. I don't mean I exactly beat her up—I was just wild—and you might say I raped my own wife, just took it away from her.

Unluckily, shortly after that night, she announced she was pregnant. Well there was nothin' for it but to have it out, so she took fifty dollars I gave her and went to a doctor and had—what do you call it?—yeah, an abortion. From that time things grew worse and worse and I finally decided we couldn't live together. So I divorced her and came back East.

He remarried, this time the nineteen-year-old daughter of an Alabama tenant farmer, "and our first baby . . . was born in the shortest period of time which could elapse between marriage and havin' a child." He went back into the cotton mills, and they had a second daughter. But "this was three and a half years after the first one. I'd learned somethin' about birth control, y'see."[13]

Whether desired or not, babies entered the families of poor whites in startlingly large numbers; and childrearing was as complex for poor whites as for the more affluent. Because both parents had to struggle just to survive, children were left to themselves when young and initiated into work routines well before their teens. Punishment tended to be physical, growing naturally from the exertion and frustration of poor white existence. One hot-tempered farm laborer regretted that he set a poor example for his children but boasted that at least he had not "spared the rod."

A sharecropper who had been next to the youngest of ten children considered his father to be the meanest man he had known. His father beat him and ran him out of the house. A female textile worker remembered her punishment for stuffing her grandmother's pipe with a mixture of tobacco and black powder. When her mother returned from her shift at the mill she administered such a flogging that her daughter remembered it years later.[14] Despite such parental judgment, poor white children seemed to have been punished no more severely than children in more affluent southern families. The region has been justly famous for its violence, and parents of all classes favor stern physical discipline.[15] Children who were so treated often remembered their parents with affection.

Maintaining self-respect was not easy for poor children. They were often "put down" for their habits, clothes, speech, or food. Mrs. L. A. House remembered when mill children attended parades in the small town of Sylacauga, Alabama, during World War II. When she heard "uptown" children making fun of the "lint heads" she intervened angrily to remind the middle-class siblings that but for the "lint heads" there would be no Sylacauga.[16] Kathleen Knight, who grew up on a tenant farm in the Mississippi delta, remembered that she felt more comfortable "with our own kind." At school the major recreation consisted of plays, and the best parts always went to the children of landowners: "And of course we didn't think much about it. We was use to taking second place."[17]

Will D. Campbell, in later years an unorthodox Southern Baptist minister, remembered when he and his brother Joe carried their lunches to school in a lard bucket, which was stored in the cloakroom until midday. Often as not their lunch consisted of fried ham, a biscuit, and a small jar of molasses. They gouged a hole in the biscuit and poured in the syrup so it would not spill. Such a lunch was no matter of pride, so Will, Joe, and the others from the lard bucket set would escape to the obscurity of a large beech tree, far enough from the brown sack, light bread, and bologna crowd so as not to be seen. One day their mother sent their lunch in a prestigious paper sack, and Will slipped in at recess and ate half a bologna sandwich. When he told his brother about the delicacy awaiting them at lunch, Joe was skeptical:

> He looked at me funny and asked me to show him which sack was ours. When I did, he confirmed that that was our place and said nothing more. His silence gave me doubts. And at lunchtime, when he hurriedly led me, not to our usual spot, but out of sight of all the other children, I knew. Joe knew that I would not willfully steal someone's lunch. And he could not tell me that I had done so by mistake. The two of us sat with a paper sack between

us and ate bologna sandwiches made out of light bread, and an orange which we halved, and two cookies. Apparently the teacher explained to the owner of the lunch that it had been taken by mistake, for we never heard it mentioned. And we never mentioned it to each other—not even when we lived to see ham and biscuit elevated to the rank of delicacy, light bread and bologna relegated to . . . dwindling status.[18]

What made such occasions excruciatingly painful was the enormous sense of pride within such families. Although degenerates could be found as well as chaotic and unstable families, what impresses most was the attempt of parents in the midst of such deprivation to instill a sense of dignity and pride in their offspring. Kathleen Knight remembered one Mississippi landlord who would not let his sharecroppers carry their own cotton to the gin. When the landlord saw her father in the wagon on his way to the gin, he told him to get back to the fields and tried to take the reins. But her father was a proud man and, picking up a pottery jug, threatened to hit his landlord if he tried to climb aboard the wagon. The landlord relented, but it was the last time her father risked his family's security for the sake of their pride. William D. Nixon, who ran a country store at Merrellton, Alabama, recounted a story concerning the wife of a tenant farmer who created a disturbance in his store over a charge she did not understand. Nixon tolerated her abusive language as long as he could, then raged: "You are a woman, and I can not talk to you, but, if you will go home and put on breeches, I'll slap your jaws." Undaunted, the woman stormed out the door with a parting shot: "I can wear the breeches." Lillie Mae Beason, explaining why her sharecropper father moved so often, reminisced: "Well, he was looking for something better. You know, he had a lot of pride. I think my dad had more pride than was really good for him. And he was always bettering himself. I can just see him now coming in and telling my mother . . . how . . . everything was just going to be rosy. He was gonna have this and this and this. He always bettered himself, he said, as he moved. I'm not so sure about it, but he said he did."[19]

But pride could not compensate for illiteracy or child labor, which were integral parts of childhood for many poor whites. By 1900, 25 percent of Alabama's textile mill workers were under the age of sixteen, and their illiteracy rates were three times as high as for nonworking children. A sample of interviews from the Federal Writers' Project is sobering. A North Carolina textile worker entered the mill when she was nine and never learned to read or write. Mrs. Tom Alsobrook worked in the Cowikee Mill in Eufaula, Alabama, began as a "spooler hand" at the age of nine, and never attended school. Her mother prepared their breakfast at five in the morning, and they left together before dawn for the six o'clock shift. After a twelve-hour day she was too tired to try to learn.[20]

Nor was the story different in the country. In the published life histories, most of the white sharecroppers, mill workers, and coal miners lacked education. Although an extreme example, one life history of a North Carolina sharecropper couple revealed that not one of their eight grandparents could read, nor any of their four parents, nor could they: "Book larnin' never come easy in our families."[21]

The extent of educational backwardness was revealed by the federal census and state illiteracy commissions, which were established early in the twentieth century. Alabama in 1890 had the fourth highest number of native-born white illiterates in the nation, 105,394 (18.84 percent of all whites in the state). Despite literacy drives, tutoring of soldiers during World War I, and "Opportunity Schools" for adult illiterates, Alabama still ranked forty-fifth of the forty-eight states in 1927; and all three states that ranked lower than Alabama in rates of literacy (Louisiana, South Carolina, and Mississippi) were southern states. A study of 172,727 draft cards turned in by Alabama men in 1917 revealed approximately 10,000 draft-age male illiterates.[22]

Why children did not attend school is a more complex matter. Among rural people and especially during summer weeding and fall harvest seasons, every child was needed in the fields. A 1918 survey of twelve Alabama counties by the National Child Labor Committee concluded that 20 percent of the daughters of farm owners worked in the fields and 32 percent of the daughters of tenants were so engaged. The sons of farm owners were absent from school 29 percent of the time; the sons of farm tenants 39 percent. The ratios for girls were 19 percent and 32 percent respectively. In one school four children aged nine, ten, twelve, and thirteen were in the first grade and were not eligible for promotion; each had been absent seventy days for farm work. A child of fifteen in the second grade had attended only two of seventy-seven days during the school term, spending the other days in farm work. The failure rate was much higher for tenants' children than for the offspring of owners.[23]

Judged by the life histories recorded by the Federal Writers' Project, such cases were not exceptional. A North Carolina sharecropper remembered putting his son to work pulling and tying tobacco at the age of six. A cash renter regretted that his son was seven years behind in school, "but I had to have him on the farm." When asked if he had attended school, Virginia coal miner M. C. Sizemore responded: "Heck no. I didn't go—I didn't finish the third grade. Back in them days there wasn't no law to make you go, and my dad, I reckon, didn't see any use for me [to go]. Course, he done wrong in it. He worked me all the time. I went to plowing when I was twelve year old. Wasn't big enough to pull a plow hardly."[24]

It is not surprising that when poor rural people moved to cities, mill towns, or mining camps, they took their ideas about family labor and education with them. Although Progressive Era reformers produced an extensive literature blaming child labor on heartless, greedy mill owners, the cause was never that simple. Contributing both to child labor and illiteracy were traditional rural attitudes of parents about work and education, family mobility which often moved children about during the school year, and belief that schooling beyond basic literacy was a waste of time. Many mill owners were only too willing to capitalize on such attitudes to establish the "family wage," which required that all able-bodied members of a family above the age of nine or ten must work in order to survive. Economic necessity reinforced traditional rural family attitudes. For children, at least initially, work was a chance to escape restrictive school discipline and earn money. As one twelve-year-old South Carolina urchin put it when explaining that he had never been to school: "Jim—he's my pal—he tried it an' he said twan't nothing but jist to be bossed by 'er stuckup woman and he cussed her out an' quit—so he did."[25]

The extent of child labor in both the textile and mining industries increased rapidly in the late nineteenth and early twentieth centuries. In 1900, 59 percent of Alabama's males and 31.3 percent of the state's females ages ten to fifteen were gainfully employed. By 1910 the figures had increased to 61.9 percent and 41.3 percent. Between 1885 and 1895 the number of male mill workers increased 31 percent; but during the same period, the number of girls below the age of eighteen increased by 158 percent and the number of boys in the same age group by 89 percent. In 1900 more than half the six hundred thousand working children in the United States lived in the South.[26]

Blame for this condition was laid on almost everyone except the children themselves. Reformer Irene Ashby blamed the mill owners; Alabama Episcopal priest Edgar G. Murphy blamed "the greed of idle parents." Some Alabama mill owners answered attacks on them by protesting that if they did not hire their adult mill workers' children under the age of twelve, the parents would move to other mills where they could obtain the extra incomes of their younger children.[27]

Such protests are easily dismissed as corporate propaganda and rationalization, which they often were; but unfortunately some poor white family histories support the contention. Julia Rhodes recounted that her father left a farm and moved into Alexander City, Alabama, hoping to provide his family a better living by putting his two older daughters to work in the cotton mill. The Birmingham Board of Education investigated the company school at Avondale Mills and found two girls, one fourteen and the other fifteen, who had been to school only two weeks in their lives. Their father was then trying to remove them from school and put them back into the mill. A Works Progress Administration worker in the 1930s remembered that when he was a boy he had attended a mill school until the seventh grade, then just before his eleventh birthday had quit to work in the mill. Because he was under age, his mother had lied about his age.[28]

By no means was this a universal attitude of poor white parents toward their children. Many of them valued education, which they viewed as a passage to a better life for their offspring. One share-renter who received only four months of education determined to keep his own children in school despite the inconvenience: "My younguns ain't never done me a speck of good. They've always been in school times the work had to be carried on; so I've had to do it all myself." One literate mill worker could not prevent his daughter from entering the mill; but at night he taught her spelling.[29] A poorly educated northern Alabama coal miner, Sam Brakefield, insisted that his thirteen children attend school and even managed to help one through the University of Southern California. A neighboring miner, John Gates, kept his son in college until the Depression forced the boy to drop out. A North Carolina sharecropper whose family had been illiterate for three generations managed to keep his five children in school through the sixth grade before they dropped out.[30]

As many oral and life histories make clear, such desires by parents were often no match for economic reality. A farm laborer family expressed the dilemma that confronted so many:

> We wanted our children to git a education because me and Pa can't neither one read nor write, and we know how not having a education can keep you out of a job, from teaching Sunday school, and from 'sociating with good people. Me and John both went to school for a few months but that won't enough for us to learn nothing. We was too pore to help the younguns through high school. When Lucy got to the sixth grade we had to stop her because they was so much work to do. . . .
>
> I'm sorry my younguns can't git a education because that is the one thing a feller has got to have to git a job. Shucks, you can't dig ditches now unless you got a high school education. I wish things was back where they useter be when a feller just had to be strong and honest and have a little horse sense.[31]

Although general economic conditions may have been the major barrier to education, specific culprits often contributed to the problem. One textile worker parent who venerated his paternalistic mill owner believed that to make a good textile worker one had to start him around the age of eight. The mill owner visited each home and learned the first name of every person—man, woman, and child. He provided a school during three months of the year, but "if he caught a child under twelve years old idle, he picked it up and put it to work. It was go to school or go to work when you lived in the mill village. That was all right with his mill families." Despite expansion of the mill, few new families were hired in that village because there were so many children growing up to take their parents' places. When a family member was sick, a younger child simply skipped school and substituted for him.[32]

Another mill worker who took enormous pride in his son's good report cards favored compulsory school attendance laws. When the mill owner called a public meeting of workers, many of them spoke against the law, complaining that they had inadequate money for clothes and books as it was. Poor people could not afford to keep their children in school beyond age fourteen anyway. Whether the families were stating their own views or had been prompted by the mill owner was uncertain. At length, the proeducation worker stood up and endorsed the compulsory attendance law. After the meeting he noticed that his boss had received his remarks with obvious disfavor, and that began an odyssey which carried him into the labor union and out of a job. And he faced one final irony: after all his efforts on behalf of his sons, both quit school following the ninth grade to work in the mill.[33]

By the time poor white children reached their teens, most had spent years performing hard physical labor in mill, mine, factory, forest, or on the land. They had often served as surrogate parents for younger brothers and sisters, and they were earning a modest income. Marriage followed as a logical extension of a youth devoid of any real childhood. Parental arguments in favor of waiting until they could afford a family were useless; if they heeded such logic they would never marry.

The ritual of courtship was as complex as all other aspects of their lives. For many poor whites Victorian innocence, even prudishness, was as pronounced as for members of the middle or upper classes. Parents were just as likely to object to a child's choice of spouse. Annie Phoebea Owens was one of eighteen children living near the Coosa River in Calhoun County, Alabama. When a young Georgian who had come to work in the foundry nearby began to court her, the family was incensed. They considered him an outsider and socially inferior to them. But love worked its magic, and Homer Flynt borrowed a horse and buggy to take his belle to the wedding. After the young couple rounded a bend which obstructed the family's view, the brash young man reached over to kiss his fiancee. She "slapped him good and hard" and reminded him that they were not yet married.[34]

June W. Odom grew up in the mill village of Cordova, Alabama, during the 1930s, the daughter of cotton mill workers. Her parents were strict members of the Church of Christ and refused to allow her to date until she was sixteen. When she finally was allowed to date, she had to return by a specified time. In her opinion, "teenagers back then . . . didn't have the same attitudes and they were not subjected to the same pressures and permissiveness and things."[35]

Her judgment was wrong. By no means were all poor white families as cohesive, as strict, or as Victorian as hers. Although textile worker W. W. Jewell could remember few divorces among his mill worker neighbors, there was a great deal of "running around going on" in the 1920s. When he arrived in Albany, Georgia, in 1919 to work in a cotton mill, there were twenty-five houses of prostitution located four or five miles from the mill village in a neighborhood surrounded by blacks. Each house contained five to ten white women, "and you could just go over there and pick you out one like you wanted" for three dollars. "But my choice was a little ole Jew girl that was out there and that was a good looking thing, I'm telling you." After "getting religion" he settled down, married, and established a stable family.[36]

The hundreds of oral histories conducted with poor whites establish no particular pattern of courtship and marriage. A white sharecropper's wife described her courtship with her husband, who was illegitimate. She met him when her family lost its tools and furniture to their landlord. He came to the auction and watched her intensely. It was "love at first sight," and a few days later they were married. Perhaps she should have spent more time courting, because following the birth of their children, her husband ran off with a sixteen-year-old girl who bore him a child and three others out of wedlock, fathered by different men. Her husband finally returned, admitting that he had "been a damn fool." She forgave his dalliance because she and the children needed him so badly to plant the tobacco crop.[37]

A poor white man on relief in the 1930s described sexual roles in a simple paragraph. He regretted his hasty courtship but had accepted the consequences: "My wife's one ain't got no easy going. She do all the house work. Washing. Ironing. Serving. Cooking. There's eight of us counting me and her. Six children. Me and Ella took a marrying notion when we wasn't no age. Without a penny laid by. Two that age ain't got no sense about what's to come. Ella ain't never throwed in my face talk of things she ought to have. Things I ain't been able to give her. She's been poor all her life."[38]

One couple living in the mountains of East Tennessee established a less formal arrangement. Calvin and Lola had been school-age sweethearts until her mother died, and she left the mountains to work in a Knoxville steam laundry. She worked ten-hour days for four dollars a week until Calvin came down from the hills and asked her to "keep house" for him: "It didn't take a powerful lot of talk. I was sick and tired of working like a slave." She vigorously defended their common-law marriage: "I ain't noways ashamed that me and Calvin has never got around to the regular kind. He's past fifty and I'm near to it and ain't neither of us ever trotted around loose like half the ones that blows about wedlock and such. We is poor but we's decent."[39]

She was right. Many poor whites who could produce a marriage certificate could not boast of a decent relationship. Jim Lauderdale, who lived near the Coosa River in eastern Alabama, fought constantly with his wife until finally he ran her and his two daughters into the textile mill at Sylacauga. Henry Kelly, who lived in a pine shack not far away, had formally divorced his wife. Moonshiner Orrie Robinson had once earned enough money to stay in a hotel with a prostitute, but she had taken all his money.[40]

George Carter also lived in Talladega County, Alabama. He was a great hulk of a man, six feet three inches tall and weighing 220 pounds. His was a perfect physique for a logger, which he had been for forty-two years when interviewed in the mid-1930s. He had never known his mother or father, who were so desperately poor they had given him and his sister away. The farmer who raised them nearly worked them to death, and Carter ran away when he was fifteen. He was caught and beaten until his jacket stuck to his bloody back. His second runaway was successful, and he found work in a circus until his boss struck him and he responded by bashing in the man's head with a sledgehammer. He took refuge in the Coosa County forests with a black man with whom he played poker, made whiskey, and raised hell. The black man was killed while trying to rape the wife of a sawmill worker, and Carter went to work in the same mill. He met a woman as poor as he was whose mother was dead and whose father "was too busy raisin' hell to mind after her," and she began to live with him. All went well until she caught him with another woman and told his boss, who warned him to clean up his life or get out of the village. He professed repentance until his boss lost the sawmill, then beat his wife for squealing on him. He deserted her for another woman in a sawmill in Shelby County and had three children by her. When the woman died in childbirth, he wasted no time finding another: "That was one place whar they was enough women to suit me, and I runned after 'em 'til my tongue was rollin' out like a damned dog's." He had more children by his new woman until he finally lost count. It was just as well because he did not take seriously the duties of parenting. When the children got older they just "drifted away." One boy was making moonshine whiskey, and a daughter had gone to work in a textile mill, where she was "runnin' after ev'ry pair of britches in sight." As for Carter, he had no intention of settling down: "I been 'round lots in my day, an' I done buried two ol' women. You couldn't give me another'n. They's too many runnin' 'bout that you don't have to feed."[41]

Nor was such conduct reserved only for males. Neeley Williams lived twelve miles south of Sylacauga on the Coosa River. She lived in a two-room pine board shanty in the 1930s and begged for food and snuff. Men all along the river had fathered her six children. Her oldest daughter had been taken away from her by child welfare workers. Her oldest son, age twenty, refused to work. When an interviewer for the Federal Writers' Project located her cabin in the 1930s, he was greeted by a naked four-year-old with a speech impediment who piped over and over in a thin voice, "Dod-dammit-dod-dammit-dod-dammit."[42]

Williams and Carter may be considered the prototype of the "poor white trash" depicted by Erskine Caldwell and William Faulkner. Descended from unstable families, crippled emotionally in childhood, such people were sexually promiscuous and unable to establish normal family relationships. But such people seem to be no more common than the rigidly strict Annie Owens or June Odom. The typical experience seems to have been a traditional family of loving parents who experienced normal if abbreviated courtships and lasting marriages.

The economic desperation of their lives was a major cause of family problems even for marriages that endured. A few hours of reading oral history transcripts dealing with poor white family life could easily convert one into a prohibitionist. Alcohol was often used as a drug that allowed the poor to forget their troubles, if only for awhile.

Alcohol abuse was especially rampant among males, and often this became a source of physical abuse and the focus of family tension. A female weaver at Cowikee Cotton Mill in Eufaula, Alabama, described her deceased husband as a good man when sober who drank himself to death: "'Fore God, he drinked enough to float a creek." Jim Lauderdale, who lived several counties north of Eufaula, fought constantly with his wife after she became a "holy roller" and objected to his bootlegging. He finally ran off his wife and two daughters. Henry Kelly, who lived nearby, was divorced and stayed drunk most of the time. A North Carolina tenant farmer's wife complained that her husband drank up the money as fast as she and the children could earn it. But she understood why he drank so much; it was "the only time he forgets that he came from pore folks." His drinking contributed to his hot temper and made it difficult for him to get along with landlords or to remain for long on any farm. Liberal New Deal activist Aubrey Williams traced his family's poverty to the 1890s, when his father, a skilled blacksmith (who "never got over the feeling of having his roots cut from under him and being adrift" after the Civil War), developed a serious drinking problem. After the family moved into Birmingham, his alcoholism became worse and they moved from house to house on the back side of the city.[43]

Although children such as Williams experienced the secondary effects of alcohol abuse, wives bore the brunt of the problem. One tenant farmer's wife ignored her husband's drinking when she married him at age sixteen. But his drinking increased, and he stayed away for days at a time during tobacco curing time, forcing her to cure the crop: "When he comes home from being gone so long and I ask him where he's been, he tells me it's none of my damned business, and that's all I ever know about it. He keeps a jug of liquor in the kitchen and he drinks when he pleases. If he wants to beat me or the children, he does, and that's all there is to it. He ain't got no mercy on nothing but mules and dogs."[44]

Many others recounted similar experiences. The wife of a North Carolina farm laborer compared her husband's drinking problem to "a hog in a bucket of slops." When drunk he would try to run his wife and children off, would "raise hell and try to fight." A mill worker drank so much he could no longer function on his job, and his wife made him move to another town "to git away from the crowd I had been drinking with." A tenant's son in the Civilian Conservation Corps complained that his father drank so much that he made "it hard on mama."[45]

Once again such testimony can easily mislead the casual student of the poor white family. For every case of alcoholism there is a comparable poor family of prohibitionists who faithfully attended a Baptist, Methodist, or Pentecostal church and opposed demon rum with a fervor that matched their scorn for landowners and mill foremen. When asked if she remembered her textile mill neighbors drinking, June Odom, who had grown up in a devoted Church of Christ family, replied: "No. Very seldom did you ever see a teenager ever drink. . . . Course, I'm sure at times they did. Just like there's an exception to every rule, but . . . there's just a different attitude with people growing up in the country, or in small towns. They aren't associated with that type of thing like you find in cities or larger places as much, not near as much. They're not around it, so therefore they never really think about it."[46]

Obviously Mrs. Odom remembered an idyllic world quite dissimilar from W. W. Jewell's whoretown in Albany, Georgia. But Jewell's world was no more typical than Odom's. A cotton mill worker who had been addicted to both alcohol and drugs was converted to Christianity and attended the church regularly despite inadequate clothes. Another mill worker believed it unchristian to attend movies because that was "the devil's territory": "If eternity should come and you'd be caught on the devil's territory what hope could you have?"[47] Many poor whites attended church with as much regularity as the more affluent, although sharecroppers, who were often deeply religious, sometimes avoided churches consisting largely of landowners because they felt underdressed and uncomfortable. In mill towns and mining camps, this problem was often eliminated by denominations establishing multiple congregations, one for "uptown" or management people and another for mill workers or miners. By the early twentieth century poor whites showed increasing preference for Pentecostal or Holiness churches, which were usually lumped together under the derisive label of "holy roller" churches. These "hard time" churches affirmed the basic worth of poor whites; their emphasis on God's universal love and their jeremiads on materialism often provided the cement that held troubled families together and gave them a sense of dignity denied by their material circumstances.

Even the family's sense of the dignity of labor suggests the danger of generalizing. As hard as it may be to understand how families could take pride in their labor in dusty fields, steamy cotton mills, or damp coal mines, they often did so. Northern Alabama coal miner Bennie Amerson described mine explosions that killed hundreds and paralyzing strikes that left his family destitute, then explained why he remained a miner: "It sort of gets a fellow when he follows it awhile." Mrs. Lee Snipes began working in a Eufaula cotton mill when she was a small girl. At first, pay was low, hours long, and conditions wretched. But a new owner bought the mill, installed five new commodes ("all cleaned every day"), and laid marble floors in the bathrooms. He installed running ice water and purchased different colored uniforms for each department. Work shifts were reduced to eight hours, and now her work was "such happiness": "It used to be we were just factory folks or 'lint heads.' Now we are 'mill operatives' and we hold our heads high. All work is honorable, you know, and we are proud of ours." She was proud of Donald Comer, who owned the mill, and there had been no "strike or trouble in any of the mills. We would all fight for him, not against him." Explaining his own devotion to the work ethic and his scorn for those who did not share his views, a white tenant ridiculed neighbors who blamed their poverty on World War I, the tariff, or "an act of God": "I say it's laziness, mental and physical laziness."[48]

In an effort to find culprits, historians have sometimes traced the problems of the poor white family to external exploiters whose avarice and greed imposed the family wage, institutionalized child labor, drove despondent workers to alcoholism, and turned mill villages into concentration camps. Such a view may be ideologically appealing, and it has some basis in fact. But it is both superficial and simplistic. Poor white families were quite capable of surviving poverty intact. Many mill families, especially females, found the social outlets and living conditions far superior to sharecropping and rejected unionism for reasons that had little to do with antiunion management tactics. Many rural family heads little valued education and regularly removed their children from school to hoe weeds or harvest cotton. Although the family wage pattern of mill and mine villages intensified pressure on women and children to obtain industrial jobs, many family heads applied as much pressure as mill or mine owners. Although a decent wage for adult male workers would have eliminated much child labor, it would not have solved the problem entirely.

As for patterns of childrearing, courtship, sexuality, and marriage, differences between southern poor white and middle-class families were minimal. Abundant evidence of internal chaos and disintegration mocks the notion of simpler times when nuclear families cohered in warmth, love, and Victorian innocence. But families with traditional values and sex roles did exist in large numbers among the poor of the South. Their patterns of courtship might be shorter and less structured, their marriage ceremonies less elaborate, and their childrearing more casual; but their demonstrable affection, their dreams of a better life for their offspring, their pride in a day's work well done, and their loyalty to the extended family refute many stereotypes about them. John William DeForest and Saffold Berney both could have learned much history by paying closer attention to the poor white family.

Notes

1. James Davidson, "The Post-Bellum Poor-White as Seen by J. W. DeForest," *Southern Folklore Quarterly* 24 (June 1960): 102–7.

2. Saffold Berney, *Hand-Book of Alabama* (Birmingham: Roberts and Son, 1892), pp. 482–83.

3. Alabama Farm Tenancy Committee, *Farm Tenancy in Alabama* (Wetumpka, Ala.: Wetumpka Printing Co., 1944), pp. 9–16.

4. Wyley D. Ward, *The Folks from Pea Ridge in Covington and Conecuh Counties, Alabama* (Huntsville, Ala.: N.p., 1973), pp. 167–68.

5. H. C. Nixon, "Changing Background of Southern Politics," *Social Forces* 11 (October 1932): 17.

6. Interview with Mrs. E. J. Alexander, Federal Writers' Project, Reel 1, "Life Histories," Folders 110–84, microfilm, originals in the Southern Historical Collection, University of North Carolina, Chapel Hill.

7. Alabama Farm Tenancy Committee, *Farm Tenancy in Alabama*, p. 12.

8. Interview with Jack Kytle, Federal Writers' Project, Reel 1.

9. Federal Writers' Project, *These Are Our Lives* (Chapel Hill: University of North Carolina Press, 1939), pp. 32, 368. For a debate on the dangers of oral history sources, see Leonard Rapport, "How Valid Are the Federal Writers' Project Life Stories: An Iconoclast among the 'True Believers,'" *Oral History Review* 7 (1979): 6–17; and Tom E. Terrill and Jerrold Hirsch, "Replies to Leonard Rapport," *Oral History Review* 8 (1980): 81–92.

10. Interview with Julia Rhodes, Federal Writers' Project, Reel 1.

11. Interview with Sam Cash, ibid.

12. Federal Writers' Project, *These Are Our Lives*, pp. 5–7.

13. Ibid., pp. 399–403.

14. Ibid., pp. 16, 31, 135.

15. See John S. Reed, *The Enduring South: Subcultural Persistence in Mass Society* (Lexington, Mass.: D. C. Heath, 1972).

16. Oral History with Mrs. L. A. House, July 10, 1974, Samford Oral History Collection, Samford University, Birmingham, Ala.

17. Oral History with Kathleen Knight, January 27, 1975, Samford Oral History Collection.

18. Will D. Campbell, *Brother to a Dragonfly* (New York: Seabury Press, 1977), pp. 49–50.

19. Oral History with Kathleen Knight; Herman C. Nixon, *Possum Trot: Rural Community, South* (Norman: University of Oklahoma Press, 1941), p. 47; Oral History with Lillie Mae Beason, January 3, 1976, Samford Oral History Collection.

20. Federal Writers' Project, *These Are Our Lives*, p. 146; interview with Mrs. Tom Alsobrook, Federal Writers' Project, Reel 1.

21. Tom E. Terrill and Jerrold Hirsch, eds., *Such as Us: Southern Voices of the Thirties* (Chapel Hill: University of North Carolina Press, 1978), p. 58.

22. U.S., Census Office, *Report on Population of the Unites States, Eleventh Census, 1890, Part II* (Washington, D.C.: U.S. Government Printing Office, 1897), pp. 530–31; Alabama, State Department of Education, *Report on Illiteracy by Division of Exceptional Education, 1927* (Birmingham: Birmingham Printing Co., 1927), p. 4; Alabama, State Department of Education, *Report of*

Special Drive against Illiteracy among Men of Draft Age, 1918 (Montgomery: Brown Printing Co., 1918), p. 5.

23. James J. Doster, "Education," and Eva Joffee, "Rural School Attendance," in Edward N. Clopper, ed., *Child Welfare in Alabama: An Inquiry by the National Child Labor Committee under the Auspices and with the Cooperation of the University of Alabama* (New York: National Child Labor Committee, 1918), pp. 105–23.

24. Federal Writers' Project, *These Are Our Lives*, pp. 33, 55.

25. An excellent examination of textile worker poor white attitudes toward child labor, education, and social control is found in David Carlton's study *Mill and Town in South Carolina, 1880–1920* (Baton Rouge: Louisiana State University Press, 1982), pp. 76–209; quote on p. 177.

26. U.S. Census Bureau, *Population, 1910*, vol. 4 (Washington, D.C.: U.S. Government Printing Office, 1914), p. 75; Shirley Garrett Schoonover, "Alabama's Quest for Social Justice during the Progressive Era" (M.A. thesis, Auburn University, 1970), p. 40.

27. Irene M. Ashby, "The Fight against Child Labor in Alabama," *American Federationist* 8 (May 1901): 150–57; clippings from February 7, October 30, 1901, in Edgar G. Murphy Papers, Southern Historical Collection, University of North Carolina, Chapel Hill.

28. Interview with Julia Rhodes; *Survey*, January 6, 1912, p. 1323; Federal Writers' Project, *These Are Our Lives*, pp. 387–88.

29. Federal Writers' Project, *These Are Our Lives*, pp. 38, 132.

30. Interviews with Sam Brakefield and John Gates, Federal Writers' Project, Reel 1; Terrill and Hirsch, eds., *Such as Us*, p. 62.

31. Federal Writers' Project, *These Are Our Lives*, pp. 8, 15.

32. Terrill and Hirsch, eds., *Such as Us*, pp. 148–49.

33. Ibid., pp. 173–80.

34. Oral History with Lillie Mae Beason.

35. Oral History with June W. Odom, December 2, 1974, Samford University Oral History Collection.

36. Oral History with W. W. Jewell, February 18, 1982, Auburn University Oral History Collection, Auburn, Alabama.

37. Federal Writers' Project, *These Are Our Lives*, pp. 32–36.

38. Ibid., p. 368.

39. Terrill and Hirsch, eds., *Such as Us*, p. 124.

40. Interviews with Jim Lauderdale, Henry Kelly, and Orrie Robinson, Federal Writers' Project, Reel 1.

41. Interview with George Carter, ibid.

42. Interview with Neeley Williams, ibid.

43. Interviews with Mrs. Champion, Jim Lauderdale, and Henry Kelly, ibid.; Terrill and Hirsch, eds., *Such as Us*, p. 59; John Salmond, *A Southern Rebel: The Life and Times of Aubrey Willis Williams, 1890–1965* (Chapel Hill: University of North Carolina Press, 1983), pp. 3–5.

44. Terrill and Hirsch, eds., *Such as Us*, pp. 97–98.

45. Federal Writers' Project, *These Are Our Lives*, pp. 6, 85, 413.
46. Oral History with June W. Odom.
47. Federal Writers' Project, *These Are Our Lives*, pp. 150, 218.
48. Interviews with Bennie Amerson and Mrs. Lee Snipes, Federal Writers' Project, Reel 1; Federal Writers' Project, *These Are Our Lives*, p. 57.

Contributors

BARBARA L. BELLOWS is assistant professor of history at Middlebury College and the coauthor of *God and General Longstreet: Essays on the Civil War and the Lost Cause* (1982).

KATHLEEN C. BERKELEY is an assistant professor of history at the University of North Carolina at Wilmington. Her most current published works include "Elizabeth Avery Meriwether, 'An Advocate for Her Sex': Feminism and Conservativism and the Post–Civil War South," *Tennessee Historical Quarterly* (Winter 1984).

CAROL K. BLESER is professor of American history at Colgate University. She is the author of *The Hammonds of Redcliffe* and is currently working on a book-length study of marriages in the mid-nineteenth-century South.

ORVILLE VERNON BURTON is associate professor of history at the University of Illinois. He has written a book on family history entitled *In My Father's House Are Many Mansions: Family and Community in Edgefield, South Carolina*.

CATHERINE CLINTON teaches southern history and women's history at Harvard University. She is author of *The Other Civil War: American Women in the Nineteenth Century* (1984) and is currently at work on a study of women on southern plantations during the Civil War and Reconstruction.

THOMAS G. DYER is a member of the faculty of the University of Georgia in higher education and history and is the editor of the *Georgia Historical Quarterly*. His most recent work is *The University of Georgia: A Bicentennial History, 1785–1985* (1985).

245

J. WAYNE FLYNT is head of the history department at Auburn University. Among his publications is *Dixie's Forgotten People: The South's Poor Whites* (1979).

WALTER J. FRASER, JR., is head of the department of history at Georgia Southern College. He is coeditor of *From the Old South to the New: Essays on the Transitional South* (1981) and *The Southern Enigma: Essays on Race, Class, and Folk Culture* (1983).

JOSEPH F. KETT is professor of history at the University of Virginia. His major publications include *Rites of Passage: Adolescence in America, 1790–Present* (1977).

THEDA PERDUE is associate professor of history at Clemson University. She is the author of *Slavery and the Evolution of Cherokee Society,* and she is working on a study of changing sexual roles among the Cherokee Indians.

R. FRANK SAUNDERS, JR., is professor of history at Georgia Southern College. His most recent publication is *Swamp Water and Wiregrass: Historical Sketches of Coastal Georgia* (1984).

STEVEN M. STOWE is on the faculty of the Pennsylvania State University College of Medicine in Hershey, Pennsylvania. He is presently completing a study of planter class culture and family life in the antebellum South.

JON L. WAKELYN is professor of history at the Catholic University of America. He is author of *The Politics of a Literary Man* (1973) and is coeditor of *Catholic Life in the Old South* (1983). He is at work on a history of higher education in the Old South.

LORENA S. WALSH is a research fellow at the Colonial Williamsburg Foundation, Williamsburg, Virginia. Her research interests include the agriculture and economy of the colonial Chesapeake and family and community history in that region.

BERTRAM WYATT-BROWN is professor of history at the University of Florida. He is the author of *Southern Honor: Ethics and Behavior in the Old South* (1982) and the forthcoming *Yankee Saints and Southern Sinners.*

246

Index